HMH

HMH Guide to **Success in Math** for the **SAT**®

Printed in the U.S.A.

ISBN 978-1-328-56905-9

$PrintCode

$AutomatedPO B C D E F G

Contents

The math section of the SAT® test assesses a variety of skills that are organized into four domains. Each domain is divided into several content dimensions, and each content dimension has a number of skills associated with it. The purpose of this publication is to provide practice on these skills using the two question types on the SAT® test: multiple choice and grid-in. For each skill, there is a two-page practice test that includes sample questions with worked-out solutions as well as practice questions. An answer sheet for each practice test is provided for you to record your answers.

The skills listed in the Table of Contents below and on the practice tests are paraphrases of the wording of the skills identified in the College Board publication *Test Specifications for the Redesigned SAT®* (pages 137–145).

Heart of Algebra

Gridding In Answers

You should record your answers on the answer sheet provided for each practice test. For the grid-in portion of a test, each numerical answer needs to be entered in a grid. Though not required, writing your answer in the boxes provided at the top of the grid is recommended. Each grid includes four boxes, one above each of the four columns of circles. Write just one character in each box. Notice the characters (fraction bar, decimal point, digits) shown along the left side of the grid. Below each box, you should fill in the circle that is to the right of the character you have written in that box. When fewer than four boxes are needed, be sure to leave the unused columns blank.

Things to remember when gridding in numerical answers:

1) Credit for a question is given only if the correct circles have been filled in.
2) Mark only one circle in each column, completely filling that circle.
3) The grid does not support negative numbers, so no question has a negative answer.
4) For answers with fewer than four characters, the answer can start in any column. If your answer is 3, use any of the four columns; if your answer is $\frac{2}{7}$, use either the first three columns or the last three columns to grid the answer. *[See Figures 1 & 2.]*
5) A mixed number result must be gridded as an improper fraction or as its decimal equivalent. A result of $2\frac{4}{5}$ should be gridded as either $\frac{14}{5}$ or 2.8. *[See Figure 3.]*
6) Decimal numbers less than 1 must be gridded without a leading zero. If your result is 0.5, you must grid it as just .5 (without a 0 in the ones place). *[See Figure 4.]*
7) If your result is a decimal with more than 3 digits (and no rounding instructions were given), then fill the grid with four characters by either rounding the final digit or truncating the decimal at this digit. Both answers will be accepted. *[See Figure 5; the answer .167 would also be accepted.]*

Figure 1

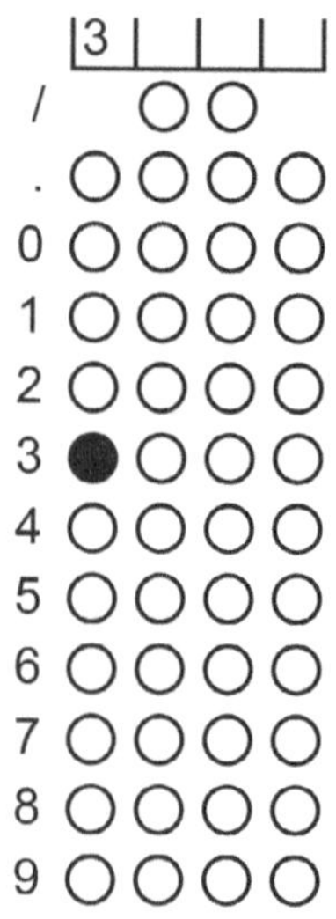

Figure 2

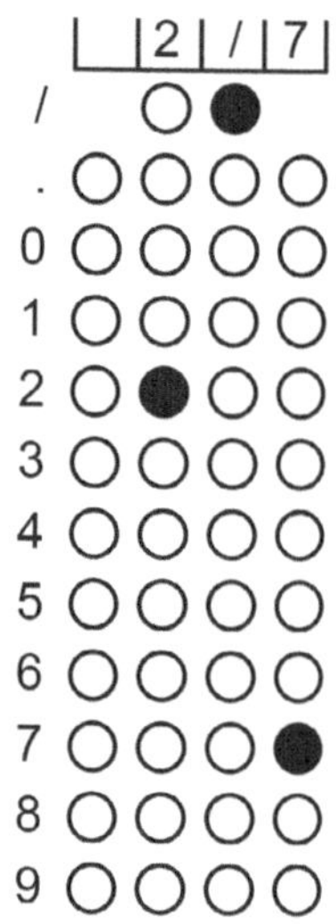

Figure 3

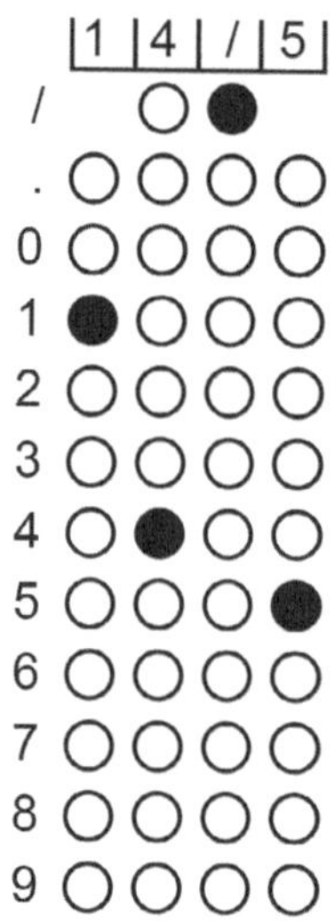

Figure 4

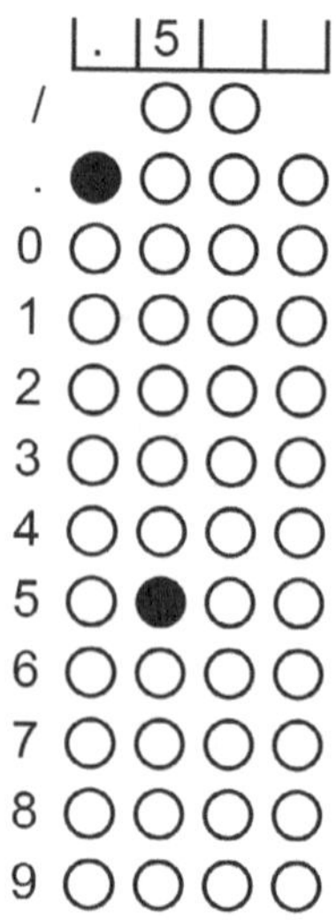

Figure 5

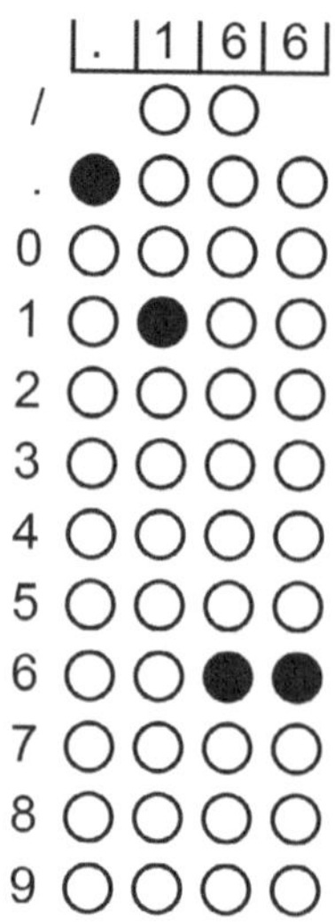

Name ______________________ Date ______________ Class ______________

Use linear equations in one variable to solve problems in a variety of contexts.

SAMPLE MULTIPLE CHOICE

An airline charges its passengers for each piece of checked baggage. The base charge is \$30 per piece. There is a surcharge of \$1.75 for each pound p that a bag weighs over 50 pounds. Jim paid \$54.50 to check a suitcase. The equation $54.50 = 30 + 1.75p$ models the number of pounds that his suitcase exceeded 50 pounds in weight. What was the weight, in pounds, of Jim's suitcase?

A) 70

B) 68

C) 66

D) 64

Isolate the variable p to solve for the number of pounds over 50 pounds.

$$54.50 = 30 + 1.75p$$
$$24.50 = 1.75p$$
$$\frac{24.50}{1.75} = p$$
$$14 = p$$

Add to find the total weight:

$$14 + 50 = 64$$

So, the bag weighed 64 pounds.

The correct answer is D. A ○ B ○ C ○ D ●

1

A moving company charges \$425 for the first 4 hours of loading items, plus a rate of \$65 per hour for any additional time needed. Crystal paid a loading fee of \$620. The equation $425 + 65h = 620$ models the number of extra hours h spent loading. How many hours did it take to load her items?

A) 3 C) 7

B) 5 D) 9

2

Rose opened a savings account with \$100. She deposited the same amount to the account each month. After 6 months, there is \$1,000 in her account. The equation $100 + 6d = 1{,}000$ models the amount d she deposited each month. How much money did she add to the account each month? Assume that the account earns simple interest accrued once annually on the date the account was opened.

A) \$150 C) \$130

B) \$140 D) \$120

3

Three books are stacked on a desk. The top of the pile of books is $32\frac{3}{4}$ inches above the floor and each of the books is $1\frac{1}{4}$ inches thick. The equation $h + 1\frac{1}{4} \bullet 3 = 32\frac{3}{4}$ models the height h of the desk. What is the height, in inches, of the desk?

A) $36\frac{1}{2}$ C) $30\frac{1}{4}$

B) 32 D) 29

4

An electrician charges a fee of \$150 plus \$70 per hour. The total bill for a job is \$255. The equation $150 + 70h = 255$ models the number of hours h spent on the job. How many hours did the electrician work on this job?

A) 1.5 C) 2.5

B) 2 D) 3

Name ______________________ Date ______________ Class______________

SAMPLE GRID-IN

$$35 = 0.75t + 8$$

The equation above models the number of tickets t that a student purchases at the state fair. Admission is \$8, and tickets to play games are \$0.75 each. The student spends \$35 total. How many tickets does the student purchase?

Isolate the variable t to solve for the number of tickets.

$$35 = 0.75t + 8$$
$$27 = 0.75t$$
$$\frac{27}{0.75} = t$$
$$36 = t$$

So, the student purchases 36 tickets.

Grid in 36.

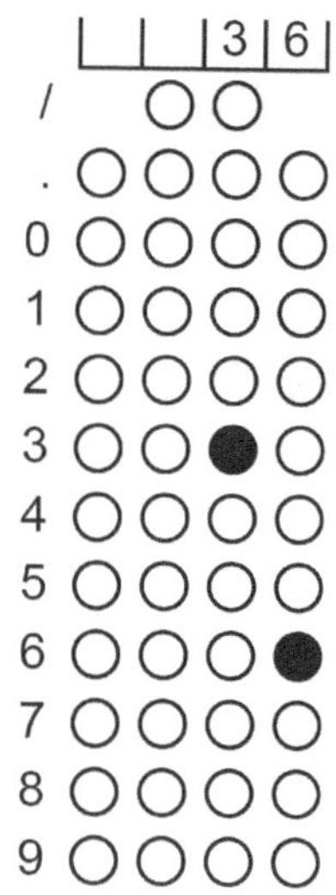

Time-Saving Tip:

Change 0.75 to a fraction before solving the equation. Since 3 is a factor of 27, multiplying 27 by $\frac{4}{3}$ can be done mentally; no calculator is needed.

$$35 = \frac{3}{4}t + 8$$
$$27 = \frac{3}{4}t$$
$$\frac{4}{3} \cdot 27 = t$$
$$36 = t$$

5

Deanna paid \$18 for a taxicab ride. The equation modeling the number of miles m she rode is $4.50 + 2.25m = 18$. How many miles did Deanna travel in the taxicab?

6

$$500 = 200 + 75x$$

The equation above models the number of hours x that a band played at a party where the total charge was \$500. How many hours did the party last?

7

The equation $1{,}500 + 750m = 18{,}750$ represents the number of months m that Jon has been paying rent at his apartment. How many months has Jon been renting the apartment?

8

The owners of an apple orchard invite the public to come and pick their own apples. The price for the apples is \$0.75 per pound. Jenna paid a total of \$14 for the bag of apples she picked and a container of apple butter priced at \$3.80. The equation $14 = 0.75p + 3.80$ models the number of pounds of apples p she picked. How many pounds of apples did Jenna pick? Assume that no sales tax was charged.

9

$$7d + 46 = 228$$

The equation above models the number of days d that it takes a squirrel to eat the remainder of the acorns it had collected and stored in a hole in a decayed tree. How many days did it take the squirrel to eat all of the remaining acorns in this location?

Name ______________________ Date ______________ Class ______________

Use linear equations in one variable to solve problems in a variety of contexts.

ANSWER SHEET

1. A B C D
   ○ ○ ○ ○

2. A B C D
   ○ ○ ○ ○

3. A B C D
   ○ ○ ○ ○

4. A B C D
   ○ ○ ○ ○

5. | | | | |
   / ○ ○
   . ○ ○ ○ ○
   0 ○ ○ ○ ○
   1 ○ ○ ○ ○
   2 ○ ○ ○ ○
   3 ○ ○ ○ ○
   4 ○ ○ ○ ○
   5 ○ ○ ○ ○
   6 ○ ○ ○ ○
   7 ○ ○ ○ ○
   8 ○ ○ ○ ○
   9 ○ ○ ○ ○

6. | | | | |
   / ○ ○
   . ○ ○ ○ ○
   0 ○ ○ ○ ○
   1 ○ ○ ○ ○
   2 ○ ○ ○ ○
   3 ○ ○ ○ ○
   4 ○ ○ ○ ○
   5 ○ ○ ○ ○
   6 ○ ○ ○ ○
   7 ○ ○ ○ ○
   8 ○ ○ ○ ○
   9 ○ ○ ○ ○

7. | | | | |
   / ○ ○
   . ○ ○ ○ ○
   0 ○ ○ ○ ○
   1 ○ ○ ○ ○
   2 ○ ○ ○ ○
   3 ○ ○ ○ ○
   4 ○ ○ ○ ○
   5 ○ ○ ○ ○
   6 ○ ○ ○ ○
   7 ○ ○ ○ ○
   8 ○ ○ ○ ○
   9 ○ ○ ○ ○

8. | | | | |
   / ○ ○
   . ○ ○ ○ ○
   0 ○ ○ ○ ○
   1 ○ ○ ○ ○
   2 ○ ○ ○ ○
   3 ○ ○ ○ ○
   4 ○ ○ ○ ○
   5 ○ ○ ○ ○
   6 ○ ○ ○ ○
   7 ○ ○ ○ ○
   8 ○ ○ ○ ○
   9 ○ ○ ○ ○

9. | | | | |
   / ○ ○
   . ○ ○ ○ ○
   0 ○ ○ ○ ○
   1 ○ ○ ○ ○
   2 ○ ○ ○ ○
   3 ○ ○ ○ ○
   4 ○ ○ ○ ○
   5 ○ ○ ○ ○
   6 ○ ○ ○ ○
   7 ○ ○ ○ ○
   8 ○ ○ ○ ○
   9 ○ ○ ○ ○

Name ______________________ Date ____________ Class ____________

Model a real-world situation with a linear equation in one variable, solve the equation, and interpret the solution.

SAMPLE MULTIPLE CHOICE

A hotel charges $6,400 for an 80-person reception. The cost includes $1,000 for the room in addition to the cost of food. How much did the hotel charge per person for the cost of food?

A) $92.50

B) $80

C) $70

D) $67.50

Let x be the cost of food per person. Represent the situation with a verbal model.

Total cost		Room rental		Cost of food per person		Number of people
$6,400	=	$1,000	+	x	•	80

Write an equation and solve for x.

$$6,400 = 1,000 + x(80)$$
$$6,400 = 1,000 + 80x$$
$$5,400 = 80x$$
$$67.50 = x$$

The correct answer is D. A ○ B ○ C ○ D ●

1

Bruce weighs 190 pounds. He wants to lose weight until he weighs 165 pounds. He plans to lose 1.5 pounds per week for x weeks. Which equation represents this situation?

A) $165 = 190 - 1.5x$

B) $165 - 1.5x = 190$

C) $165 = 1.5x - 190$

D) $1.5x - 165 = 190$

2

A new cell phone contract with unlimited talk and text costs $39.95 per month in addition to the cost of a new phone. The new phone costs $450, and the entire contract costs $1,408.80. Which equation represents the number of months n covered by the contract?

A) $39.95n - 450 = 1,408.8$

B) $450 + 39.95n = 1,408.8$

C) $450n + 39.95 = 1,408.8$

D) $450 = 1,408.8n + 39.95$

3

The maximum permissible gross weight of a vehicle allowed to cross a small bridge is 20 tons. A truck weighs 4 tons when empty. The driver, who weighs 200 pounds, must determine the greatest number of 78-pound bags of cement his truck can carry without exceeding the weight limit. Since 1 ton = 2,000 pounds, he solves the equation $78b + 8,200 = 40,000$. What does the result $b \approx 407.69$ mean in this situation?

A) He should have 408 bags loaded.

B) He should have 407 bags loaded.

C) He should take a different route.

D) A smaller person should drive.

4

Mercedes currently has 32 gemstones in her collection. Every month, she adds the same number of gemstones g to the collection. Six months ago, there were 14 gemstones in her collection. Which equation models this situation?

A) $6g + 32 = 14$

B) $14 - 6g = 32$

C) $32 = 14 + 6g$

D) $6g - 14 = 32$

Name ________________________ Date ______________ Class ______________

SAMPLE GRID-IN

Marissa works at a manufacturing company. She is paid a weekly salary of \$640 plus \$24 for every hour h of overtime worked beyond 40 hours. Last week, she earned \$724. How many hours of overtime did Marissa work last week?

Represent the situation with a verbal model.

Weekly salary \$640	+	Overtime hourly pay rate \$24	•	Hours of overtime h	=	Total earnings \$724

Write an equation and solve for h.

$$640 + 24h = 724$$
$$24h = 84$$
$$h = \frac{84}{24}$$
$$h = 3.5$$

So, Marissa worked 3.5 hours of overtime last week.

Grid in 3.5.

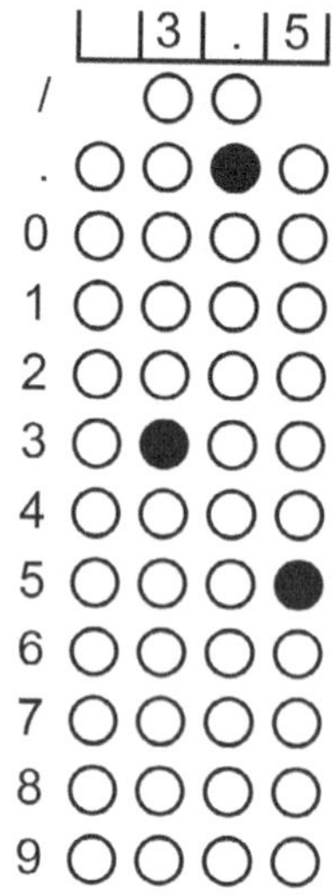

5

Kwasi is buying a new car priced at \$18,700. He pays \$1,600 now and takes a 60-month interest-free loan to pay the remaining amount. How much will his monthly payment be for the car?

6

A digital music subscription charges a monthly access fee of \$5 to download music at \$0.49 per song. Last month, Sarah spent \$28.03 on music. How many songs did she download?

7

Membership at a local gym costs \$20 per month. Members can work with personal trainers for an additional fee per session. Jamal spent \$240 his first month and met with a personal trainer 4 times. How much did each session with a personal trainer cost?

8

Roberta eats a cup of yogurt and bowl of soup every day for lunch. If her favorite yogurt costs \$2.50 per cup and her favorite soup costs \$3.65 per bowl, how many lunches can she buy for \$50?

9

While on vacation, Phoebe rents a motorized scooter for a base fee plus \$0.25 for every mile she rides it. When she returns the scooter, her bill is \$25. How much was the base fee if she rode the scooter 32 miles?

10

Tomas pays a monthly fee to rent a post office box. He paid \$6 to have the lock mechanism replaced when he started the rental. After 18 months, he had paid a total of \$95.10. How much is the monthly fee, in dollars?

Name ______________________ Date ______________ Class ______________

Model a real-world situation with a linear equation in one variable, solve the equation, and interpret the solution.

ANSWER SHEET

1. A B C D

2. A B C D

3. A B C D

4. A B C D

5. Grid-in: / . 0 1 2 3 4 5 6 7 8 9

6. Grid-in: / . 0 1 2 3 4 5 6 7 8 9

7. Grid-in: / . 0 1 2 3 4 5 6 7 8 9

8. Grid-in: / . 0 1 2 3 4 5 6 7 8 9

9. Grid-in: / . 0 1 2 3 4 5 6 7 8 9

10. Grid-in: / . 0 1 2 3 4 5 6 7 8 9

Name ______________________ Date ______________ Class ______________

Use the structure of a linear equation in one variable to solve the equation efficiently.

SAMPLE MULTIPLE CHOICE

What value of x satisfies the equation $\frac{x+1}{12}+\frac{5}{6}=-\frac{2}{3}$?

A) −22
B) −19
C) −8
D) −3

Notice that the equation contains fractions with denominators 12, 6, and 3. The least common multiple of these three numbers is 12. Multiply both sides of the equation by 12 to produce an equivalent equation that no longer involves any fractions. Solve the resulting equation for x.

$$\frac{x+1}{12}+\frac{5}{6}=-\frac{2}{3}$$
$$12\left(\frac{x+1}{12}+\frac{5}{6}\right)=12\left(-\frac{2}{3}\right)$$
$$(x+1)+2(5)=4(-2)$$
$$x+1+10=-8$$
$$x=-19$$

The correct answer is B. A ○ B ● C ○ D ○

1

What value of m satisfies the equation $-\frac{1}{2}(25m-6)=10m-2$?

A) $-\frac{2}{45}$
B) $\frac{1}{45}$
C) $\frac{2}{9}$
D) $\frac{5}{9}$

2

The equation $300+1{,}492d=60{,}000$ models the number of days d it will take for the number of bees in a bee colony to reach 60,000. The keepers plan to split the colony after the hive reaches a mature bee count of 60,000. Assuming that no bees die in the days it takes to reach 60,000, find the approximate number of days the beekeepers have to wait to split the hive.

A) 40
B) 70
C) 200
D) 600

3

What value of x satisfies the equation $0.1875+0.875x=0.75x-0.5$?

A) −5.5
B) −2.2
C) 2.2
D) 2.5

4

If $10x+64=8(9)$, what is the value of $0.3(5x+32)$?

A) 5.4
B) 7.2
C) 10.8
D) 21.6

5

The current population of a town is 35,000. It is projected to increase by 2,500 people per year. The expression $35{,}000+2{,}500n$ gives the population of the town after n years. If the town will be reclassified as a city when its population reaches 100,000 people, in how many years will that occur?

A) 2
B) 2.6
C) 20
D) 26

Name ____________________ Date ____________ Class ____________

SAMPLE GRID-IN

If $19d + 68$ is 12 less than 137, what is the value of $38d$?

Rewrite "12 less than 137" as $137 - 12 = 125$.

Set the expression equal to 125 and solve for $19d$.

$$19d + 68 = 125$$
$$19d = 125 - 68$$
$$19d = 57$$

Since $38d$ is two times $19d$,

$$38d = 2(19d)$$
$$= 2(57)$$
$$= 114$$

Grid in 114.

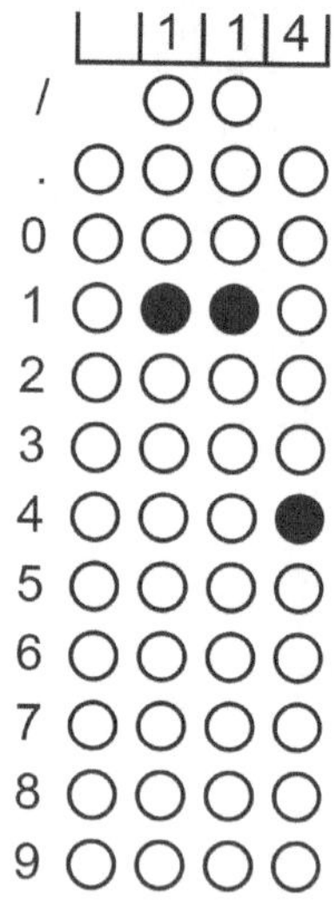

6

If $30c - 16$ is the difference of -97 and -99, what is $5c$?

7

The expression $-76 + 92a$ is equal to the square root of 2,704. What is the value of $23a$?

8

The cost of a class trip can be modeled by the expression $378 + 12s$, where s is the number of students on the trip. The school budget for the trip is \$2,898. If the school separates the students into groups of 6, how many groups of 6 students can go on the trip?

9

If $-15h - 26$ is equal to twice as much as 87, what is $-45h$?

10

Given $-41(-11 + p) + 33 - 3p = -38$, find the value of $p - 11$.

11

$$-4(8r + 18) - 200 = -32\left(-\frac{9}{4} - r\right) + 4$$

Given the equation above, find the value of the expression $-32r - 72$.

12

If $-3(12v + 1) - 36v + 64 = 72v - 17$, what is the value of $36v$?

13

$$-\frac{1}{2}(36n - 10) - 3(5n - 6) = -(n - 7)$$

Given the equation above, find the value of $16n$.

Name ______________________ Date ______________ Class ______________

Use the structure of a linear equation in one variable to solve the equation efficiently.

ANSWER SHEET

1. A B C D
2. A B C D
3. A B C D
4. A B C D
5. A B C D

6. / . 0 1 2 3 4 5 6 7 8 9

7. / . 0 1 2 3 4 5 6 7 8 9

8. / . 0 1 2 3 4 5 6 7 8 9

9. / . 0 1 2 3 4 5 6 7 8 9

10. / . 0 1 2 3 4 5 6 7 8 9

11. / . 0 1 2 3 4 5 6 7 8 9

12. / . 0 1 2 3 4 5 6 7 8 9

13. / . 0 1 2 3 4 5 6 7 8 9

Name ______________________ Date ____________ Class ______________

Interpret a linear equation in one variable in context, and define the conditions affecting the number of solutions.

SAMPLE MULTIPLE CHOICE

$$-15+9(10-2x)=-3(6x)+\_\_\_\_\_$$

Fill in the missing term so that the equation has infinitely many solutions.

A) 90

B) 75

C) $9x$

D) $-18x$

For there to be infinitely many solutions, the two sides of the equation must be identical.

Simplify both sides of the equation.

$$-15+9(10-2x)=-3(6x)+\_\_\_\_\_$$
$$-15+90-18x=-18x+\_\_\_\_\_$$
$$75-18x=-18x+\_\_\_\_\_$$

There is no need to simplify any further; it can be seen that the missing term is 75.

The correct answer is B. A ○ B ● C ○ D ○

1

$$75+3(\_\_\_+18)=14x+7(4x+9)$$

Which term, when inserted at the blank line, would result in an equation that has no solutions?

A) -43

B) 14

C) $14x$

D) $42x$

2

$$(x+4)-4(-5-x)=\frac{1}{15}(75x)-2$$

How many solutions does the equation above have?

A) Infinitely many solutions

B) A unique solution: $x=-4.1$

C) A unique solution: $x=45$

D) No solutions

3

The expression $45+0.05t$ gives the total charges per month, in dollars, for a cellular plan where t is the total number of text messages sent during the month. Which of the following could be the total amount for a monthly bill?

A) \$43

B) \$52.60

C) \$60.24

D) \$77.61

4

$$26.2=6.5h$$

The equation above gives the number of hours h it takes for a runner to finish a 26.2-mile marathon. What is the runner's speed, in miles per hour?

A) 0.25

B) 4.03

C) 6.5

D) 8.06

5

$$16-h-4^2=-9(h+4)-2(-18-4h)$$

How many solutions does the equation above have?

A) No solutions

B) Infinitely many solutions

C) A unique solution: $h=18$

D) A unique solution: $h=-2$

6

To install new recessed lighting in a home, an electrician charges a trip fee plus a set amount per light. She uses the expression $25+275x$ to calculate the cost to install x new lights. Which of the following could be the total amount she charges a homeowner for a job?

A) \$3,050

B) \$2,335

C) \$1,730

D) \$275

Name ____________________ Date ____________ Class ____________

SAMPLE GRID-IN

$$P = 2.4t + 314$$

The population *P*, in millions, of the United States is modeled by the equation shown above where *t* is the number of years since 2012. In what year does the model indicate that the population of the United States reached 326 million people?

For $P = 326$ (million), the equation becomes $326 = 2.4t + 314$. Solve this equation for *t*:

$$326 = 2.4t + 314$$
$$12 = 2.4t$$
$$5 = t$$

Add 5 years to the year 2012:

$$2012 + 5 = 2017$$

So, the model predicts that the U.S. population reached 326 million in 2017.

Grid in 2017.

Time-Saving Tip: The coefficient of the variable *t* means that every year the population increased by 2.4 million. Recognizing that the increase is $326 - 314 = 12$ (million), dividing 12 by 2.4 gives $t = 5$ years: $2012 + 5$, or 2017.

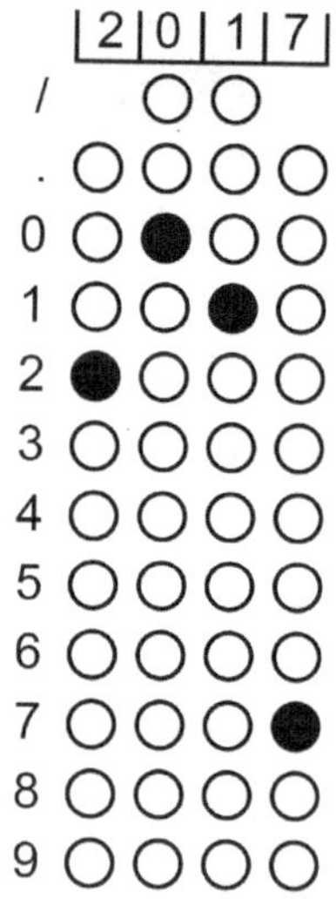

7

$$11y - 5(4 - y) = 3(y - 17) + \_\_\_$$

For the equation above, give the value needed for the equation to have the unique solution $y = -2$.

8

$$12(8c - 1) + \_\_\_ = 7(9c) + 11(3c + 2)$$

What constant is needed on the left side for the equation to have infinitely many solutions?

9

A chimney-cleaning company charges a trip fee plus an hourly rate for their service. The equation $30(2x + 1) = 420$ models the number of hours *x* spent on a recent job. What is the hourly rate, in dollars, charged by the company?

10

$$6(4 - z) + 2(3z + 10) = 7(z + \_\_\_) + z$$

For the equation above, give the value needed for the equation to have the unique solution $z = -5$.

11

$$60x + 738 = 5{,}238$$

The monthly cost to produce *x* chairs at a factory is modeled by the equation above. What are the fixed costs for operating the factory?

12

The equation $84 - 2.8t = 42$ models the amount of time *t*, in hours, it takes to pump half of the oil (in millions of gallons) from an oil tanker. What is the rate, in millions of gallons per hour, at which the pump removes the oil?

13

$$5(9w - 2) - (15w + 2) = 8$$

What value of *w* is a unique solution to this equation?

14

$$8v - (-5v - 6) = 9v + 1 + 4v + \_\_\_$$

In the equation above, what value added to the right side will create an equation with infinitely many solutions?

Name ______________________ Date ______________ Class ______________

Interpret a linear equation in one variable in context, and define the conditions affecting the number of solutions.

ANSWER SHEET

1. A B C D ○○○○
2. A B C D ○○○○
3. A B C D ○○○○
4. A B C D ○○○○
5. A B C D ○○○○
6. A B C D ○○○○

7. (grid-in: / ○○; . ○○○○; 0–9 ○○○○)

8. (grid-in: / ○○; . ○○○○; 0–9 ○○○○)

9. (grid-in: / ○○; . ○○○○; 0–9 ○○○○)

10. (grid-in: / ○○; . ○○○○; 0–9 ○○○○)

11. (grid-in: / ○○; . ○○○○; 0–9 ○○○○)

12. (grid-in: / ○○; . ○○○○; 0–9 ○○○○)

13. (grid-in: / ○○; . ○○○○; 0–9 ○○○○)

14. (grid-in: / ○○; . ○○○○; 0–9 ○○○○)

Name ______________________ Date ____________ Class ____________

Proficiently solve a linear equation in one variable.

SAMPLE MULTIPLE CHOICE	
If $a(x+2)=9$ and $a=\frac{3}{2}$, what is the value of x? A) 3 B) 4 C) 6 D) 7	Substitute $\frac{3}{2}$ for a to get $\frac{3}{2}(x+2)=9$. Then solve for x: $\frac{2}{3}\bullet\frac{3}{2}(x+2)=\frac{2}{3}\bullet 9$ $x+2=6$ $x+2-2=6-2$ $x=4$ The correct answer is B. A B C D ○●○○

1

Solve the equation
$25.25n-84=42-37.75n$ for n.

A) -2

B) 2

C) 3

D) 4

2

$$-3\left(\frac{y}{6}-\frac{5}{3}\right)=\frac{1}{4}(2y+8)$$

Solve the equation above for y.

A) -3

B) -1

C) 3

D) 5

3

Determine the value of b if
$4.8(b+3)=3.2(b-7)$.

A) -23

B) -2.3

C) 2.3

D) 23

4

What is the value of w if
$2(3w-5)-22=-6(7+w)$?

A) $-\frac{5}{6}$

B) 1.2

C) 3

D) 5

5

Find the value of s if $\frac{s}{20}+\frac{3}{4}=\frac{6}{5}$.

A) -3

B) 3

C) 5

D) 9

6

If $\frac{4-2m}{3}=\frac{12}{k^2}+\frac{5m}{k+2}$ and $k=4$, what is the value of m?

A) $-\frac{7}{2}$

B) $-\frac{2}{7}$

C) $\frac{7}{18}$

D) $\frac{18}{7}$

Name ______________________ Date ____________ Class ____________

SAMPLE GRID-IN	
Given the equation $5y-9(2-2y)=4y+1$, solve for y.	Begin by using the Distributive Property on the left side and then combine like terms.

$$5y-9(2-2y)=4y+1$$
$$5y-18+18y=4y+1$$
$$23y-18=4y+1$$

Next, add or subtract terms to isolate the variable on one side of the equation. Finally, solve for y.

$$23y-18=4y+1$$
$$19y=19$$
$$y=1$$

The correct answer is 1.

Grid in 1.

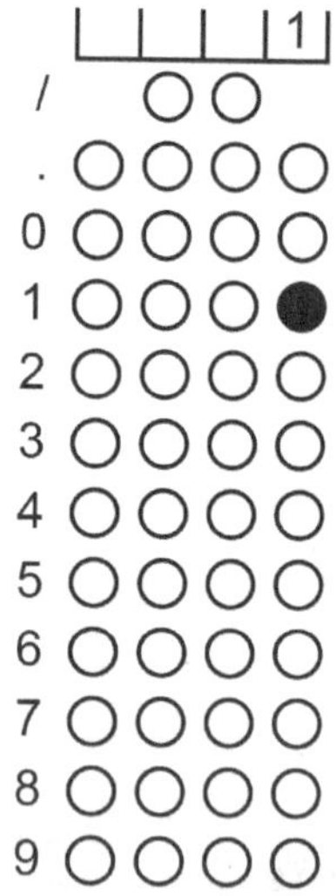

7

Find the value of x in the equation $57.5x-56.2=39.2x+17$.

8

Solve for x in the equation below.

$$\frac{5}{3}(x-9)=-\frac{3}{5}(x-9)$$

9

Given the equation

$$12\left(\frac{3}{4}u+\frac{2}{3}\right)=15\left(\frac{8}{5}-\frac{7}{3}u\right),$$

what is the value of u?

10

Determine the value of n if $6(25n-7)=8(12n+15)$.

11

If $\frac{x+1}{0.7x+21}=\frac{3}{0.1x+3}$, what is the value of x?

12

$$\frac{5}{2}x+\frac{1}{4}=4x-\frac{1}{4}$$

Solve for x in the equation above.

13

Find the value of m in the equation $\frac{2m+1}{6}+\frac{3m}{8}=\frac{3m-7}{4}$.

14

If $6x+2=2a+9-3x$ and $a=10$, what is the value of x?

Name ______________________ Date ______________ Class ______________

Proficiently solve a linear equation in one variable.

ANSWER SHEET

1. A B C D
2. A B C D
3. A B C D
4. A B C D
5. A B C D
6. A B C D
7. / . 0 1 2 3 4 5 6 7 8 9
8. / . 0 1 2 3 4 5 6 7 8 9
9. / . 0 1 2 3 4 5 6 7 8 9
10. / . 0 1 2 3 4 5 6 7 8 9
11. / . 0 1 2 3 4 5 6 7 8 9
12. / . 0 1 2 3 4 5 6 7 8 9
13. / . 0 1 2 3 4 5 6 7 8 9
14. / . 0 1 2 3 4 5 6 7 8 9

Name ______________________ Date ____________ Class ____________

Write and use linear functions to solve problems representing real-world situations.

SAMPLE MULTIPLE CHOICE

John is painting signs for the garden club. He has already painted 12 signs. He can paint 2 signs in 3 hours. At this rate, how many signs will he have painted in all after working for 4.5 more hours?

A) 14

B) 14.5

C) 15

D) 15.5

Write a function f to represent the situation. Let t represent the number of hours that John works.

$$f(t) = \frac{2}{3}t + 12$$

Substitute and solve.

$$f(t) = \frac{2}{3}t + 12$$

$$f(t) = \frac{2}{3}(4.5) + 12$$

$$f(t) = 3 + 12$$

$$f(t) = 15$$

John will have painted 15 signs.

The correct answer is C. A ○ B ○ C ● D ○

1

Hayden has carved 5 inches of a wooden chain. He can carve 2 inches per week. After 3 more weeks of carving, how many inches long will the wooden chain be?

A) 6

B) 7

C) 9

D) 11

2

Katie is knitting scarves for charity. She has 21 inches of a scarf completed. She can knit an additional 3 inches each day. How many additional days will it take her to complete a 48-inch scarf?

A) 4

B) 9

C) 12

D) 16

3

Human hair grows approximately 1.25 cm per month. Tim's hair is currently 8 cm in length. At this rate, how many centimeters long will his hair be in 6 months if he does not get a haircut?

A) 9.25

B) 10

C) 15.5

D) 16.75

4

There are 4 inches of snow on the ground when a storm begins. The storm brings snow at a rate of 2.5 inches per hour. If the storm lasts 4 hours, how many inches of snow will be on the ground when it ends?

A) 10

B) 12

C) 14

D) 16

Name ______________________ Date ______________ Class______________

SAMPLE GRID-IN

$$f(s) = 3{,}500 - 190s$$

The function above models the altitude of a high-speed skier skiing at a steady rate of 190 feet per second downhill from an altitude of 3,500 feet. What is the altitude of the skier after 15 seconds?

Evaluate the function when $s = 15$.

$$f(s) = 3{,}500 - 190s$$
$$f(15) = 3{,}500 - 190(15)$$
$$= 3{,}500 - 2{,}850$$
$$= 650$$

So, the altitude of the skier is 650 feet after 15 seconds.

Grid in 650.

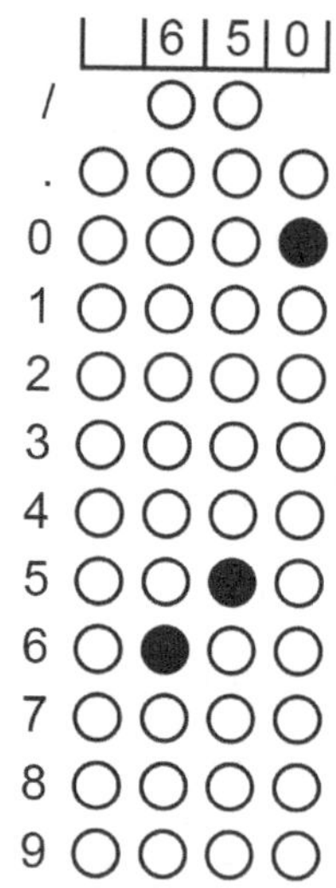

5

The function $f(h) = 65h + 300$ represents the cost of an emergency plumbing repair, where h is the number of hours the plumber takes to make the repair. Antoine had several pipes burst in cold weather and paid a plumber $625 for an emergency repair. How many hours did the plumber take to make the repair?

6

Workers on a farm have cleared 2 acres of land. If they can clear land at a rate of two-thirds of an acre per week, how many total acres will the workers have cleared after working for 6 more weeks?

7

In 2018, a small town had 34 miles of utility lines to service. Each year, the town adds 0.4 mile of utility lines. Assuming the build rate will remain constant, in what year will the town have a total of 40 miles of utility lines?

8

Michaela feeds her cat dry cat food. A full bag of food contains 48 ounces of meat. How many ounces of meat does her cat receive each day if the bag is one-third full and this amount is enough food for 4 days?

9

A book donation box contains 120 books. It had 48 books 6 days ago. Assuming the fill rate was constant, how many more days will it take to reach the maximum capacity of 300 books?

10

An elevator has an “up” speed of 12 meters per second. The elevator is called to the top floor from its location on the fourth floor, 14 meters from the ground level. It takes 13 seconds for the elevator to reach the top floor. What is the height of the top floor above the ground level?

Name ______________________ Date ______________ Class ______________

Write and use linear functions to solve problems representing real-world situations.

ANSWER SHEET

1. A B C D

2. A B C D

3. A B C D

4. A B C D

5. Grid-in: / . 0 1 2 3 4 5 6 7 8 9

6. Grid-in: / . 0 1 2 3 4 5 6 7 8 9

7. Grid-in: / . 0 1 2 3 4 5 6 7 8 9

8. Grid-in: / . 0 1 2 3 4 5 6 7 8 9

9. Grid-in: / . 0 1 2 3 4 5 6 7 8 9

10. Grid-in: / . 0 1 2 3 4 5 6 7 8 9

Name ______________________ Date ______________ Class ______________

Determine a linear function that models a relationship between two quantities.

SAMPLE MULTIPLE CHOICE

At the end of 2014, a county had 64 miles of paved bike trails. At the end of 2018, the same county had 72 miles of paved bike trails. Assuming that new bike trails were paved at a constant rate, which function models the relationship between the number of miles of paved bike trails and the year x?

A) $f(x) = 2x - 3{,}964$

B) $f(x) = 2{,}014 + 2x$

C) $f(x) = 1{,}768 + 4x$

D) $f(x) = 3{,}964 - 2x$

Use the given information to identify two points. Then find the slope between them.

$$(2014,\ 64) \text{ and } (2018,\ 72)$$

$$m = \frac{y_2 - y_1}{x_2 - x_1} = \frac{72 - 64}{2018 - 2014} = \frac{8}{4} = 2$$

Substitute 2 for m in $f(x) = mx + b$. Use the point $(2014, 64)$ to find b.

$$f(x) = mx + b$$
$$64 = 2(2014) + b$$
$$64 = 4{,}028 + b$$
$$-3{,}964 = b$$

So, the correct function is $f(x) = 2x - 3{,}964$.

The correct answer is A. A ● B ○ C ○ D ○

1

In 2006, a town had 4,545 residents. The same town had 4,865 residents in 2016. Assuming the population grew at a constant rate, which function models the relationship between the population of the town and the year x?

A) $f(x) = 32x - 4{,}545$

B) $f(x) = 32x + 2{,}006$

C) $f(x) = 32x - 59{,}647$

D) $f(x) = 32x - 4{,}865$

2

Two days after it was filled, 190 gumballs remained in a gumball machine. It still held 154 gumballs three days later. If gumballs are bought at a constant rate, which function models the relationship between the number of gumballs and the number of days x since it was filled?

A) $f(x) = -12x - 2{,}468$

B) $f(x) = 12x - 3$

C) $f(x) = 2x - 190$

D) $f(x) = -12x + 214$

3

A snowstorm began at 11:30 A.M. and snowed continuously until 7:30 P.M. During that time, 9 inches of snow fell. Assuming the snow fell at a steady rate, which function models the relationship between the inches of snow and the number of hours x since the storm began?

A) $f(x) = 1.125x$

B) $f(x) = 8x$

C) $f(x) = 9 - 1.125x$

D) $f(x) = \frac{8}{9}x$

4

A marathon runner reaches the eighth mile in 92 minutes and the eighteenth mile after 207 minutes. Assuming the runner maintains a constant pace, which function models the relationship between the distance run and the time t, in minutes, since the start of the marathon?

A) $f(t) = \frac{2}{23}t$

B) $f(t) = 11.5t$

C) $f(t) = 26 - t$

D) $f(t) = 8 + 11.5t$

Name ______________________________ Date ______________ Class______________

SAMPLE GRID-IN

An airplane is descending at a steady rate while approaching an airport for landing. Five minutes after beginning its descent, the plane is at an altitude of 16,500 feet. Ten minutes later, the altitude of the plane is 11,250 feet. How many minutes total since the plane began its descent will it take for the plane to reach an altitude of 750 feet?

Let x be the number of minutes since the plane began its decent and then $f(x)$ is the altitude of the plane. Use the points (5, 16500) and (15, 11250) to find the slope of the line between them.

$$m = \frac{16,500 - 11,250}{5 - 15} = -525$$

Substitute for m in $f(x) = mx + b$. Use the point (15, 11250) to find b.

$$f(x) = mx + b$$
$$11,250 = -525(15) + b$$
$$11,250 = -7,875 + b$$
$$19,125 = b$$

So the function is $f(x) = -525x + 19,125$.

Substitute 750 for $f(x)$ and solve for x.

$$750 = -525x + 19,125$$
$$525x = 18,375$$
$$x = \frac{18,375}{525} = 35$$

So, it will take the plane 35 minutes.

Grid in 35.

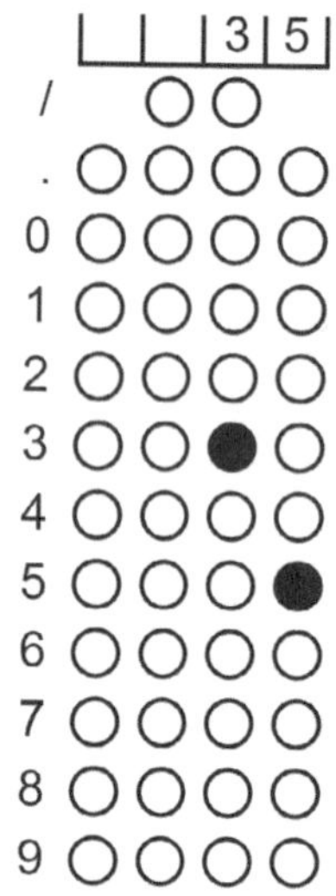

5

After the second snowstorm of the winter, a city has 15,370 pounds of road salt remaining. After the fifth snowstorm, the city has 7,786 pounds of road salt remaining. On average, how many pounds of road salt did the city use for each snowstorm?

6

During a heat wave, a small pond evaporates at constant rate. On day 5 of the heat wave, the pond holds 5,780 gallons of water. On day 14, the pond holds 5,168 gallons. If this heat wave continues, how many total days would it take for the pond to dry out completely?

7

Rick bought a truck to use for making deliveries at work. After 15 days, the truck's odometer reading was 2,408. After 40 days, the odometer reading was 5,958. His delivery route is the same every day. What was the odometer reading on the truck when he bought it?

8

After 3 months living in an apartment, the electric meter read 6,754 kilowatt-hours. After 8 months, the meter read 7,794 kilowatt-hours. What was the reading on the meter when the tenant moved in? Assume her electric usage was the same each month.

Name ______________________ Date ____________ Class ____________

Determine a linear function that models a relationship between two quantities.

ANSWER SHEET

1. A B C D

2. A B C D

3. A B C D

4. A B C D

5.
/
.
0
1
2
3
4
5
6
7
8
9

6.
/
.
0
1
2
3
4
5
6
7
8
9

7.
/
.
0
1
2
3
4
5
6
7
8
9

8.
/
.
0
1
2
3
4
5
6
7
8
9

Name ________________________ Date ______________ Class ______________

Calculate the inputs and/or outputs for a linear function for a real-world situation, and interpret the meaning.

SAMPLE MULTIPLE CHOICE

$$f(t) = -4t + 360$$

The function above models the location of a service elevator descending from the top of a 360-foot vertical shaft at a rate of 4 feet per second, where *t* is the number of seconds the elevator descends. Given an input of 40, what does the corresponding output represent? (Note: In this context, the domain is $0 \le t \le 90$.)

A) The distance the elevator descended

B) The distance the elevator still needs to descend

C) The time the elevator has descended

D) The time the elevator will take to descend

Begin by considering the slope, which represents the change in distance over time, or the rate of descent. The *y*-intercept represents the initial height, or the top of the shaft. Next, calculate $f(t)$ when $t = 40$.

$$f(t) = -4(40) + 360$$
$$f(t) = -160 + 360$$
$$f(t) = 200$$

Finally, interpret the meaning of this result.

When $t = 40$ seconds, the elevator is 200 feet above the base of the elevator shaft.

The correct answer is B. A ○ B ● C ○ D ○

Questions 1–4 refer to the following information.

In Virginia, the fine for exceeding the speed limit by *s* miles per hour (mph) in a residential area is assessed using the function $f(s) = 8s + 200$.

1

Suppose the output is 320. What does the corresponding input represent?

A) Driving 52.5 mph in a residential zone

B) The fine for speeding in a 15 mph zone

C) Exceeding the speed limit by 15 mph

D) Speeding in a 40 mph zone

2

What does the output represent when the input is 8?

A) A \$264 fine for speeding

B) A \$288 fine for speeding

C) The fine for driving 288 mph

D) The fine for driving 264 mph

3

What does the constant 200 represent?

A) A \$200 alternate ticket option

B) A \$200 addition to yearly car insurance costs

C) The maximum fine for a speeding ticket

D) An additional \$200 charge added to the fee per mile per hour over the speed limit

4

Why is an output of 200 unrealistic in this context?

A) A \$200-dollar ticket is not enough to discourage speeding.

B) A driver will not get a speeding ticket if they are 0 mph over the limit.

C) There is no such thing as a \$200 bill.

D) Most cars cannot reach 200 mph.

Name ______________________ Date ______________ Class______________

SAMPLE GRID-IN

$f(x) = 30x + 25$

The function above models the cost, in dollars, for loam and to have it delivered. The price is determined by adding a $25 delivery charge to the cost for x cubic yards of loam. If Tony's bill is $445, how many cubic yards of loam did he have delivered?

Since $f(x)$ represents the total cost (the bill), replace $f(x)$ with 445 and solve for x.

$$f(x) = 30x + 25$$
$$445 = 30x + 25$$
$$420 = 30x$$
$$14 = x$$

So, Tony had 14 cubic yards of loam delivered.

Grid in 14.

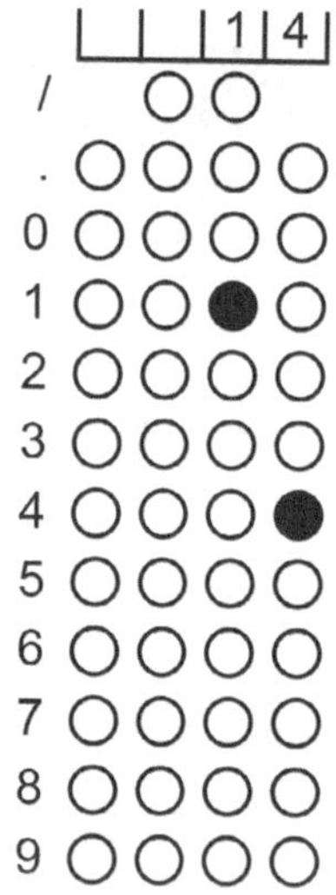

Questions 5–7 refer to the following information.

The continuing cost (in dollars) of buying and using a certain model of printer is determined by the cost of the printer and the cost of buying x toner cartridges for it. The function modeling the continuing cost is given below.

$$f(x) = 49.5x + 239$$

5

What is the cost, in dollars, of the printer?

6

What is the value of the output, in dollars, when the input is 4?

7

What is the value of the input when the output is $536?

8

Emergency repair costs on a refrigerant leak are determined by combining a service fee and the total hourly cost of the time needed to fix the leak. How much is the service fee if Elena pays $375 for 3 hours of work at $85 per hour?

9

Cathy purchased a new sofa for her apartment. She made a $250 down payment on a $1,120 sofa and is using 6 months of interest-free financing to pay off the remaining amount. How much must Cathy pay each month to finish paying for the sofa in 6 months?

10

A doggy daycare center charges $14 per day plus an initial fee of $80 for a health exam on the first day. Marti just paid her bill of $710. How many days did she have her dog at the center?

Name ______________________ Date ______________ Class ______________

Calculate the inputs and/or outputs for a linear function for a real-world situation, and interpret the meaning.

ANSWER SHEET

1. A B C D

2. A B C D

3. A B C D

4. A B C D

5.
/
.
0
1
2
3
4
5
6
7
8
9

6.
/
.
0
1
2
3
4
5
6
7
8
9

7.
/
.
0
1
2
3
4
5
6
7
8
9

8.
/
.
0
1
2
3
4
5
6
7
8
9

9.
/
.
0
1
2
3
4
5
6
7
8
9

10.
/
.
0
1
2
3
4
5
6
7
8
9

Name ________________ Date ________ Class ________

Connect various representations of linear functions by deriving one from the other.

SAMPLE MULTIPLE CHOICE

x	$f(x)$
0	2
2	8
4	14
6	20

Which function models the data given in the table above?

A) $f(x) = 2x + 3$

B) $f(x) = 3x + 2$

C) $f(x) = 3x + 3$

D) $f(x) = 2x + 2$

The general form of a linear equation is $f(x) = mx + b$. To find the value of b, look for a value in the table where $x = 0$:

$$f(0) = 2, \text{ so } b = 2.$$

To find m, substitute 2 for x and solve for m.

$$f(x) = mx + b$$
$$f(2) = m(2) + 2$$
$$8 = 2m + 2$$
$$6 = 2m$$
$$3 = m$$

Substitute for m.

$$f(x) = mx + 2$$
$$f(x) = 3x + 2$$

The correct answer is B. A ○ B ● C ○ D ○

1

Which function represents the data given in the table below?

x	$f(x)$
1	3
2	1
3	–1

A) $f(x) = 2x + 5$

B) $f(x) = 2x - 5$

C) $f(x) = -2x - 5$

D) $f(x) = -2x + 5$

2

What happens to the graph of the linear function $y = mx + b$ if the value of b is increased?

A) The graph becomes steeper.

B) The graph becomes less steep.

C) The graph is translated upward.

D) The graph is translated downward.

3

Which group includes three points that all satisfy the function below?

$$f(x) = \frac{x}{2} + 6$$

A) $(0, 6)$, $(2, 8)$, and $(4, 10)$

B) $(2, 7)$, $(4, 8)$, and $(6, 9)$

C) $(0, 8)$, $(2, 6)$, and $(4, 4)$

D) $(2, 6)$, $(4, 8)$, and $(4, 4)$

4

The points $(0, -4)$, $(2, 0)$, and $(4, 4)$ would all be on the graph of which of these functions?

A) $f(x) = -2x - 4$

B) $f(x) = 2x - 2$

C) $f(x) = 2x - 4$

D) $f(x) = -2x + 4$

Name ______________________ Date ______________ Class ______________

SAMPLE GRID-IN

For the function whose graph is shown below, what is the y-value that corresponds to an x-value of -7?

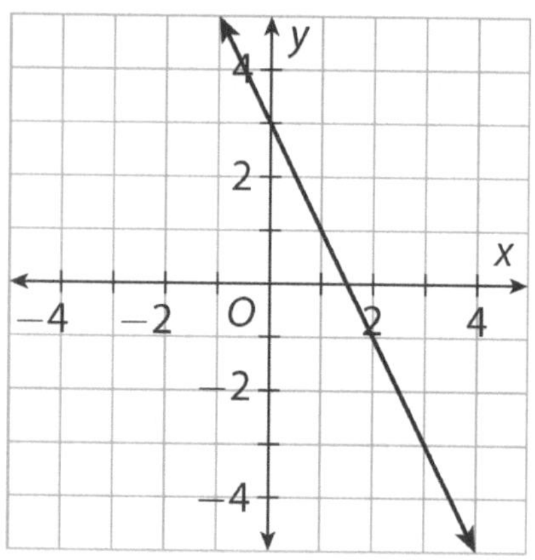

Since the x-axis does not show $x = -7$, write the equation of the line in the form $y = mx + b$.

From the graph, it can be seen that the slope m is -2 and the y-intercept b is 3. So, the equation of the line is $y = -2x + 3$.

Use the equation to find the value of y when $x = -7$.

$$y = -2(-7) + 3$$

$$y = 14 + 3$$

$$y = 17$$

The y-value is 17 when $x = -7$.

Grid in 17.

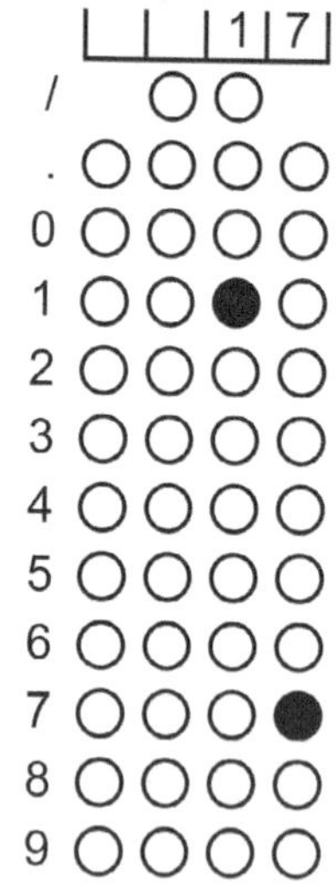

Questions 5–7 refer to the following information.

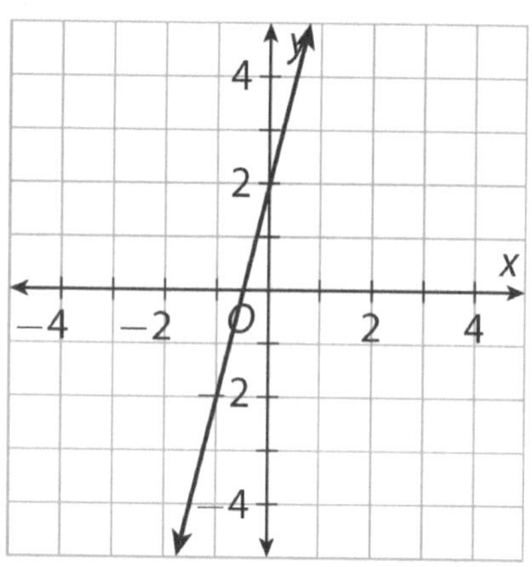

The equation of the linear function graphed above can be written in the form $y = mx + b$.

5

What is the value of m for the function shown in the graph?

6

What is the value of b for the function shown in the graph?

7

What is the x-value that corresponds to a y-value of 16?

8

The table below shows four ordered pairs (x, y) that satisfy a linear function. What is the y-intercept of the graph of the function?

x	−3	1	7	10
y	−4.5	7.5	25.5	34.5

9

The table below shows four ordered pairs (x, y) that satisfy a linear function. What is the x-intercept of the graph of the function?

x	−4	−1	0	2
y	13.75	6.25	3.75	−1.25

Name ______________________ Date ____________ Class ____________

Connect various representations of linear functions by deriving one from the other.

ANSWER SHEET

1. A B C D
○ ○ ○ ○

2. A B C D
○ ○ ○ ○

3. A B C D
○ ○ ○ ○

4. A B C D
○ ○ ○ ○

5. [| | | |]
/ ○ ○
. ○ ○ ○ ○
0 ○ ○ ○ ○
1 ○ ○ ○ ○
2 ○ ○ ○ ○
3 ○ ○ ○ ○
4 ○ ○ ○ ○
5 ○ ○ ○ ○
6 ○ ○ ○ ○
7 ○ ○ ○ ○
8 ○ ○ ○ ○
9 ○ ○ ○ ○

6. [| | | |]
/ ○ ○
. ○ ○ ○ ○
0 ○ ○ ○ ○
1 ○ ○ ○ ○
2 ○ ○ ○ ○
3 ○ ○ ○ ○
4 ○ ○ ○ ○
5 ○ ○ ○ ○
6 ○ ○ ○ ○
7 ○ ○ ○ ○
8 ○ ○ ○ ○
9 ○ ○ ○ ○

7. [| | | |]
/ ○ ○
. ○ ○ ○ ○
0 ○ ○ ○ ○
1 ○ ○ ○ ○
2 ○ ○ ○ ○
3 ○ ○ ○ ○
4 ○ ○ ○ ○
5 ○ ○ ○ ○
6 ○ ○ ○ ○
7 ○ ○ ○ ○
8 ○ ○ ○ ○
9 ○ ○ ○ ○

8. [| | | |]
/ ○ ○
. ○ ○ ○ ○
0 ○ ○ ○ ○
1 ○ ○ ○ ○
2 ○ ○ ○ ○
3 ○ ○ ○ ○
4 ○ ○ ○ ○
5 ○ ○ ○ ○
6 ○ ○ ○ ○
7 ○ ○ ○ ○
8 ○ ○ ○ ○
9 ○ ○ ○ ○

9. [| | | |]
/ ○ ○
. ○ ○ ○ ○
0 ○ ○ ○ ○
1 ○ ○ ○ ○
2 ○ ○ ○ ○
3 ○ ○ ○ ○
4 ○ ○ ○ ○
5 ○ ○ ○ ○
6 ○ ○ ○ ○
7 ○ ○ ○ ○
8 ○ ○ ○ ○
9 ○ ○ ○ ○

Name ________________ Date ________ Class ________

Use two input/output pairs or one input/output pair and the rate of change to find the rule for a linear function.

SAMPLE MULTIPLE CHOICE

Which rule do the ordered pairs (x, y) given below satisfy?

$(-5, -44)$ and $(2, 40)$

A) $y = 5x + 30$

B) $y = 8x - 4$

C) $y = 16x + 8$

D) $y = 12x + 16$

Calculate the slope of the line passing through the given points $(-5, -44)$ and $(2, 40)$.

$$m = \frac{40 - (-44)}{2 - (-5)} = \frac{84}{7} = 12$$

Substitute the value of m and the point $(-5, -44)$ into an equation in slope-intercept form and solve for b.

$$\begin{aligned} y &= mx + b \\ -44 &= 12(-5) + b \\ -44 &= -60 + b \\ 16 &= b \end{aligned}$$

So, the function rule is $y = 12x + 16$.

The correct answer is D. A ○ B ○ C ○ D ●

1

Which rule do the ordered pairs (x, y) given below satisfy?

$(-2, -19)$ and $(3, 21)$

A) $y = 7x$

B) $y = 8x - 3$

C) $y = 6x + 3$

D) $y = 10x + 1$

2

Which rule is satisfied by the two ordered pairs (x, y) given below?

$(3, 6.5)$ and $(1, 5.5)$

A) $y = \frac{x}{2} + 5$

B) $y = 2x + 0.5$

C) $y = 3x - 2.5$

D) $y = \frac{x}{2} + 5.5$

3

Which rule is satisfied by the two ordered pairs (x, y) given below?

$(-2, 7)$ and $(4, -11)$

A) $y = -2x - 3$

B) $y = 3x - 1$

C) $y = -3x + 1$

D) $y = -5x - 3$

4

Which rule do the ordered pairs (x, y) given below satisfy?

$(-4, -2)$ and $(3, -9)$

A) $y = -3x$

B) $y = -x - 6$

C) $y = 2x + 3$

D) $y = -2x - 10$

Name ______________________ Date ______________ Class______________

SAMPLE GRID-IN	
Find the y-intercept of a function with a constant rate of change of 5 that has an output of 22 when the input is 4.	For a function, the input is the independent variable and the output is the dependent variable. Begin by writing a function rule that is satisfied by the ordered pair (4, 22) and which has the given rate of change (slope) of 5. Substitute 5 for m and the point (4, 22) into the slope-intercept form of a function. Solve for b. $y = mx + b$ $22 = 5(4) + b$ $22 = 20 + b$ $2 = b$ So, the y-intercept is 2. Grid in 2.

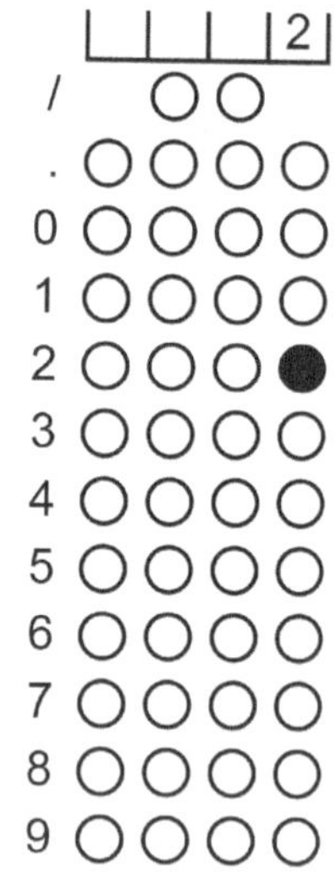

5

Find the y-intercept of a function with a constant rate of change of -2 that has an output of -5.5 when the input is 3.

6

Find the y-intercept of a function with a constant rate of change of $\frac{1}{2}$ that has an output of 13.5 when the input is 3.

7

What is the slope of the linear function that is satisfied by the two ordered pairs (x, y) given below?

$$(-7, -21) \text{ and } (5, 18)$$

8

Find the y-intercept of a function with a constant rate of change of 18 that has an input of 4 when the output is 98.

9

Find the y-intercept of a function that has an input of 3 when the output is 155 and a constant rate of change of 35.

10

In a linear function, two unique inputs both have an output of 15. What is the slope of this function?

11

Find the y-intercept of a function that has an input of -2 when the output is 55 and has a constant rate of change of 20.

12

Find the y-intercept of a function that has an input of 6 when the output is -29 and has a constant rate of change of -8.

Name ______________________ Date ______________ Class ______________

Use two input/output pairs or one input/output pair and the rate of change to find the rule for a linear function.

ANSWER SHEET

1. A B C D

2. A B C D

3. A B C D

4. A B C D

5.
/
.
0
1
2
3
4
5
6
7
8
9

6.
/
.
0
1
2
3
4
5
6
7
8
9

7.
/
.
0
1
2
3
4
5
6
7
8
9

8.
/
.
0
1
2
3
4
5
6
7
8
9

9.
/
.
0
1
2
3
4
5
6
7
8
9

10.
/
.
0
1
2
3
4
5
6
7
8
9

11.
/
.
0
1
2
3
4
5
6
7
8
9

12.
/
.
0
1
2
3
4
5
6
7
8
9

Name ______________________ Date ______________ Class______________

Write and use a linear equation in two variables to solve problems representing real-world situations.

SAMPLE MULTIPLE CHOICE

A local hot sauce company buys jalapeño peppers for $1.27 per pound and habaneros for $6.85 per pound. If the company buys $135 worth of peppers and buys 16 pounds of habaneros, how many pounds of jalapeño peppers did the company buy?

A) 15

B) 20

C) 21

D) 50

Let j be the number pounds of jalapeños and h be the number of pounds of habaneros the company buys. Write a linear equation using the variables.

$$1.27j + 6.85h = 135$$

Substitute 16 for h and solve for j.

$$\begin{aligned} 1.27j + 6.85h &= 135 \\ 1.27j + 6.85(16) &= 135 \\ 1.27j + 109.6 &= 135 \\ 1.27j &= 25.4 \\ j &= 20 \end{aligned}$$

So, the company bought 20 pounds of jalapeño peppers.

The correct answer is B. A ○ B ● C ○ D ○

1

Finn spent the winter riding a stationary bike and using a rowing machine. He burned 360 calories per hour on the bike and 525 calories per hour on the rowing machine. In two weeks, he burned a total of 9,435 calories. If he spent 16 hours on the bike, how many hours did he spend using the rowing machine?

A) 7

B) 17

C) 23

D) 26

2

A landscaping company bought two types of decorative pavers for $337. One type of paver costs $6, and the other costs $11. If the company bought 17 of the $11 pavers, how many $6 pavers did they buy?

A) 60

B) 45

C) 28

D) 25

3

A school buys boxes of black dry erase markers for $7.49 and boxes containing dry erase markers in assorted colors for $10.99. The school spends a total of $265.72 on dry erase markers and buys 12 boxes of black markers. How many boxes of markers in assorted colors did the school buy?

A) 16

B) 24

C) 28

D) 35

4

A manufacturing company makes $5 for every functional toy it produces but loses $2 for every defective toy. In one week, the company made $23,789 and produced 4,775 functional toys. How many defective toys were produced that week?

A) 21

B) 43

C) 86

D) 172

Name ______________________ Date ____________ Class ____________

SAMPLE GRID-IN

A groomer charges \$19 to wash a small dog and \$26 to wash a large dog. On Wednesday, the groomer earned \$370 and washed 4 large dogs. How many small dogs did the groomer wash?

Write a linear equation with s as the number of small dogs and ℓ as the number of large dogs.

$$19s + 26\ell = 370$$

Substitute 4 for ℓ and solve for s.

$$19s + 26\ell = 370$$
$$19s + 26(4) = 370$$
$$19s + 104 = 370$$
$$19s = 266$$
$$s = 14$$

So, the groomer washed 14 small dogs.

Grid in 14.

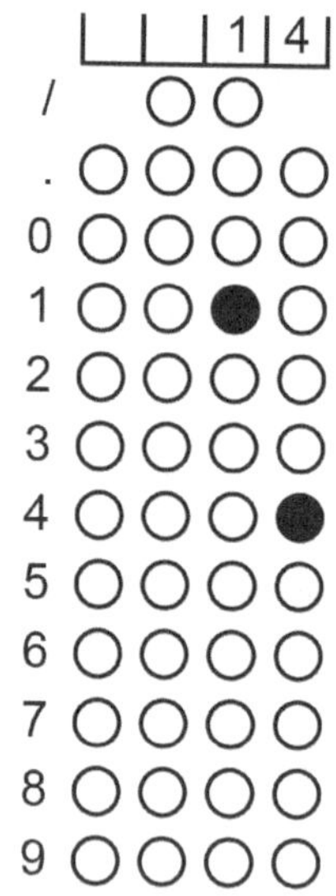

5

At a skating rink, adult tickets cost \$5 and youth tickets cost \$3. Yesterday, the revenue from ticket sales was \$402 and 18 of the tickets were adult tickets. How many youth tickets were sold?

6

A landscaping company stocks lilac bushes and mock orange bushes to make privacy screens for customers. The company sells lilac bushes for \$32.76 and mock orange bushes for \$18.46. A customer spent \$555.10 on a group of bushes, which included 13 lilac bushes. How many mock orange bushes did the customer buy?

7

Carlton is making 10 small gift baskets and 10 large gift baskets. He has 12.5 pounds of chocolate to use in the 20 baskets. He uses 0.75 pound of chocolate in each of the larger baskets. How much chocolate, in pounds, can he put in each of the smaller baskets?

8

The Hernandez family drove 575 miles for a vacation. They traveled at the speed limit on roads with speed limits of 55 and 75 miles per hour. If they drove at 55 miles per hour for 5 hours, how many hours did the Hernandez family drive at 75 miles per hour?

9

On a business trip, Mykala rented a car for 3 days. The rental agency she used charges \$28.95 per day and \$0.35 per mile for their rentals. If the total charge was \$143.55, how many miles did she drive the rental car?

10

As of March 2018, the largest flag ever flown from a flagpole was raised on December 2, 2011. It was a rectangular flag with a perimeter of 188.6 meters. Each shorter side of the flag was 34.3 meters long. What was the length, in meters, of each of the longer sides of the flag?

Name ______________________ Date ______________ Class ______________

Write and use a linear equation in two variables to solve problems representing real-world situations.

ANSWER SHEET

1. A B C D
○ ○ ○ ○

2. A B C D
○ ○ ○ ○

3. A B C D
○ ○ ○ ○

4. A B C D
○ ○ ○ ○

5.
/ ○○
. ○○○○
0 ○○○○
1 ○○○○
2 ○○○○
3 ○○○○
4 ○○○○
5 ○○○○
6 ○○○○
7 ○○○○
8 ○○○○
9 ○○○○

6.
/ ○○
. ○○○○
0 ○○○○
1 ○○○○
2 ○○○○
3 ○○○○
4 ○○○○
5 ○○○○
6 ○○○○
7 ○○○○
8 ○○○○
9 ○○○○

7.
/ ○○
. ○○○○
0 ○○○○
1 ○○○○
2 ○○○○
3 ○○○○
4 ○○○○
5 ○○○○
6 ○○○○
7 ○○○○
8 ○○○○
9 ○○○○

8.
/ ○○
. ○○○○
0 ○○○○
1 ○○○○
2 ○○○○
3 ○○○○
4 ○○○○
5 ○○○○
6 ○○○○
7 ○○○○
8 ○○○○
9 ○○○○

9.
/ ○○
. ○○○○
0 ○○○○
1 ○○○○
2 ○○○○
3 ○○○○
4 ○○○○
5 ○○○○
6 ○○○○
7 ○○○○
8 ○○○○
9 ○○○○

10.
/ ○○
. ○○○○
0 ○○○○
1 ○○○○
2 ○○○○
3 ○○○○
4 ○○○○
5 ○○○○
6 ○○○○
7 ○○○○
8 ○○○○
9 ○○○○

Name ______________________ Date ______________ Class ______________

Write a linear equation in two variables to model a relationship between two quantities.

SAMPLE MULTIPLE CHOICE

To translate a document into English, Hamsa charges \$80 for the first 2 hours and \$35 for each additional hour. Which of the following expresses the amount T, in dollars, Hamsa charges if it takes her x hours to translate a document, where $x > 2$?

A) $T = 80x + 35$

B) $T = 35x + 10$

C) $T = 35x + 80$

D) $T = 35x$

Represent the situation with a verbal model.

Total charge T	=	Charge for first 2 hrs \$80	+	Charge per hour after first 2 hrs \$35	•	Number of hours after first 2 hrs $(x-2)$

Write an equation and simplify:

$$T = 80 + 35(x-2)$$
$$T = 80 + 35x - 70$$
$$T = 35x + 10$$

The correct answer is B. A ○ B ● C ○ D ○

1

To join an online learning community, you start with a one-month trial for the discounted price of \$25. If you choose to continue beyond the trial, you then pay a \$39 monthly fee. Which of the following expresses the cost C, in dollars, for the online learning community membership for x months, where $x > 1$?

A) $C = 39x + 14$

B) $C = 25x + 14$

C) $C = 39x + 25$

D) $C = 39x - 14$

2

Caroline is saving money to buy a car. She saves \$150 in the first 2 months and then \$350 each month after that. How many months does it take for Caroline to save the money to buy a used car for \$2,250?

A) 6

B) 7

C) 8

D) 9

3

Darin receives a \$3,000 commission for the first 10 cars he sells and \$450 for each additional car he sells. Which of the following expresses the commission C, in dollars, Darin receives if he sells x cars in a month, where $x > 10$?

A) $C = 450x + 1{,}500$

B) $C = 350x - 1{,}500$

C) $C = 450x - 1{,}500$

D) $C = 450x + 3{,}000$

4

Uriel has challenged himself to memorize 100 words. It takes him 3 days to memorize the first 25 words, and he continues to memorize words at a rate of 15 words per day. How many days does it take Uriel to finish his challenge?

A) 4

B) 8

C) 14

D) 25

Name ______________________ Date ____________ Class____________

SAMPLE GRID-IN

In Shanghai, a taxi charges 14 yuan for the first 3 kilometers and 4 yuan for each additional kilometer. If James paid 36.4 yuan for his taxi ride, how many kilometers did he travel?

Let C be the cost of the taxi ride and x be the distance in kilometers James traveled. From the description, the cost is 14 yuans plus 4 yuans per kilometer after the first 3 kilometers.

The following equation models the cost of the taxi.

$$C = 14 + 4(x - 3)$$

Substitute 36.4 for C and solve for x.

$$36.4 = 14 + 4(x - 3)$$
$$36.4 = 14 + 4x - 12$$
$$36.4 = 2 + 4x$$
$$34.4 = 4x$$
$$8.6 = x$$

So, James traveled 8.6 kilometers.

Grid in 8.6.

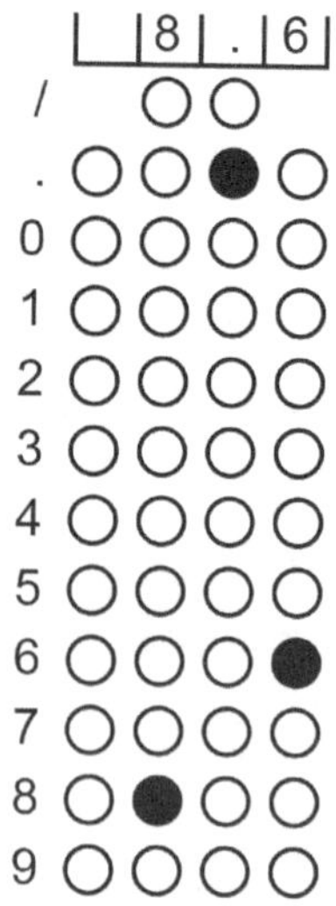

5

A company is printing 1,700 promotional flyers for their second anniversary sale. In the first 2 hours, the company prints 900 flyers and continues to print flyers at a rate of 200 flyers an hour. How long does it take the company to print the 1,700 flyers they want for advertising the sale?

6

Each contestant in a cooking contest has 180 minutes to prepare 5 different meals. Brittany spent 30 minutes on her first meal. How many minutes should she spend on each of the remaining meals to finish the contest? Assume she spends the same amount of time on each meal.

7

Nancy is collecting seashells on the beach, and she wants to have 50 seashells for her friends. Nancy found 23 seashells in the first 2 hours. If she has to leave the beach in 3 hours, how many seashells does she need to find each hour to reach her goal? Assume she collects the same number of seashells every hour.

8

Karl has joined a weight-loss program and set a goal of losing 42 pounds. He managed to lose 27 pounds in the first 3 months and continues to lose 3 pounds per month. When Karl reaches his goal, how many months will he have been on the weight-loss program?

Name ______________________ Date ____________ Class ____________

Write a linear equation in two variables to model a relationship between two quantities.

ANSWER SHEET

1. A B C D
○ ○ ○ ○

2. A B C D
○ ○ ○ ○

3. A B C D
○ ○ ○ ○

4. A B C D
○ ○ ○ ○

5. | | | | |
/ ○ ○
. ○ ○ ○ ○
0 ○ ○ ○ ○
1 ○ ○ ○ ○
2 ○ ○ ○ ○
3 ○ ○ ○ ○
4 ○ ○ ○ ○
5 ○ ○ ○ ○
6 ○ ○ ○ ○
7 ○ ○ ○ ○
8 ○ ○ ○ ○
9 ○ ○ ○ ○

6. | | | | |
/ ○ ○
. ○ ○ ○ ○
0 ○ ○ ○ ○
1 ○ ○ ○ ○
2 ○ ○ ○ ○
3 ○ ○ ○ ○
4 ○ ○ ○ ○
5 ○ ○ ○ ○
6 ○ ○ ○ ○
7 ○ ○ ○ ○
8 ○ ○ ○ ○
9 ○ ○ ○ ○

7. | | | | |
/ ○ ○
. ○ ○ ○ ○
0 ○ ○ ○ ○
1 ○ ○ ○ ○
2 ○ ○ ○ ○
3 ○ ○ ○ ○
4 ○ ○ ○ ○
5 ○ ○ ○ ○
6 ○ ○ ○ ○
7 ○ ○ ○ ○
8 ○ ○ ○ ○
9 ○ ○ ○ ○

8. | | | | |
/ ○ ○
. ○ ○ ○ ○
0 ○ ○ ○ ○
1 ○ ○ ○ ○
2 ○ ○ ○ ○
3 ○ ○ ○ ○
4 ○ ○ ○ ○
5 ○ ○ ○ ○
6 ○ ○ ○ ○
7 ○ ○ ○ ○
8 ○ ○ ○ ○
9 ○ ○ ○ ○

Name ______________________ Date ______________ Class ______________

For a linear equation in two variables, interpret the parts of the equation and its solution based on the context.

SAMPLE MULTIPLE CHOICE

$$m = 0.1p + 5$$

A library holds a summer reading program where participants earn money for every page that they read during the summer. The equation above models the amount m, in dollars, earned for reading p pages. What could the 5 in the model possibly represent?

A) The age limit to join the program
B) The total number of participants
C) A \$5 limit on the total earnings
D) A \$5 initial reward for participating

The equation gives the total earnings m, in dollars, made from reading p pages. If a participant joins the program but has not yet read any pages, then $p = 0$. Substitute this into the equation.

$$m = 0.1(0) + 5$$
$$m = 0 + 5$$
$$m = 5$$

Without reading any pages, the initial amount the participant earns is \$5.

The correct answer is D. A B C D ○ ○ ○ ●

1

$$w = 48{,}600 - 1{,}500(t - 6)$$

The amount of water w, in gallons, left in a pool after being drained for t hours can be modeled by the equation above. At what rate is water draining from the pool, in gallons per hour?

A) 6
B) 1,500
C) 7,500
D) 9,000

2

$$s = 312m + 2{,}484$$

The amount of maple syrup s, in gallons, sold by a grocery store chain can be modeled by the equation above, where m is the number of years after 2012. What does 3732 represent in the ordered pair $(m,\ s) = (4,\ 3732)$?

A) The fourth year after 2012
B) The fifth year after 2012
C) The number of gallons sold in 2015
D) The number of gallons sold in 2016

3

$$P = 2\ell + 4(\ell - 3)$$

The perimeter P of a rectangle with length ℓ is given by the equation above. What is the width of the rectangle in terms of ℓ?

A) 2ℓ
B) 4ℓ
C) $\ell - 3$
D) $2\ell - 6$

4

$$s = 13t + 20(1 - t)$$

A fishing boat leaves the harbor at a speed of 13 knots and increases its speed to 20 knots when it reaches the open ocean. Assuming the boat changed speed instantly, the average speed of the boat s, in knots, during the first hour can be modeled by the equation above, where t is the amount of time in hours that the boat traveled at a speed of 13 knots. If the average speed of the boat was 18.32 knots, how long (in hours) did it spend traveling at a speed of 20 knots?

A) 0.24
B) 0.28
C) 0.76
D) 1.68

Name ______________________ Date ______________ Class______________

SAMPLE GRID-IN	
$c = 81x + 600$ The equation above gives the total cost c, in dollars, of producing x tires. What is the cost of producing 35 tires?	Substitute $x = 35$ into the given equation and simplify. $c = 81x + 600$ $c = 81(35) + 600$ $c = 2{,}835 + 600$ $c = 3{,}435$ The cost of producing 35 tires is \$3,435. Grid in 3435.

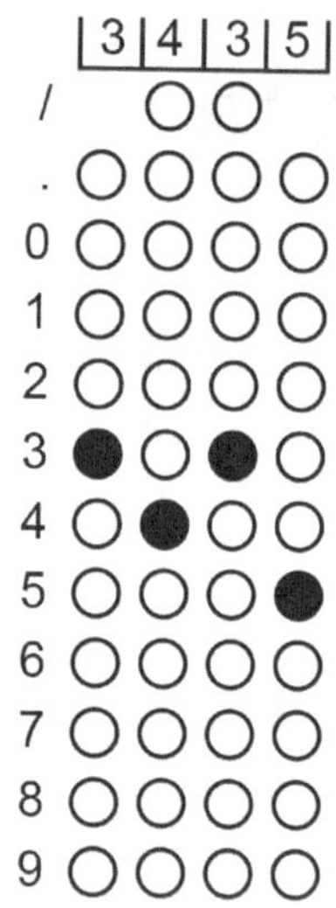

5

$$C = 18v + 12$$

The cost C, in dollars, to renew the registration permit for a car in a city is given by the equation above, where v is the current value of the car in thousands of dollars. If the cost of the registration for a car is \$174, what is the current value, in dollars, of the car?

6

$$p = 0.774d$$

The equation above models the value p, in British pounds, of d U.S. dollars on May 1, 2017. How much was \$5,000 worth in British pounds on that date? Round to the nearest British pound. Ignore currency symbols when gridding your response.

7

$$t = 480x + 1{,}358$$

The tuition t, in dollars, for x credit hours at a certain college during the summer session can be found using the equation above. How much does a student pay per credit hour?

8

$$a = 3{,}500 - 55t$$

The terminal velocity for a skydiver in a stable, abdomen-to-earth position is about 55 meters per second. The equation above gives the altitude a, in meters, of a skydiver t seconds after reaching terminal velocity. The parachute must be deployed at an altitude of 760 meters. To the nearest tenth of a second, how long does the skydiver get to fall at terminal velocity before deploying the parachute?

9

The perimeter P of a particular triangle can be calculated using the equation $P = 7s + 4$, where s is the length of the shortest side. Find the perimeter of a similar triangle for which $s = 8$.

10

$$C = 25 + 0.15d$$

A sales representative earns a total commission C, in dollars, for a sale of d dollars. How much does the representative make if no sales are made? Ignore the dollar sign when gridding your response.

Name ______________________ Date ____________ Class ____________

For a linear equation in two variables, interpret the parts of the equation and its solution based on the context.

ANSWER SHEET

1. A B C D
2. A B C D
3. A B C D
4. A B C D
5. / . 0 1 2 3 4 5 6 7 8 9
6. / . 0 1 2 3 4 5 6 7 8 9
7. / . 0 1 2 3 4 5 6 7 8 9
8. / . 0 1 2 3 4 5 6 7 8 9
9. / . 0 1 2 3 4 5 6 7 8 9
10. / . 0 1 2 3 4 5 6 7 8 9

Name ______________________ Date ______________ Class______________

Connect various representations of linear equations in two variables by deriving one from the other.

SAMPLE MULTIPLE CHOICE

x	3	5	7	9
y	33	43	53	63

Use the table to write a linear equation in slope-intercept form.

A) $y = 3x + 10$

B) $y = 2(x + 3) + 33$

C) $y = 5x + 18$

D) $y = 10(x - 5) + 43$

An equation in slope-intercept form has the form $y = mx + b$. Use the slope formula and any two points shown in the table to find m.

$$m = \frac{43 - 33}{5 - 3} = \frac{10}{2} = 5$$

Substitute for m in the slope-intercept form and use any point from the table to find the value of b.

$$y = mx + b$$
$$43 = 5(5) + b$$
$$43 = 25 + b$$
$$18 = b$$

So, the equation is $y = 5x + 18$.

The correct answer is C. A B ● D

1

$$r = -14s + 8$$

Use the equation above to determine the unknown value of s in the table below.

s	–1	3	?
r	22	–34	–118

A) –7

B) 5

C) 7

D) 9

2

Using the equation $t = 0.6(z - 12) + 18$, determine which two points lie on the graph of the equation. The ordered pairs are in the form (z, t).

A) $(-3, 9)$, $(7, 15)$

B) $(0, 2)$, $(2, 8)$

C) $(3, -2)$, $(7, 2)$

D) $(-5, -5)$, $(1, -2)$

3

If the equation of the line graphed below is written in the form $y = mx + b$, what is the value of b?

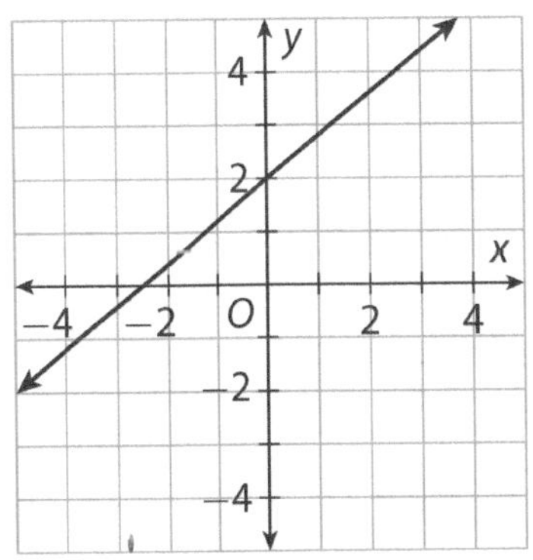

A) –3

B) –2.5

C) 2

D) 5

4

Which is the equation of the line shown in the graph for Question 3?

A) $y = -0.4x + 2$

B) $y = \frac{2}{3}x - 2.5$

C) $y = 0.8x + 2$

D) $y = -\frac{5}{3}x - 3$

Name ____________________ Date ____________ Class ____________

SAMPLE GRID-IN

Given the graphs of lines A and B below, what constant must you add to the equation of line B to obtain the equation of line A?

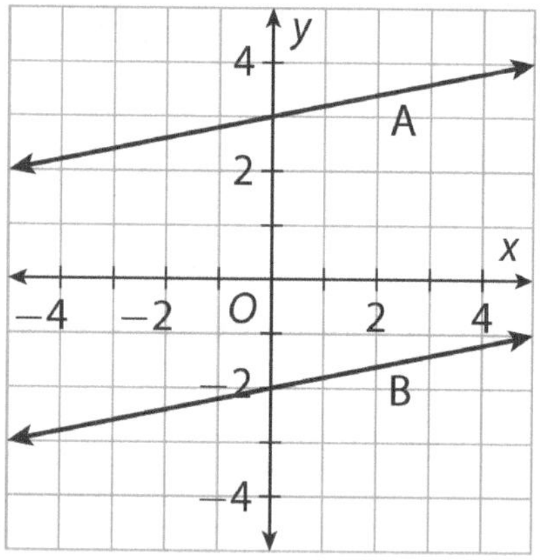

From the graph, both lines have slope $\frac{1}{5}$.

The y-intercept of line A is 3 and the y-intercept of line B is −2. So, the equation of line A is

$y = \frac{1}{5}x + 3$ and the equation of line B is $y = \frac{1}{5}x - 2$.

To obtain the equation of line A from the equation of line B, add 5.

$$y = \frac{1}{5}x - 2 + 5 = \frac{1}{5}x + 3$$

So, the constant 5 must be added.

Grid in 5.

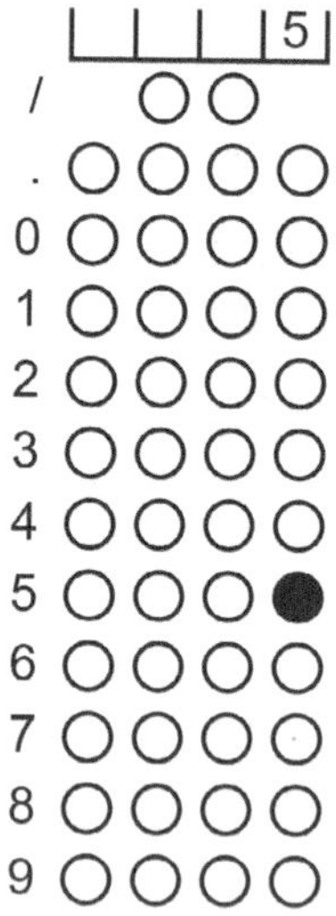

5

A mail carrier is able to deliver to 77 mailboxes per hour and has 449 mailboxes on her route. The number of mailboxes p she has left after t hours can be modeled by an equation of the form $p = mt + b$. What is the value of b?

6

What is the slope of the line that passes through the points in the table below?

x	−2	−1	1
y	1.6	2.1	3.1

7

Determine the unknown value in the table.

x	−2	−1	0	1
y	−1.4	0.6	?	4.6

8

Where will the graph of the line $s = -3(t - 7) - 12$ cross the t-axis?

9

Examine the graph of line F below. If the equation of line F is written in the form $y = mx + b$, what is the value of mb?

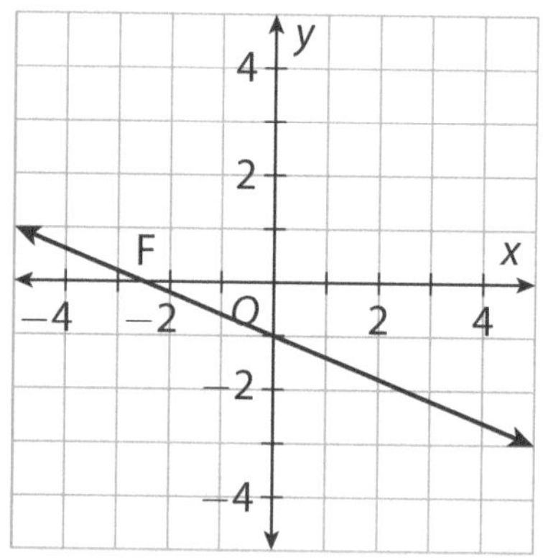

Name ______________________ Date ______________ Class ______________

Connect various representations of linear equations in two variables by deriving one from the other.

ANSWER SHEET

1. A B C D ○ ○ ○ ○

2. A B C D ○ ○ ○ ○

3. A B C D ○ ○ ○ ○

4. A B C D ○ ○ ○ ○

5. Grid-in

/		○	○	
.	○	○	○	○
0	○	○	○	○
1	○	○	○	○
2	○	○	○	○
3	○	○	○	○
4	○	○	○	○
5	○	○	○	○
6	○	○	○	○
7	○	○	○	○
8	○	○	○	○
9	○	○	○	○

6. Grid-in

/		○	○	
.	○	○	○	○
0	○	○	○	○
1	○	○	○	○
2	○	○	○	○
3	○	○	○	○
4	○	○	○	○
5	○	○	○	○
6	○	○	○	○
7	○	○	○	○
8	○	○	○	○
9	○	○	○	○

7. Grid-in

/		○	○	
.	○	○	○	○
0	○	○	○	○
1	○	○	○	○
2	○	○	○	○
3	○	○	○	○
4	○	○	○	○
5	○	○	○	○
6	○	○	○	○
7	○	○	○	○
8	○	○	○	○
9	○	○	○	○

8. Grid-in

/		○	○	
.	○	○	○	○
0	○	○	○	○
1	○	○	○	○
2	○	○	○	○
3	○	○	○	○
4	○	○	○	○
5	○	○	○	○
6	○	○	○	○
7	○	○	○	○
8	○	○	○	○
9	○	○	○	○

9. Grid-in

/		○	○	
.	○	○	○	○
0	○	○	○	○
1	○	○	○	○
2	○	○	○	○
3	○	○	○	○
4	○	○	○	○
5	○	○	○	○
6	○	○	○	○
7	○	○	○	○
8	○	○	○	○
9	○	○	○	○

Name ______________________ Date ______________ Class ______________

Find an equation for a line given two points, a point and the slope, or a point and a parallel or perpendicular line.

SAMPLE MULTIPLE CHOICE

Determine the equation for a line in the *xy*-plane that passes through the points $(-2,2)$ and $(2,6)$.

A) $y=x-4$

B) $y=-x-4$

C) $y=x+4$

D) $y=x-2$

First, calculate the slope of the line using the slope formula. Using $(x_1,y_1)=(-2,2)$ and $(x_2,y_2)=(2,6)$:

$$m=\frac{y_2-y_1}{x_2-x_1}=\frac{6-2}{2-(-2)}=\frac{4}{4}=1$$

Now use the point-slope form of the equation of a line. Substitute the slope *m* and the point (x_1,y_1) into the equation.

$$y-y_1=m(x-x_1)$$
$$y-2=1(x-(-2))$$
$$y-2=x+2$$
$$y=x+4$$

The correct answer is C. A ○ B ○ C ● D ○

1

What is the equation of a line in the *xy*-plane that passes through the point $(15,\ 2)$ and has a slope of $\frac{1}{6}$?

A) $y=-6x-2$

B) $y=\frac{1}{6}x-\frac{1}{2}$

C) $y=3x-4$

D) $y-\frac{1}{6}x+2$

2

Determine the equation for a line that passes through the points $(0,\ 4)$ and $(5,-2)$.

A) $y=-6x+4$

B) $y=-\frac{5}{6}x+4$

C) $y=-5x-2$

D) $y=-\frac{6}{5}x+4$

3

What is the equation of a line that passes through the point $(-2,-3)$ and is parallel to the line $-x+2y=0$?

A) $y=\frac{1}{2}x-2$

B) $y=-2x+1$

C) $y=-2x-1$

D) $y=\frac{1}{2}x+2$

4

Write the equation for a line that passes through the point $(-2,4)$ and is perpendicular to the line $-2x+5y=1$.

A) $y-4=-\frac{5}{2}(x-2)$

B) $y+4=5(x+2)$

C) $y-4=-\frac{5}{2}(x+2)$

D) $y+2=5(x-2)$

Name ______________________ Date ______________ Class ______________

SAMPLE GRID-IN

Find the value of a so that the line with equation $ax + y = -6$ is perpendicular to the line whose equation is $y = \frac{1}{3}x + 5$.

The equation of the second line is in slope-intercept form, $y = mx + b$, where m is the slope. So, the slope of the second line is $\frac{1}{3}$.

Since perpendicular lines have slopes that are opposite reciprocals, the slope of the first line must be -3.

Now, rewrite the equation of the first line in slope-intercept form.

$$ax + y = -6$$

$$y = -ax - 6$$

The slope is $-a$, which is equal to -3.

$$-a = -3$$

$$a = 3$$

So, the value of a is 3.

Grid in 3.

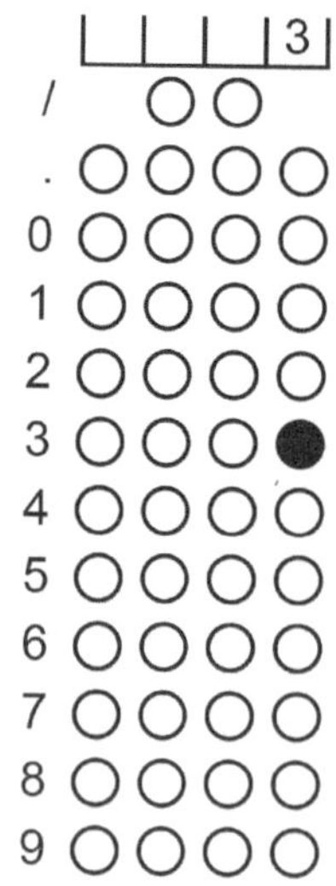

5

Find the slope of a line that is parallel to the line $4x - 5y = 20$.

6

A line passes through the origin and the point $(-4, y_1)$. Assuming this line is perpendicular to the line $-2x + 3y = 7$, what is the value of y_1?

7

A line in the xy-plane passes through the points $(13, 8)$ and $(2, 0)$. What is the slope of a line that is parallel to this line?

8

A line passes through the origin and the point $\left(-\frac{1}{2}, y_1\right)$. Assuming this line is parallel to the line $3x + 2y = 4$, what is the value of y_1?

9

The line $3x + by = 18$ passes through the point $(16, 6)$. What is the slope of this line?

10

What is the slope of a line that is perpendicular to the line passing through the points $(2, -12.5)$ and $(0, -1.5)$?

11

What is the slope of a line that passes through the point $(2, -5)$ and is parallel to the line $-3x + 2y = -9$?

12

Find the slope of a line that is perpendicular to the line $8x + 7y = 16$.

Name ____________________ Date ______________ Class ______________

Find an equation for a line given two points, a point and the slope, or a point and a parallel or perpendicular line.

ANSWER SHEET

1. A B C D
○ ○ ○ ○

2. A B C D
○ ○ ○ ○

3. A B C D
○ ○ ○ ○

4. A B C D
○ ○ ○ ○

5.
/ ○ ○
. ○ ○ ○ ○
0 ○ ○ ○ ○
1 ○ ○ ○ ○
2 ○ ○ ○ ○
3 ○ ○ ○ ○
4 ○ ○ ○ ○
5 ○ ○ ○ ○
6 ○ ○ ○ ○
7 ○ ○ ○ ○
8 ○ ○ ○ ○
9 ○ ○ ○ ○

6.
/ ○ ○
. ○ ○ ○ ○
0 ○ ○ ○ ○
1 ○ ○ ○ ○
2 ○ ○ ○ ○
3 ○ ○ ○ ○
4 ○ ○ ○ ○
5 ○ ○ ○ ○
6 ○ ○ ○ ○
7 ○ ○ ○ ○
8 ○ ○ ○ ○
9 ○ ○ ○ ○

7.
/ ○ ○
. ○ ○ ○ ○
0 ○ ○ ○ ○
1 ○ ○ ○ ○
2 ○ ○ ○ ○
3 ○ ○ ○ ○
4 ○ ○ ○ ○
5 ○ ○ ○ ○
6 ○ ○ ○ ○
7 ○ ○ ○ ○
8 ○ ○ ○ ○
9 ○ ○ ○ ○

8.
/ ○ ○
. ○ ○ ○ ○
0 ○ ○ ○ ○
1 ○ ○ ○ ○
2 ○ ○ ○ ○
3 ○ ○ ○ ○
4 ○ ○ ○ ○
5 ○ ○ ○ ○
6 ○ ○ ○ ○
7 ○ ○ ○ ○
8 ○ ○ ○ ○
9 ○ ○ ○ ○

9.
/ ○ ○
. ○ ○ ○ ○
0 ○ ○ ○ ○
1 ○ ○ ○ ○
2 ○ ○ ○ ○
3 ○ ○ ○ ○
4 ○ ○ ○ ○
5 ○ ○ ○ ○
6 ○ ○ ○ ○
7 ○ ○ ○ ○
8 ○ ○ ○ ○
9 ○ ○ ○ ○

10.
/ ○ ○
. ○ ○ ○ ○
0 ○ ○ ○ ○
1 ○ ○ ○ ○
2 ○ ○ ○ ○
3 ○ ○ ○ ○
4 ○ ○ ○ ○
5 ○ ○ ○ ○
6 ○ ○ ○ ○
7 ○ ○ ○ ○
8 ○ ○ ○ ○
9 ○ ○ ○ ○

11.
/ ○ ○
. ○ ○ ○ ○
0 ○ ○ ○ ○
1 ○ ○ ○ ○
2 ○ ○ ○ ○
3 ○ ○ ○ ○
4 ○ ○ ○ ○
5 ○ ○ ○ ○
6 ○ ○ ○ ○
7 ○ ○ ○ ○
8 ○ ○ ○ ○
9 ○ ○ ○ ○

12.
/ ○ ○
. ○ ○ ○ ○
0 ○ ○ ○ ○
1 ○ ○ ○ ○
2 ○ ○ ○ ○
3 ○ ○ ○ ○
4 ○ ○ ○ ○
5 ○ ○ ○ ○
6 ○ ○ ○ ○
7 ○ ○ ○ ○
8 ○ ○ ○ ○
9 ○ ○ ○ ○

Name ______________________ Date ______________ Class______________

Write and use a system of two linear equations in two variables to solve problems in real-world situations.

SAMPLE MULTIPLE CHOICE

The admission prices for a high school football game are \$5 for students and \$8 for adults. For the opening game, the school collected \$1,210 from the sale of 170 tickets to the game. How many adult tickets were sold?

A) 50

B) 60

C) 120

D) 240

First, define the unknowns.

s = number of student tickets sold

a = number of adult tickets sold

Next, write two equations that model the given information.

$$s + a = 170$$
$$5s + 8a = 1{,}210$$

Solve the first equation for s. Substitute for s in the second equation and solve the resulting equation for a.

$$5(170 - a) + 8a = 1{,}210$$
$$850 - 5a + 8a = 1{,}210$$
$$3a = 360$$
$$a = 120$$

So, 120 adult tickets were sold.

The correct answer is C. A ○ B ○ C ● D ○

1

At a local fair, a hamburger costs \$5 and a sausage costs \$4. A concession stand raises \$267 and sells 59 items. How many sausages did the concession stand sell?

A) 12

B) 14

C) 28

D) 31

2

The admission to a fundraiser at a local club is \$5 for members and \$8 for non-members. The club raised \$378. The number of members attending was 8 more than the number of non-members. How many non-members attended the fundraiser?

A) 12

B) 18

C) 26

D) 36

3

Bananas cost \$0.58 per pound and apples cost \$1.18 per pound. Beth bought a total of 7 pounds of bananas and apples this week at a total cost of \$5.86. How many pounds of bananas did she buy?

A) 1

B) 2

C) 3

D) 4

4

A store earns \$25 for each item it sells but loses \$10 for every defective item returned. In one day, the store earns \$1,725. That day, the number of defective items returned was one-fifth the number of items sold. How many items were sold that day?

A) 15

B) 60

C) 75

D) 90

Name ______________________ Date ____________ Class ____________

SAMPLE GRID-IN

The members of a running group are ordering performance shirts to wear during workouts. Some members want short-sleeve shirts, while others want long-sleeve shirts. Short-sleeve shirts cost $24, and long-sleeve shirts cost $35. The group spends a total of $343 for 12 shirts. How many long-sleeve shirts were ordered?

First, define the unknowns.

x = number of short-sleeve shirts

y = number of long-sleeve shirts

Next, write two equations modeling the given information.

$$x + y = 12$$
$$24x + 35y = 343$$

Now solve the first equation for x. Substitute for x in the second equation and solve the resulting equation for y.

$$24(12 - y) + 35y = 343$$
$$288 + 11y = 343$$
$$y = 5$$

So, the team ordered 5 long-sleeve shirts.

Grid in 5.

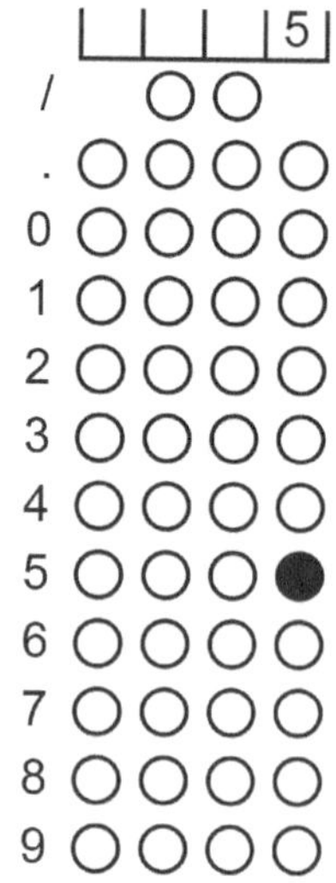

5

A soccer team is ordering jerseys for the upcoming season, and each player is selecting the number for the back of their jersey. Two-digit numbers cost $24.50 per shirt and one-digit numbers cost $23.75 per shirt. The team pays $267.25 in all for 11 jerseys. How many players have two-digit numbers?

6

A lacrosse team is ordering jackets for the upcoming season, and players must choose either an orange or a white jacket. Orange costs $67.50 per jacket, and white costs $59.95 per jacket. Ten players order jackets for a total of $629.70. How many white jackets were ordered?

7

For service calls, one electrician charges an initial fee of $100 plus an additional $65 per hour of labor. A second electrician charges an initial fee of $50 plus an additional $85 per hour of labor. After how many hours of labor would the two electricians charge the same amount?

8

A service organization is hosting a fund-raising dinner with a former astronaut as the speaker. Guests could order roast duck or a vegetarian meal. The roast duck dinner costs $63, and the vegetarian dinner costs $42. The organization raised $7,728. Twice as many guests ordered the roast duck than ordered the vegetarian meal. How many guests ordered the roast duck?

Name ________________________ Date ______________ Class ______________

Write and use a system of two linear equations in two variables to solve problems in real-world situations.

ANSWER SHEET

1. A B C D

2. A B C D

3. A B C D

4. A B C D

5.

/
.
0
1
2
3
4
5
6
7
8
9

6.

/
.
0
1
2
3
4
5
6
7
8
9

7.

/
.
0
1
2
3
4
5
6
7
8
9

8.

/
.
0
1
2
3
4
5
6
7
8
9

Name ______________________ Date ______________ Class ______________

Write a system of linear equations in two variables, and interpret solutions in terms of context when appropriate.

SAMPLE MULTIPLE CHOICE

The admission to a concert in the park is \$5 for children and \$8 for adults. The park employees at the ticket booth collected \$2,655 from 447 attendees. How many more children than adults attended?

A) 27
B) 140
C) 167
D) 307

Let c represent the number of children at the concert and let a represent the number of adults.

Write two equations in terms of c and a.

$$c + a = 447$$
$$5c + 8a = 2,655$$

Solve the first equation for c: $c = 447 - a$

Substitute the result into the other equation and solve for a.

$$5(447 - a) + 8a = 2,655$$
$$2,235 + 3a = 2,655$$
$$3a = 420$$
$$a = 140$$

Now use this value to find the value of c.

$$c = 447 - 140 = 307$$

Finally, find the difference: $307 - 140 = 167$

So, there were 167 more children than adults at the concert.

The answer is C. A ○ B ○ C ● D ○

1

The admission to a play in the park is \$7 for children and \$12 for adults. The park collected \$321 from 33 attendees. How many more adults than children attended the play?

A) 3
B) 11
C) 15
D) 18

2

The daily entrance fee at a town pool is \$3 for children and \$8 for adults. During one weekday, a total of \$223 was collected at the pool. On that day, there were 23 more children than adults. How many people paid for admission to the pool that day?

A) 14
B) 37
C) 51
D) 60

3

The entry fee for a road race is \$15 with an \$8 discount for senior citizens. The race had 162 entrants and collected \$2,094. How many senior citizens entered the race?

A) 22
B) 42
C) 78
D) 120

4

A table has 4 legs, and a stool has 3 legs. A woodworker makes 143 legs and assembles 44 individual pieces of furniture. If each table is sold with 3 stools, how many complete sets did he make?

A) 3
B) 9
C) 11
D) 12

Name ____________________ Date ____________ Class ____________

SAMPLE GRID-IN

The student council is decorating the cafeteria for a graduation event. Black balloon bouquets cost $16.99, and red bouquets cost $9.99. The group spends $281.76 and buys 3 times as many red bouquets as black bouquets. How many red balloon bouquets did they buy?

Let b represent the number of black balloon bouquets and let r represent the number of red balloon bouquets. Write two equations in terms of b and r.

$$r = 3b$$
$$16.99b + 9.99r = 281.76$$

Substitute the expression for r from the first equation into the second equation and solve for b.

$$16.99b + 9.99(3b) = 281.76$$
$$46.96b = 281.76$$
$$b = 6$$

Use this value to calculate the value of r.

$$r = 3(6) = 18$$

So, they bought 18 red balloon bouquets.

Grid in 18.

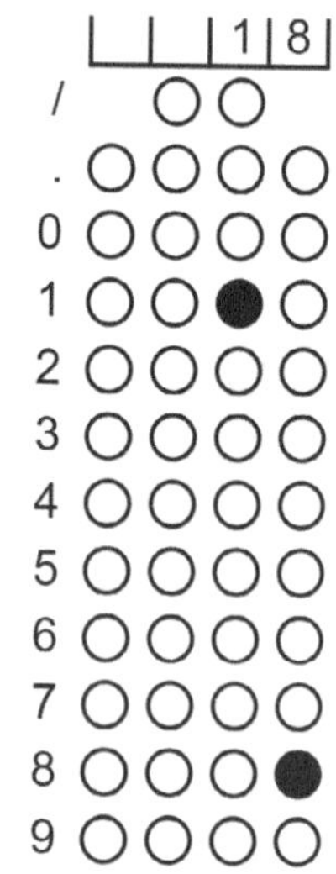

5

The student council is decorating the cafeteria for a dance. Red-and-white patterned streamers cost $1.99 per roll and solid black streamers cost $0.99 per roll. The group spends $17.87 for 13 rolls. How much more did they spend on red-and-white patterned streamers than on black streamers? Ignore the dollar sign when gridding your response.

6

After a fundraiser, the science club purchased new equipment for their classroom. They spent $302.00 on graduated cylinders costing $5.62 each and Erlenmeyer flasks costing $12.29 each. They bought a total of 30 items. How many more Erlenmeyer flasks than graduated cylinders were they able to purchase?

7

A machinist is making gears of two different sizes. The smaller gears each have 26 teeth and the larger gears each have 65 teeth. He completes 11 gears in one day, and these gears have a total of 403 teeth. How many teeth in all did he shape on smaller gears that day?

8

A local farm sells raw milk by the liter and by the gallon at a farmers' market held each Saturday. A liter costs $2.50, and a gallon costs $6. The farm fills 40 containers for the market and sells them all for a total of $177. What is the difference between the number of liter containers and the number of gallon containers that were filled and sold?

Name ______________________ Date ______________ Class ______________

Write a system of linear equations in two variables, and interpret solutions in terms of context when appropriate.

ANSWER SHEET

1. A B C D

2. A B C D

3. A B C D

4. A B C D

5.

/
.
0
1
2
3
4
5
6
7
8
9

6.

/
.
0
1
2
3
4
5
6
7
8
9

7.

/
.
0
1
2
3
4
5
6
7
8
9

8.

/
.
0
1
2
3
4
5
6
7
8
9

Name ______________________ Date ______________ Class ______________

Connect various representations of systems of linear equations by deriving one from the other.

SAMPLE MULTIPLE CHOICE

What is the solution to the system represented in the table below?

x	y_1	y_2
–2	–3	–8
0	1	–2
2	5	4
4	9	10
6	13	16

A) (3,0) C) (3,7)

B) (3,5) D) (3,9)

First determine the equations for the system.

$$y_1 = 2x + 1$$
$$y_2 = 3x - 2$$

For the solution of the system, $y_1 = y_2$. Use this fact to find the corresponding value of x.

$$2x + 1 = 3x - 2$$
$$1 + 2 = 3x - 2x$$
$$3 = x$$

Substitute 3 for x in either equation: $y_1 = 2(3) + 1 = 7$

So, the solution to the system is (3, 7).

The correct answer is C. A B C D ○ ○ ● ○

1

What is the solution to the system represented in the table below?

x	y_1	y_2
–2	–4	–6
0	2	–4
2	8	–2

A) (–6,–8) C) (–1,–3)

B) (–3,–7) D) (1,–3)

2

Which line is parallel to the lines shown?

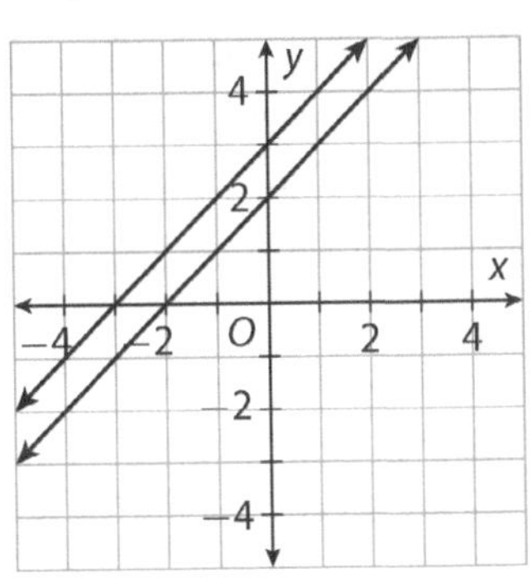

A) $2y = x - 4$ C) $y + x = 3$

B) $y - 2x = 2$ D) $y - x = -3$

3

The equation of one of the lines in the system graphed in the figure below is $2y - 3x = -6$. What is an equation of the other line?

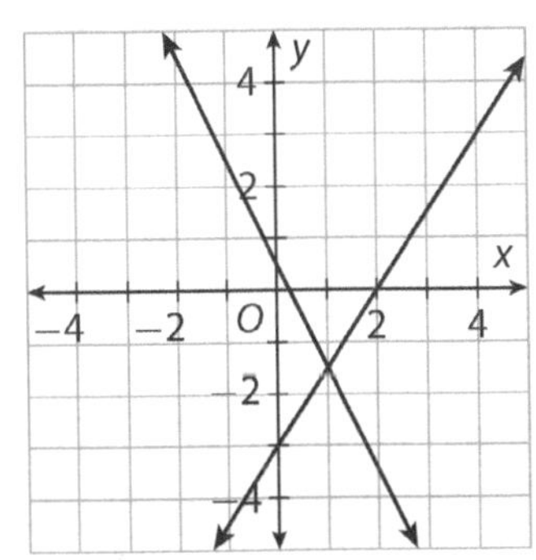

A) $4y - 5x = 1$ C) $2y + 4x = 1$

B) $3y + 4x = 9$ D) $y - 2x = -3$

4

If the equations $2x + y = 2$ and $-x + y = -1$ are graphed in the same plane, where will their graphs intersect?

A) (2,–4) C) (–1, 0)

B) (1, 0) D) (0, 1)

Name ______________________ Date ______________ Class ______________

SAMPLE GRID-IN

What is the sum of the slopes of the lines in the system represented in the graph below and the line $y = 2x + 5$?

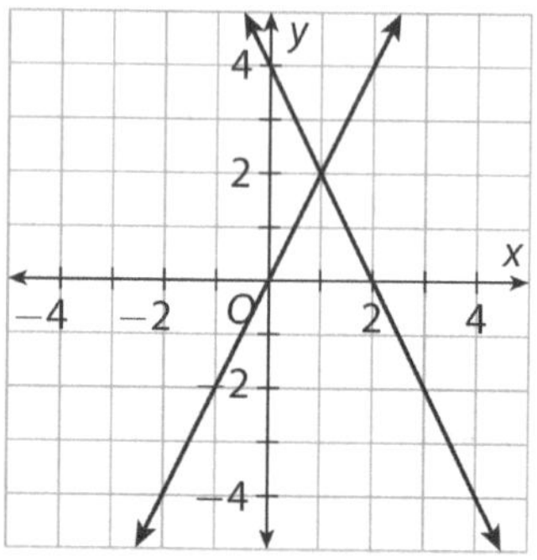

On the graph, the *y*-coordinate for one line decreases by 2 units as *x* increases 1 unit, so the slope is –2.

The *y*-coordinate of the other line on the graph increases by 2 units as *x* increases 1 unit, so the slope is 2.

The slope of the line $y = 2x + 5$ is 2.

$$-2 + 2 + 2 = 2$$

So, the sum of the slopes is 2.

Grid in 2.

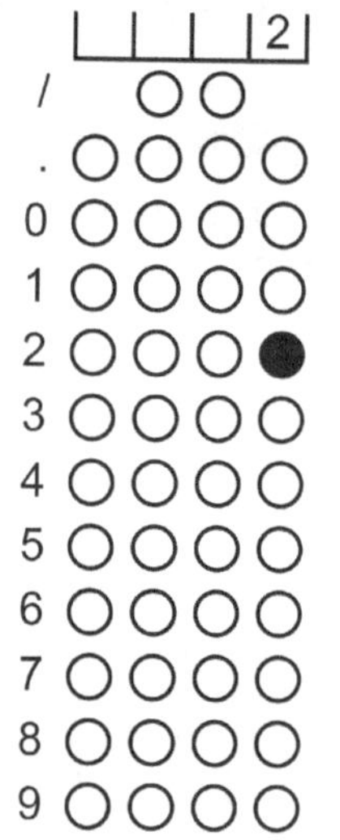

5

What is the sum of the slopes of the lines in the system represented in the graph below?

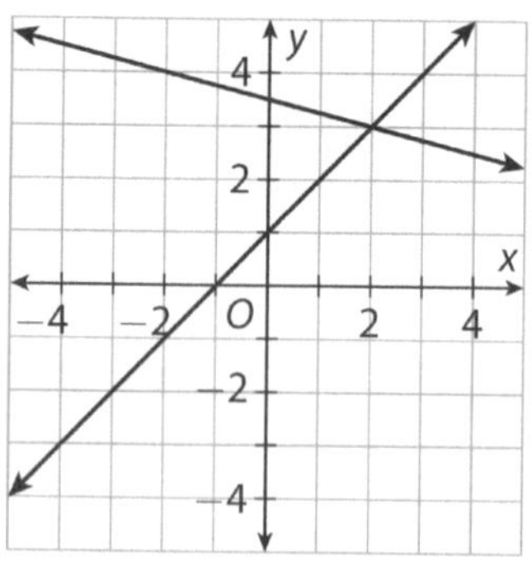

6

What is the *y*-value of the solution to the system consisting of the line represented in the table below and the line $4y + 7x = 40$?

x	y
–4	1
0	2
4	3

7

What is the sum of the *y*-intercepts of the lines in the system represented in the graph below and the *y*-intercept of the line $y = 5x + 3$?

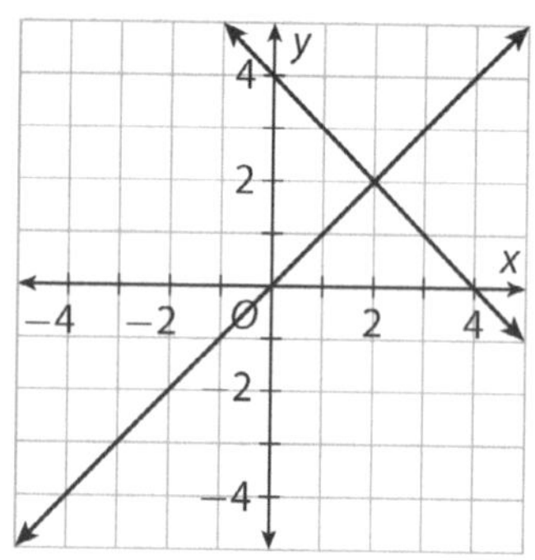

8

What is the *y*-value of the solution to the system represented in the table below?

x	y_1	y_2
6	1.5	6
7	2	2
8	2.5	–2
9	3	–6

Name ______________________ Date ______________ Class ______________

Connect various representations of systems of linear equations by deriving one from the other.

ANSWER SHEET

1. A B C D

2. A B C D

3. A B C D

4. A B C D

5. / . 0 1 2 3 4 5 6 7 8 9

6. / . 0 1 2 3 4 5 6 7 8 9

7. / . 0 1 2 3 4 5 6 7 8 9

8. / . 0 1 2 3 4 5 6 7 8 9

Name ______________________ Date ____________ Class____________

Utilize algebraic structure to efficiently solve a system of two linear equations in two variables.

SAMPLE MULTIPLE CHOICE

Solve this system of two equations.

$$y = 3x + 2$$
$$y = 5x - 6$$

A) (0,4)

B) (4,14)

C) (2,8)

D) No solution

Set the expressions for *y* equal and solve the resulting equation for *x*.

$$3x + 2 = 5x - 6$$
$$8 = 2x$$
$$4 = x$$

Substitute the value of *x* into either given equation and find the value of *y*.

$$y = 3x + 2$$
$$y = 3(4) + 2$$
$$y = 14$$

So, the solution to the system is (4, 14).

The correct answer is B. A ○ B ● C ○ D ○

1

Solve this system of two equations.

$$y = 4x - 1$$
$$y = x + 2$$

A) (0,−1) C) (1,3)

B) (0,2) D) No solution

2

Solve the given system.

$$-4x + 3y = -1$$
$$5x - 3y = -1$$

A) (−3,−2) C) (2,3)

B) (−2,−3) D) No solution

3

Solve the system of equations.

$$y = -2x - 4$$
$$y = 3x + 6$$

A) (−2,0) C) (0,−2)

B) (0,2) D) No solution

4

Solve the system of equations.

$$0.75y = -2x - 2$$
$$8 - 7x = 0.75y$$

A) (8,2) C) (2,−8)

B) (−8,−2) D) No solution

5

Solve the given system.

$$-4x + y = 22$$
$$3x - y = -17$$

A) (−5,2) C) (−2,5)

B) (5,−2) D) No solution

6

Solve this system of two equations.

$$-2x + y = -8$$
$$-2x + y = 3$$

A) (0,−8) C) (0,−3)

B) (−3,−8) D) No solution

Name ____________________ Date ____________ Class ____________

SAMPLE GRID-IN

What is the value of $x + y$ for the system shown below?

$$-2x + 5y = 1$$
$$3x - 4y = 9$$

The system of equations can be solved algebraically using substitution and then the values for x and y could be added. The process of solving either equation for one of the variables and then substituting the expression into the other equation involves several steps of careful calculation.

Time-Saving Tip: Much less time is needed to answer the question if one recognizes that when the two equations are added together, their sum is the equation $x + y = 10$.

This result shows the value of the quantity $x + y$ directly. The answer to the question is 10.

Grid in 10.

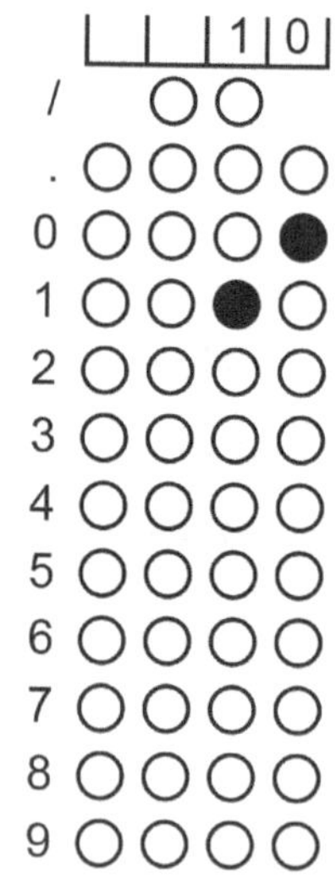

7

What is the value of $7y$ for the given system?

$$9x + 4y = 21$$
$$-9x + 3y = 0$$

8

What is the y-coordinate of the solution to the given system?

$$5x + 2y = 18$$
$$5x + y = 14$$

9

What is the value of xy for the given system?

$$y = -x$$
$$y = x$$

10

What is the x-coordinate of the solution to the given system?

$$y = 2.9x - 26.3$$
$$y = 1.9x + 19.7$$

11

What is the value of $3x + y$ for the given system?

$$6x - 5y = 28$$
$$x - 2y = 7$$

12

What is the value of $x + y$ for the given system?

$$3x + 2y = 24$$
$$2x + 3y = 6$$

Name ____________________ Date ____________ Class ____________

Utilize algebraic structure to efficiently solve a system of two linear equations in two variables.

ANSWER SHEET

1. A B C D ○ ○ ○ ○
2. A B C D ○ ○ ○ ○
3. A B C D ○ ○ ○ ○
4. A B C D ○ ○ ○ ○
5. A B C D ○ ○ ○ ○
6. A B C D ○ ○ ○ ○

7.
```
  |_|_|_|_|
/    ○ ○
. ○ ○ ○ ○
0 ○ ○ ○ ○
1 ○ ○ ○ ○
2 ○ ○ ○ ○
3 ○ ○ ○ ○
4 ○ ○ ○ ○
5 ○ ○ ○ ○
6 ○ ○ ○ ○
7 ○ ○ ○ ○
8 ○ ○ ○ ○
9 ○ ○ ○ ○
```

8.
```
  |_|_|_|_|
/    ○ ○
. ○ ○ ○ ○
0 ○ ○ ○ ○
1 ○ ○ ○ ○
2 ○ ○ ○ ○
3 ○ ○ ○ ○
4 ○ ○ ○ ○
5 ○ ○ ○ ○
6 ○ ○ ○ ○
7 ○ ○ ○ ○
8 ○ ○ ○ ○
9 ○ ○ ○ ○
```

9.
```
  |_|_|_|_|
/    ○ ○
. ○ ○ ○ ○
0 ○ ○ ○ ○
1 ○ ○ ○ ○
2 ○ ○ ○ ○
3 ○ ○ ○ ○
4 ○ ○ ○ ○
5 ○ ○ ○ ○
6 ○ ○ ○ ○
7 ○ ○ ○ ○
8 ○ ○ ○ ○
9 ○ ○ ○ ○
```

10.
```
  |_|_|_|_|
/    ○ ○
. ○ ○ ○ ○
0 ○ ○ ○ ○
1 ○ ○ ○ ○
2 ○ ○ ○ ○
3 ○ ○ ○ ○
4 ○ ○ ○ ○
5 ○ ○ ○ ○
6 ○ ○ ○ ○
7 ○ ○ ○ ○
8 ○ ○ ○ ○
9 ○ ○ ○ ○
```

11.
```
  |_|_|_|_|
/    ○ ○
. ○ ○ ○ ○
0 ○ ○ ○ ○
1 ○ ○ ○ ○
2 ○ ○ ○ ○
3 ○ ○ ○ ○
4 ○ ○ ○ ○
5 ○ ○ ○ ○
6 ○ ○ ○ ○
7 ○ ○ ○ ○
8 ○ ○ ○ ○
9 ○ ○ ○ ○
```

12.
```
  |_|_|_|_|
/    ○ ○
. ○ ○ ○ ○
0 ○ ○ ○ ○
1 ○ ○ ○ ○
2 ○ ○ ○ ○
3 ○ ○ ○ ○
4 ○ ○ ○ ○
5 ○ ○ ○ ○
6 ○ ○ ○ ○
7 ○ ○ ○ ○
8 ○ ○ ○ ○
9 ○ ○ ○ ○
```

Name ______________________ Date ____________ Class____________

Determine the number of solutions for a system, and use structure to interpret parts of systems of equations.

SAMPLE MULTIPLE CHOICE

Determine the number of solutions for the following system.

$$y = 2x + 2$$
$$y = 2x - 6$$

A) 0
B) 1
C) 2
D) Infinitely many

A system has no solution if the graphs of the equations are parallel lines, one solution if the lines intersect at a single point, and infinite solutions if the lines are the same.

Notice that the slope in both equations is 2, so the lines are either parallel or the same.

Since the *y*-intercepts are different the lines cannot be the same, so the lines must be parallel. Parallel lines do not intersect. This system has 0 solutions.

The correct answer is A. A ● B ○ C ○ D ○

1

Determine the number of solutions for the following system.

$$y = 2x + 4$$
$$2y = 4x + 8$$

A) 0
B) 1
C) 2
D) Infinitely many

2

Determine the number of solutions for the system shown below.

$$y = x + 4$$
$$y = 3x - 6$$

A) 0
B) 1
C) 2
D) Infinitely many

3

Determine the number of solutions for the following system.

$$3x = y + 6$$
$$y = 3x + 2$$

A) 0
B) 1
C) 2
D) Infinitely many

4

Suppose the equations in the following system were graphed in the same *xy*-plane. At how many points will the graphs of the lines intersect?

$$3y - 2x = 3$$
$$x + 2y = 9$$

A) 0
B) 1
C) 2
D) Infinitely many

5

A 21-mile community path has distance markers along it. A jogger and a bicyclist start at opposite ends at the same time and approach each other. The following system describes their locations *y* along the path after *x* hours.

$$y = 3x$$
$$y = -12x + 21$$

What does the *x*-coordinate of the solution to this system represent?

A) The distance marker where they meet
B) The distance they travel before meeting
C) The time it takes for them to meet
D) The time it takes each of them to reach the half way point on the path

Name ______________________ Date ______________ Class ______________

SAMPLE GRID-IN

What value of b would result in the following system of equations having infinitely many solutions?

$$3y = 6x + 9$$
$$5y = 10x + b$$

Systems of linear equations have infinitely many solutions when the equations model the same line.

Notice that the terms of the first equation have a common factor of 3. Divide each term on both sides of the equation by 3.

$$\frac{3y}{3} = \frac{6x}{3} + \frac{9}{3}$$
$$y = 2x + 3$$

When this equation is multiplied by 5, the resulting x- and y-terms match those in the second equation.

$$5(y) = 5(2x + 3)$$
$$5y = 10x + 15$$

So, the value of b must be 15 for the system to have infinitely many solutions.

Grid in 15.

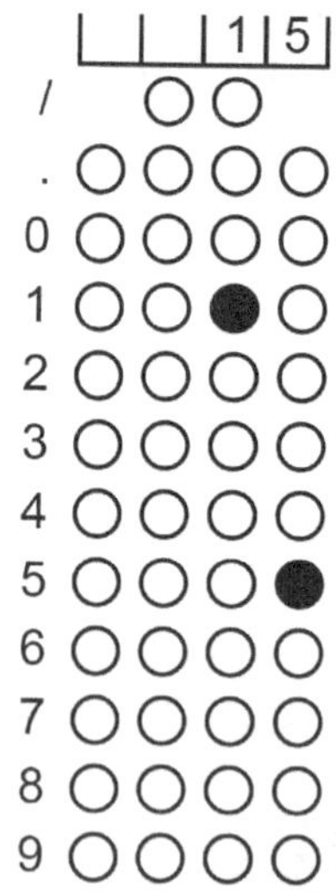

6

What value of b would result in the following system of equations having infinitely many solutions?

$$3y = 6x - 12$$
$$5y = 10x - b$$

7

What value of m would result in this system of equations having no solution?

$$4y = mx + 20$$
$$6y = 15x + 12$$

8

What value of m would make this system have infinitely many solutions?

$$3y - mx = 9$$
$$-7x + 7y = -21$$

9

The following system has one solution. What CANNOT be the value of a?

$$2y = 8x + 2$$
$$ay = 12x + 3$$

10

The following system has one solution. What CANNOT be the value of m?

$$-3y = 6x - 18$$
$$-y = mx + 6$$

11

The following system has no solution. What CANNOT be the value of b?

$$y = \frac{1}{4}x + b$$
$$y = \frac{1}{4}x + \frac{1}{2}$$

Name ______________________ Date ______________ Class ______________

Determine the number of solutions for a system, and use structure to interpret parts of systems of equations.

ANSWER SHEET

1. A B C D

2. A B C D

3. A B C D

4. A B C D

5. A B C D

6.
/
.
0
1
2
3
4
5
6
7
8
9

7.
/
.
0
1
2
3
4
5
6
7
8
9

8.
/
.
0
1
2
3
4
5
6
7
8
9

9.
/
.
0
1
2
3
4
5
6
7
8
9

10.
/
.
0
1
2
3
4
5
6
7
8
9

11.
/
.
0
1
2
3
4
5
6
7
8
9

Name ______________________ Date ______________ Class______________

Proficiently solve a system of linear equations in two variables.

SAMPLE MULTIPLE CHOICE

Jerome has \$7.95 in quarters and nickels. If the number of nickels he has is 3 more than 8 times the number of quarters, how many nickels does he have?

A) 11

B) 12

C) 99

D) 159

Let n be the number of nickels and q be the number of quarters. Use the given information to write two linear equations.

$$0.25q + 0.05n = 7.95$$
$$n = 3 + 8q$$

Substitute $3 + 8q$ for n in the first equation and solve for q.

$$0.25q + 0.05n = 7.95$$
$$0.25q + 0.05(3 + 8q) = 7.95$$
$$0.25q + 0.15 + 0.4q = 7.95$$
$$0.65q = 7.8$$
$$q = 12$$

Substitute 12 for q in the second equation.

$$n = 3 + 8(12)$$
$$n - 3 + 96 = 99$$

So, Jerome has 99 nickels.

The correct answer is C. A B C D ○ ○ ● ○

1

Lydia has \$18.70 worth of 49-cent and 34-cent stamps. The number of 49-cent stamps she has is 4 more than 5 times the number of 34-cent stamps. How many 49-cent stamps does she have?

A) 6 C) 45

B) 34 D) 49

2

Parker babysat over school vacation for two families and earned \$606. One family pays \$12 an hour and the other family pays \$15 an hour. If he babysat at the \$12 rate for 5 more than 2 times the number of hours he babysat for the other family, how many hours did he spend babysitting for \$12 an hour?

A) 14 C) 33

B) 32 D) 47

3

The Singh family drove on a trip for 1,305 miles. They traveled at the speed limit on roads with speed limits of 55 and 65 miles per hour. They traveled at 65 miles per hour for 3 more than twice the number of hours they traveled at 55 miles per hour. How many hours were spent driving at 65 miles per hour?

A) 6 C) 20

B) 15 D) 24

4

$$25a + 5.5b = 119$$
$$a + b = 11$$

Which of the following points (a, b) satisfies the system above?

A) (4,7) C) (6,5)

B) (2,9) D) (3,8)

Name ______________________ Date ____________ Class____________

SAMPLE GRID-IN

A movie theater sells adult tickets for $15 and child tickets for $10. One night they sell $635 worth of tickets to a movie. If the number of adult tickets sold is 2 more than 3 times the number of child tickets, how many adult tickets did they sell?

Write a system of two linear equations where a is the number of adult tickets and c is the number of child tickets.

$$15a + 10c = 635$$
$$a = 2 + 3c$$

Substitute $2 + 3c$ for a in the first equation and solve for c.

$$15a + 10c = 635$$
$$15(2 + 3c) + 10c = 635$$
$$30 + 45c + 10c = 635$$
$$55c = 605$$
$$c = 11$$

Substitute 11 for c in the second equation and simplify.

$$a = 2 + 3(11)$$
$$a = 2 + 33 = 35$$

So, the theater sold 35 adult tickets.

Grid in 35.

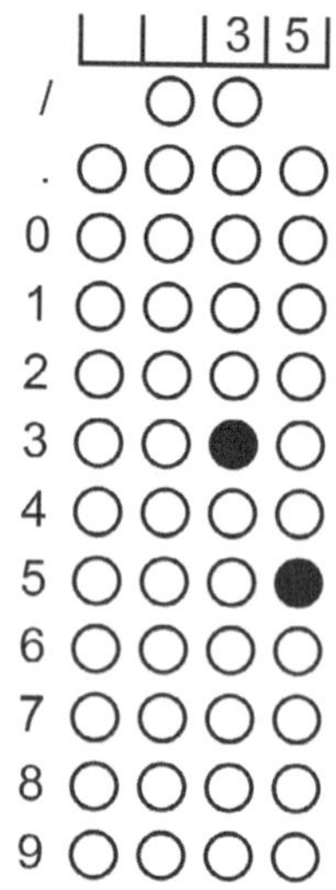

5

A landscaping company orders 2,045 pounds of grass seed. The grass seed comes in 35-pound bags and 80-pound bags. If the company ordered 43 bags of grass seed in all, how many 35-pound bags did the company order?

6

A school club spent $474 on hats and sweatshirts with the club logo on it. Hats cost $14 each and sweatshirts cost $22. If the number of sweatshirts they bought is 3 more than 4 times the number of hats, how many sweatshirts did they buy?

7

A groomer charges $17 to groom a cat and $25 to groom a dog. Last weekend he made $685 by grooming a total of 29 dogs and cats. How many dogs did he groom?

8

Hazel spent a total of $20.29 on kale and bananas to make breakfast smoothies for the cross-country team. Kale costs $1.99 per pound and the bananas cost $0.34 per pound. If the number of pounds of kale she bought was 5 less than twice the number of pounds of bananas she bought, how many pounds of kale did she buy?

9

To get ready for the upcoming summer youth softball season, a community activities director spent $708 on boxes of new softballs for game play and bags of line chalk for marking the fields. The softballs cost $75 per box of 12 balls and the chalk cost $9 per 50-pound bag. If the number of bags of chalk she bought was 4 less than the number of boxes of softballs, how many new softballs did she purchase?

Name ______________________ Date ______________ Class ______________

Proficiently solve a system of linear equations in two variables.

ANSWER SHEET

1. A B C D
○ ○ ○ ○

2. A B C D
○ ○ ○ ○

3. A B C D
○ ○ ○ ○

4. A B C D
○ ○ ○ ○

5. | | | | |

/ ○ ○
. ○ ○ ○ ○
0 ○ ○ ○ ○
1 ○ ○ ○ ○
2 ○ ○ ○ ○
3 ○ ○ ○ ○
4 ○ ○ ○ ○
5 ○ ○ ○ ○
6 ○ ○ ○ ○
7 ○ ○ ○ ○
8 ○ ○ ○ ○
9 ○ ○ ○ ○

6. | | | | |

/ ○ ○
. ○ ○ ○ ○
0 ○ ○ ○ ○
1 ○ ○ ○ ○
2 ○ ○ ○ ○
3 ○ ○ ○ ○
4 ○ ○ ○ ○
5 ○ ○ ○ ○
6 ○ ○ ○ ○
7 ○ ○ ○ ○
8 ○ ○ ○ ○
9 ○ ○ ○ ○

7. | | | | |

/ ○ ○
. ○ ○ ○ ○
0 ○ ○ ○ ○
1 ○ ○ ○ ○
2 ○ ○ ○ ○
3 ○ ○ ○ ○
4 ○ ○ ○ ○
5 ○ ○ ○ ○
6 ○ ○ ○ ○
7 ○ ○ ○ ○
8 ○ ○ ○ ○
9 ○ ○ ○ ○

8. | | | | |

/ ○ ○
. ○ ○ ○ ○
0 ○ ○ ○ ○
1 ○ ○ ○ ○
2 ○ ○ ○ ○
3 ○ ○ ○ ○
4 ○ ○ ○ ○
5 ○ ○ ○ ○
6 ○ ○ ○ ○
7 ○ ○ ○ ○
8 ○ ○ ○ ○
9 ○ ○ ○ ○

9. | | | | |

/ ○ ○
. ○ ○ ○ ○
0 ○ ○ ○ ○
1 ○ ○ ○ ○
2 ○ ○ ○ ○
3 ○ ○ ○ ○
4 ○ ○ ○ ○
5 ○ ○ ○ ○
6 ○ ○ ○ ○
7 ○ ○ ○ ○
8 ○ ○ ○ ○
9 ○ ○ ○ ○

Name ______________________ Date ______________ Class______________

Write and use linear inequalities in one or two variables to solve problems in real-world situations.

SAMPLE MULTIPLE CHOICE

$$T = 40 - 29x$$

Two mountain climbers are ascending a 2.23-mile-high summit. The temperature T, in degrees Fahrenheit, can be found for the altitude x, in miles, above the base of the summit using the equation above. At what altitudes will the climbers be in temperatures at or between 0° and 32° Fahrenheit?

A) $-0.3 \le x \le -0.27$

B) $1.1 \le x \le 1.4$

C) $1.4 \le x \le 2.23$

D) $0.28 \le x \le 1.38$

Use the given equation to find the values of x when T is between 0° and 32° Fahrenheit, inclusively. That is, find the values of x satisfying the following linear inequalities.

$$0 \le 40 - 29x \text{ and } 40 - 29x \le 32$$

Combine the two inequalities and solve for x.

$$0 \le 40 - 29x \le 32$$

$$-40 \le -29x \le -8$$

$$\frac{-40}{-29} \ge x \ge \frac{-8}{-29}$$

$$1.38 \ge x \ge 0.28$$

The correct answer is D. A ○ B ○ C ○ D ●

1

The number of grapes that are mixed in a bowl of fruit is given by $0.3(f + 6)$, where f is the total number of pieces of fruit in the bowl. If a bowl of fruit for brunch is to have between 21 and 24 grapes, inclusive, how many total pieces of fruit should be in the bowl?

A) $85 \le f \le 95$

B) $70 \le f \le 80$

C) $64 \le f \le 74$

D) $55 \le f \le 65$

2

The water capacity for a small dam is 375,000 gallons of water. On April 1, the dam contained 312,682 gallons. If runoff is entering the dam at a rate of 995 gallons of water per day d, which of the following inequalities describes when the dam is at or above its capacity?

A) $375{,}000 - 995 \le d$

B) $995d \le 62{,}318$

C) $995d + 312{,}682 \ge 375{,}000$

D) $995d \ge 687{,}682$

3

The average annual cost of owning a dog is \$695, while it is \$705 for a cat. Write an inequality that describes the number of dogs d and cats c that a pet owner can have if she is to keep the yearly costs below \$2,500.

A) $1{,}400(c + d) < 2{,}500$

B) $695c + 705d \le 2{,}500$

C) $1{,}400(c - d) \ge 2{,}500$

D) $705c + 695d < 2{,}500$

4

The maximum takeoff weight for one type of passenger plane is 171.7 metric tons. The operating weight of the airplane when empty is 90.9 metric tons, leaving 80.8 metric tons for fuel, crew, and passengers and their luggage. If 50 tons of fuel is needed, what is the maximum number of persons p (crew and passengers) allowed on board if the average person and their luggage are estimated to weigh 100 kilograms? (1 metric ton = 1,000 kilograms)

A) 308

B) 500

C) 808

D) 909

Name ______________________ Date ______________ Class ______________

SAMPLE GRID-IN

If the cost for a rental truck is \$25 per day plus 75 cents per mile driven, what is the maximum number of miles m that the rental truck can be driven each day so that the daily cost is no more than \$55?

The cost of renting the truck for m miles is given by the following expression.

$$25 + 0.75m$$

The total cost cannot exceed \$55, so solve the inequality $25 + 0.75m \leq 55$.

$$25 + 0.75m \leq 55$$
$$0.75m \leq 30$$
$$m \leq 40$$

So, the truck can be driven a maximum of 40 miles each day to stay within the daily budget of \$55.

Grid in 40.

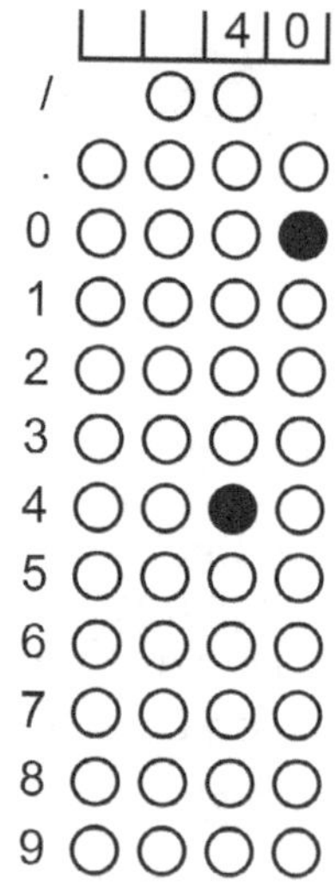

5

The yearly salary S for an employee beginning in 2014 is found in the table below, where n is the number of years after 2014. The employee receives a raise each year on the anniversary of her start date. If the employee continues working at the company, in what year will the salary first exceed \$27,000?

n	0	1	2
S	\$23,568	\$23,908	\$24,248

6

A homeowner is looking to hire an electrician to replace some switches. To replace switches, Arthur charges a trip fee of \$70 plus \$80 per switch. Jim charges a trip fee of \$50 plus \$83 per switch. What is the maximum number of switches that can be replaced if the homeowner wants to hire Jim and have the repairs cost less than what Arthur would charge?

7

Sandra raises chickens and sells the eggs. It costs her \$60 per month to raise the chickens. She sells each egg for \$0.25. What is the minimum number of eggs per month that Sandra must sell to make a profit?

8

A light-duty truck can hold up to 1,250 pounds of material in the bed of the truck. A contractor needs to transport 60-pound bags of cement mix and 20 cinder blocks that weigh 30 pounds each. What is the maximum number of bags of cement mix the contractor can transport along with all 20 cinder blocks in a single trip?

9

The revenue, in dollars, from selling w packages of wooden pencils is $5.95w$, and the cost of producing the packages is $0.2w$. Find the minimum number of packages of wooden pencils w needed in order for the profit to exceed \$42,000.

10

Your doctor recommends that you consume no more than 54 grams of protein per day. A cup of 2% milk has 8 grams of protein, and a single serving of lean ground beef has 18 grams. What is the maximum number of cups of milk you can drink if you eat 2 servings of lean ground beef? Give your answer as a whole number.

Name ______________________ Date ______________ Class ______________

Write and use linear inequalities in one or two variables to solve problems in real-world situations.

ANSWER SHEET

1. A B C D

2. A B C D

3. A B C D

4. A B C D

5.
/
.
0
1
2
3
4
5
6
7
8
9

6.
/
.
0
1
2
3
4
5
6
7
8
9

7.
/
.
0
1
2
3
4
5
6
7
8
9

8.
/
.
0
1
2
3
4
5
6
7
8
9

9.
/
.
0
1
2
3
4
5
6
7
8
9

10.
/
.
0
1
2
3
4
5
6
7
8
9

Name ______________________ Date ______________ Class______________

Create linear inequalities, and interpret their solutions in terms of the context.

SAMPLE MULTIPLE CHOICE

For a fruit bowl, there must be at least 3 more apples than oranges, and there must be at least 5 oranges. If there are 18 apples in a fruit bowl, what is the greatest number of oranges allowed?

A) 21
B) 15
C) 10
D) 3

Write an inequality for the first condition. Let A represent the number of apples, and let R represent the number of oranges.

$$A \geq 3 + R$$

It is given that there are 18 apples in the bowl, so let $A = 18$. Solve the resulting inequality for R.

$$18 \geq 3 + R$$
$$15 \geq R$$

The greatest number of oranges allowed is 15.

The correct answer is B. A ○ B ● C ○ D ○

1

Beatriz paid $18.32 at a market this morning. She had three $5 bills and some quarters. What is the least number of quarters she needed to use?

A) 1
B) 2
C) 13
D) 14

2

D'ante takes $38 with him when he goes to the amusement park. He spends $4.57 on lunch and later spends $2.63 for ice cream. After D'ante rides the Flomobile seven times at a cost of $2 per ride, what is the greatest number of times he can ride the Supertwister if it costs $3.50 per ride?

A) 6
B) 5
C) 4
D) 3

3

A couple is organizing their wedding reception. They have budgeted $2,000 for it. The location they selected charges a $100 maintenance fee plus $36 per person. What is the greatest number of people the couple can have at the reception and stay within their budget?

A) 51
B) 52
C) 53
D) 54

4

Madison is playing a game that has four rounds. In the first three rounds, she scores 76, 82, and 79 points. How many points can she score in the fourth round so that her average is below 80?

A) fewer than 83
B) no more than 83
C) at least 83
D) more than 83

5

Justin works in a clothing store. He earns $175 per week plus 6% of the total amount he sells. What is the minimum whole-number dollar amount of sales he needs to make in a week in order to earn at least $300 that week?

A) $2,083
B) $2,084
C) $2,916
D) $2,917

6

A school district predicts that there will be 1,785 new students next year. If each class has 1 teacher, what is the minimum number of new teachers the district must hire to keep the average class size under 28?

A) 62
B) 63
C) 64
D) 65

Name ________________________ Date ______________ Class______________

SAMPLE GRID-IN

A crew will install liners in pipes that are each 72 feet long. If the crew has 189 liners that are each 20 feet long, what is the greatest number of pipes the crew can fully line? Assume partial liners can be used.

Each 72-foot pipe needs $\frac{72}{20} = 3.6$ liners that are each 20 feet long. If x is the number of pipes that can be lined, then $3.6x$ represents the number of liners needed for x pipes. The total number of liners cannot exceed 189. Set up and solve an inequality.

$$3.6x \leq 189$$

$$x \leq \frac{189}{3.6}$$

$$x \leq 52.5$$

So, the greatest number of pipes is 52.

Grid in 52.

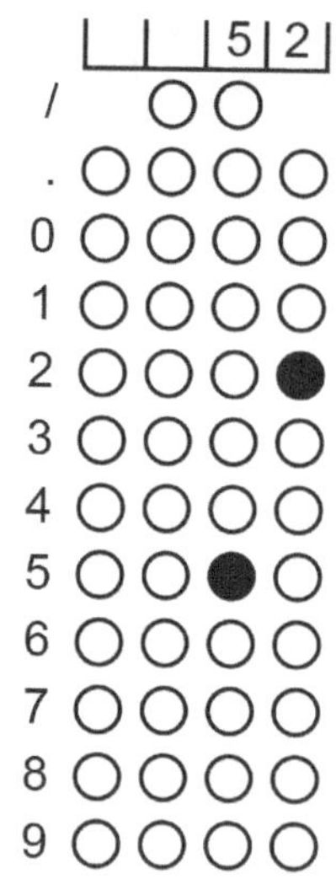

7

A car salesman earns a commission of 2.5% of the price of every new car sold. His goal is to earn at least $5,700 this month. He has already earned $3,445. If he wants to earn the rest by selling "closeout special" models at $19,900 each, what is the minimum number of closeout specials he must sell?

8

At a small factory, the weekly costs include $14,000 for labor and $4 for each item manufactured. The factory earns $18 per item. What is the minimum number of items that must be manufactured in a week for the total income to be greater than the total of the labor and per-item costs?

9

Julia is deciding between a job at a clothing store and a job at an electronics store. At the clothing store, she would earn $3,100 per month. At the electronics store, she would earn $2,000 plus a 5% commission on all of her sales that month. How many $300 television sets would she need to sell in a month to earn more at the electronics store than she would earn at the clothing store?

10

Marco wants to buy T-shirts and hats for his friends at a baseball game. He has $95 to spend. Each shirt costs $15.95, and each hat costs $12.49. If he buys 2 shirts, what is the greatest number of hats he can buy?

11

Keisha sells bracelets at a craft fair for $8 each. Her monthly fixed costs are $865, and each bracelet costs $3.45 to make. At least how many bracelets must she sell in a month to make a profit?

12

An elevator at a construction site has a maximum capacity of 5,000 pounds. The elevator operator weighs 180 pounds. Considering the weight of the elevator operator, what is the greatest number of 80-pound bags of cement mix that the elevator can hold?

13

An archery set containing a bow and three arrows costs $33.99. Additional arrows cost $2.50 each. Including the arrows in the set, what is the maximum number of arrows that can be purchased with $100 when buying one set?

Name ______________________ Date ____________ Class ____________

Create linear inequalities, and interpret their solutions in terms of the context.

ANSWER SHEET

1. A B C D
2. A B C D
3. A B C D
4. A B C D
5. A B C D
6. A B C D

7.
/
.
0
1
2
3
4
5
6
7
8
9

8.
/
.
0
1
2
3
4
5
6
7
8
9

9.
/
.
0
1
2
3
4
5
6
7
8
9

10.
/
.
0
1
2
3
4
5
6
7
8
9

11.
/
.
0
1
2
3
4
5
6
7
8
9

12.
/
.
0
1
2
3
4
5
6
7
8
9

13.
/
.
0
1
2
3
4
5
6
7
8
9

Name ______________________ Date ____________ Class ____________

Interpret components of linear inequalities in one or two variables.

SAMPLE MULTIPLE CHOICE

$$y > ax + b$$

In the xy-plane, (0, 0) is a solution to the inequality above. Which of the following relationships must be true?

A) $b > 0$

B) $b < 0$

C) $a > b$

D) $a < b$

Since (0, 0) is a solution to the inequality, substituting $x = 0$ and $y = 0$ must yield a true statement.

$$y > ax + b$$
$$0 > a(0) + b$$
$$0 > b$$
$$b < 0$$

The correct answer is B. A ○ B ● C ○ D ○

1

$$y < ax - b$$

In the xy-plane, (1, 0) is a solution to the inequality above. Which of the following relationships must be true?

A) $b > 0$

B) $b < 0$

C) $a > b$

D) $a < b$

2

If c, d, and x are all positive, which of the following inequalities must be true?

A) $cx - d > 0$

B) $cx + d > 0$

C) $-cx - d > 0$

D) $-cx + d > 0$

3

Suppose that $x < y$. If k is a nonzero constant, which of the following statements must be true?

A) $x + k > y - k$

B) $kx > y$

C) $kx < ky$

D) $x + k < y + k$

4

If $0 < a < b$, which of the following relationships must be true?

A) $a^2 < b^2$

B) $a - b > 0$

C) $\frac{1}{a} < \frac{1}{b}$

D) $ab < 0$

5

If $0 < x < y$, which of the following relationships between x and y is NOT necessarily true?

A) $\frac{y}{x} > 1$

B) $xy < 1$

C) $xy > 0$

D) $y^2 > x^2$

6

$$ax + by \leq 0$$

If the graph of the inequality above does not include any points in quadrant II, which of the following pairs of inequalities could both be true?

A) $a > 0$ and $b > 0$

B) $a > 0$ and $b < 0$

C) $a < 0$ and $b > 0$

D) $a < 0$ and $b < 0$

Name ______________________ Date ______________ Class______________

SAMPLE GRID-IN

Suppose that $1 < x < y < 15$, where x and y are both integers. What is the greatest possible value of xy?

The greatest possible value of xy occurs from using the greatest possible values of x and y that satisfy the given inequality. Since y is an integer strictly less than 15, its greatest possible value is 14. Similarly, since x is an integer strictly less than y, its greatest possible value when y equals 14 is 13. Multiply these two values:

$$xy = 13(14) = 182$$

So, the greatest possible product is 182.

Grid in 182.

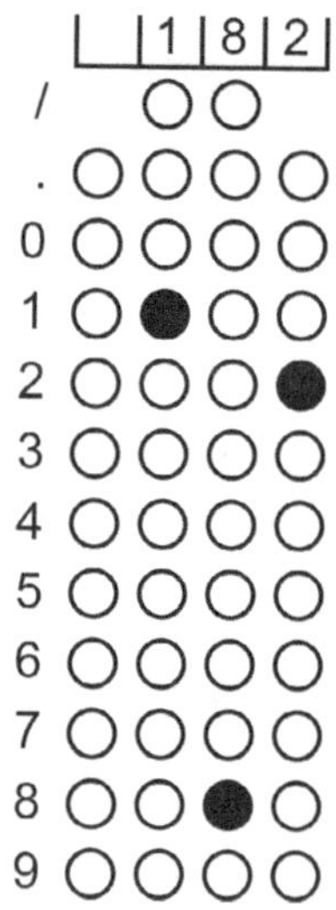

7

Suppose that $12 \le m < n < 20$, where m and n are both integers. What is the least possible value of $m + n$?

8

$$17 \le x \le k$$

If x and k are both integers, for what value of k does the inequality above have exactly one solution for x?

9

If $2 \le x \le 7$ and $3 \le y \le 12$, what is the greatest possible product of xy and $\frac{y}{x}$?

10

If $4r - 1 \ge 7$, what is the least possible value of $8r + 1$?

11

$$y \le -2x + 7$$

How many ordered-pair solutions (x, y) of the inequality above have coordinates that are both positive integers?

12

$$y < -\frac{1}{3}x + 8$$

$$ax + by < c$$

If the two inequalities above have the same graph and $c > 0$, what is the value of $\frac{a}{b}$?

13

Suppose that $p \le 9$ and that $30 \le p + q \le 37$. What is the least possible value of q?

14

$$0 \le \frac{2}{3}x + b \le 18$$

What is the least possible value of b for which the inequality above is not satisfied by any positive value of x?

Name ____________________ Date ____________ Class ____________

Interpret components of linear inequalities in one or two variables.

ANSWER SHEET

1. A B C D ○ ○ ○ ○
2. A B C D ○ ○ ○ ○
3. A B C D ○ ○ ○ ○
4. A B C D ○ ○ ○ ○
5. A B C D ○ ○ ○ ○
6. A B C D ○ ○ ○ ○

7. Grid-in: / ○○; . ○○○○; 0–9 ○○○○

8. Grid-in: / ○○; . ○○○○; 0–9 ○○○○

9. Grid-in: / ○○; . ○○○○; 0–9 ○○○○

10. Grid-in: / ○○; . ○○○○; 0–9 ○○○○

11. Grid-in: / ○○; . ○○○○; 0–9 ○○○○

12. Grid-in: / ○○; . ○○○○; 0–9 ○○○○

13. Grid-in: / ○○; . ○○○○; 0–9 ○○○○

14. Grid-in: / ○○; . ○○○○; 0–9 ○○○○

Name ______________________ Date ______________ Class______________

Connect various representations of linear inequalities in one or two variables by deriving one from the other.

SAMPLE MULTIPLE CHOICE

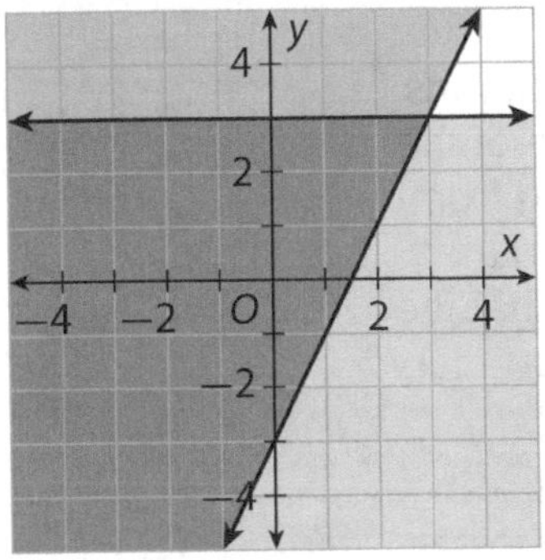

The figure above shows the graph of a system of linear inequalities. What are the inequalities?

A) $y \geq 2x - 3$ and $y \geq 3$

B) $y \geq 2x - 3$ and $y \leq 3$

C) $y \leq 2x - 3$ and $y \geq 3$

D) $y \leq 2x - 3$ and $y \leq 3$

The solution of a system of linear inequalities is the region that is common to the solutions of the individual inequalities.

First consider the oblique line. The shaded region is above this solid line, meaning that the *y*-values satisfying the system are on or above this line. Therefore, the first inequality is $y \geq 2x - 3$.

Now consider the solid horizontal line. The shaded region is below this solid line, meaning that the *y*-values satisfying the system are on or below this line. Therefore, the second inequality is $y \leq 3$.

The correct answer is B. A ○ B ● C ○ D ○

1

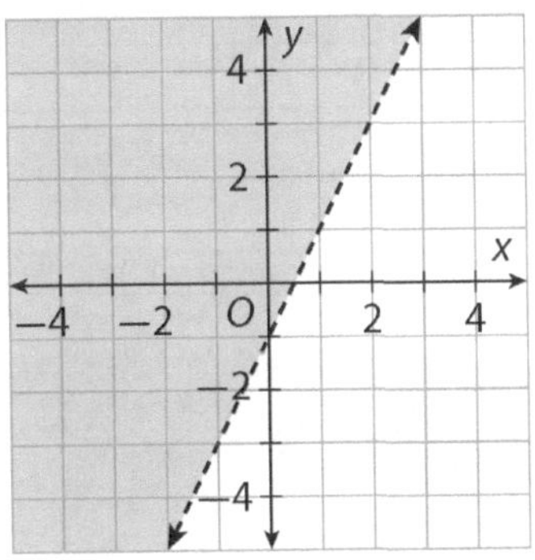

The figure above shows the graph of a linear inequality in two variables. Which of the following represents the linear inequality?

A) $2x - y < 1$

B) $2x - y > 1$

C) $2x + y < 1$

D) $2x + y > 1$

2

The table below shows several solutions (x, y) of a linear inequality in two variables. Which of the following could NOT be the linear inequality?

x	0	–1	7	–2
y	6	4	–1	5

A) $3x + 5y > 15$

B) $y > 2x + 3$

C) $x \geq -8$

D) $3x + 4y < 27$

3

The table below shows several solutions (x, y) of a linear inequality in two variables. Which of the following could be the linear inequality?

x	–10	4	6	–7
y	–8	–10	–8	2

A) $x - 2y < -11$

B) $x - 2y > -11$

C) $x - 2y \leq -11$

D) $x - 2y \geq -11$

Name ______________________ Date ____________ Class ____________

SAMPLE GRID-IN

y	least x	greatest x
–5	0	36
–3	1	28
–1	2	20

The table shows the least and greatest x-coordinates of points that satisfy a system of linear inequalities for selected y-coordinates. What is the greatest value of y for which the ordered pair (x, y) satisfies the system?

Notice that as the y-values increase, the least x-values increase and the greatest x-values decrease. This means that the boundary of the solution region has an inverted-V shape.

The values in the first two columns of the table show that the slope of the portion of the boundary rising from left to right is 2. The values in the first and last columns show that the slope of the portion of the boundary falling from left to right is $-\frac{1}{4}$.

The lines intersect at (4, 3). Points with greater y-coordinates are not in the solution region.

So, the greatest y-value of an ordered pair solution is 3.

Grid in 3.

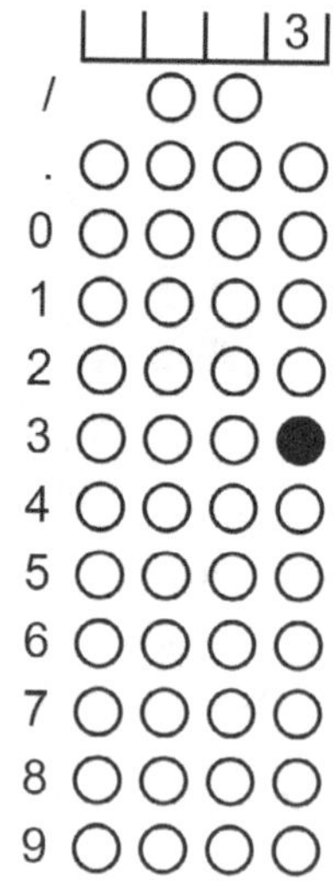

4

The table at the right shows the least and greatest y-coordinates of points that satisfy a system of linear inequalities for selected x-coordinates. What is the greatest value of x for which the ordered pair (x, y) satisfies the system?

x	least y	greatest y
0	–3	22
1	0	20
2	3	18

5

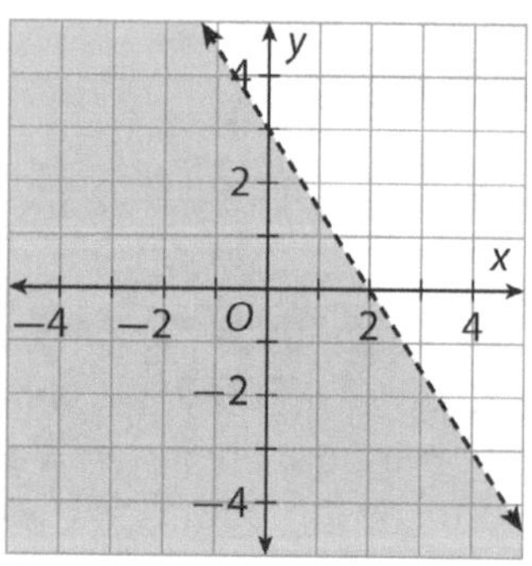

The graph above shows the solution of the linear inequality $3x + By < 6$. What is the value of B?

6

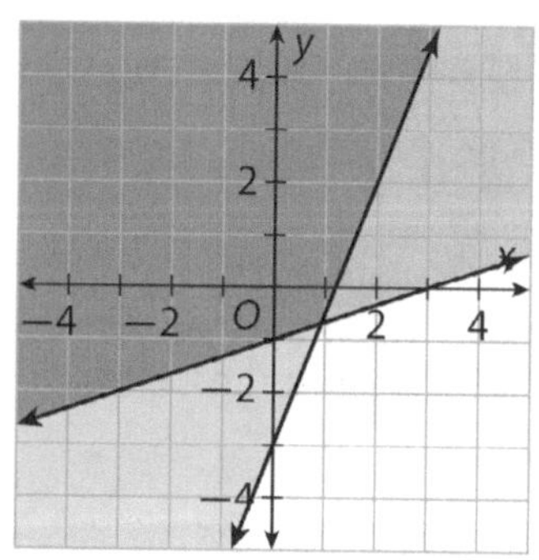

The graph above shows the solution of a system of linear inequalities of the form $-x + ky \geq -3$ and $\frac{5}{2}x - y \leq k$. What is the value of k?

Name ________________________ Date ____________ Class____________

Connect various representations of linear inequalities in one or two variables by deriving one from the other.

ANSWER SHEET

1. A B C D
○ ○ ○ ○

2. A B C D
○ ○ ○ ○

3. A B C D
○ ○ ○ ○

4. | | | | |

/		○	○	
.	○	○	○	○
0	○	○	○	○
1	○	○	○	○
2	○	○	○	○
3	○	○	○	○
4	○	○	○	○
5	○	○	○	○
6	○	○	○	○
7	○	○	○	○
8	○	○	○	○
9	○	○	○	○

5. | | | | |

/		○	○	
.	○	○	○	○
0	○	○	○	○
1	○	○	○	○
2	○	○	○	○
3	○	○	○	○
4	○	○	○	○
5	○	○	○	○
6	○	○	○	○
7	○	○	○	○
8	○	○	○	○
9	○	○	○	○

6. | | | | |

/		○	○	
.	○	○	○	○
0	○	○	○	○
1	○	○	○	○
2	○	○	○	○
3	○	○	○	○
4	○	○	○	○
5	○	○	○	○
6	○	○	○	○
7	○	○	○	○
8	○	○	○	○
9	○	○	○	○

Name ______________________ Date ______________ Class______________

Interpret a point in the solution set of a linear inequality or system of linear inequalities.

SAMPLE MULTIPLE CHOICE

Which of the following ordered pairs is NOT a solution of the inequality $3x - 4y \geq 12$?

A) $(0,-3)$

B) $(2,-1)$

C) $(-2,-5)$

D) $(-1,-4)$

A solution of the inequality must satisfy the inequality. Substitute the coordinates of the point for x and y in the inequality, and determine if a true statement results.

$(0,-3)$: $3(0)-4(-3)\overset{?}{\geq}12$; $12\overset{?}{\geq}12$; True

$(2,-1)$: $3(2)-4(-1)\overset{?}{\geq}12$; $10\overset{?}{\geq}12$; False

$(-2,-5)$: $3(-2)-4(-5)\overset{?}{\geq}12$; $14\overset{?}{\geq}12$; True

$(-1,-4)$: $3(-1)-4(-4)\overset{?}{\geq}12$; $13\overset{?}{\geq}12$; True

So, the only ordered pair that does not satisfy the inequality is $(2,-1)$.

The correct answer is B. A ○ B ● C ○ D ○

1

Which of the following numbers is NOT a solution of $2x - 7 < 5x + 2$?

A) -4

B) -2

C) -1

D) 0

2

Which of the following is the solution set of the inequality $4x + 1 \geq 4x - 7$?

A) $x \geq 1$

B) $x \geq -7$

C) $x \geq 0$

D) All real numbers

3

Consider the inequality $y + 2x < -1$. Which of the following possible values of y in the ordered pair $(-4, y)$ satisfies the inequality?

A) 12

B) 10

C) 8

D) 6

4

$$y \geq 3x - 2$$
$$x - 4y > -8$$

Consider the system of inequalities shown above. If the system is graphed in the xy-plane, which of the following points is NOT in the solution region?

A) $(0,0)$

B) $(4,-1)$

C) $(-4,-1)$

D) $(0,-1)$

5

If the system of inequalities below is graphed in the xy-plane, which quadrant contains NO solutions of the system?

$$x + y > 1$$
$$x \geq -1$$

A) Quadrant I

B) Quadrant II

C) Quadrant III

D) Quadrant IV

Name ______________________ Date ____________ Class____________

SAMPLE GRID-IN

$$3x - 8 > -2$$
$$\frac{1}{2}x + 3 < 5$$

Consider the system of linear inequalities above. What whole number x satisfies the system?

Both inequalities must be satisfied. Solve each one for x, and then determine the value of x that is in both solutions.

$3x - 8 > -2$	AND	$\frac{1}{2}x + 3 < 5$
$3x > 6$		$\frac{1}{2}x < 2$
$x > 2$		$x < 4$

The only whole number that is both greater than 2 and less than 4 is 3.

Grid in 3.

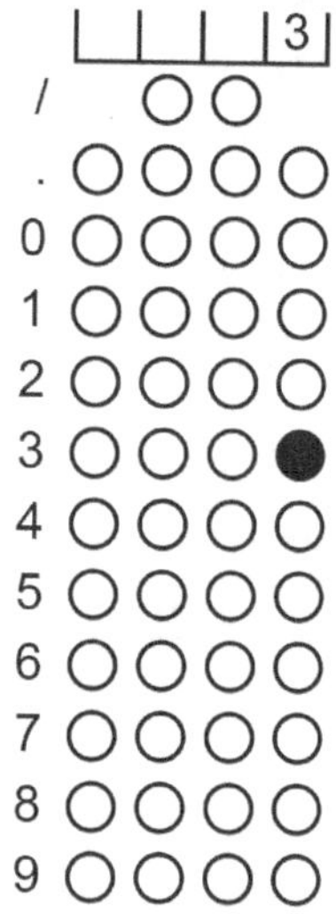

6

What is the greatest integer value of x in the ordered pair $(x, 1)$ for which the point lies in the solution region of the graph of the system of inequalities $y \le 2x - 1$ and $y < -\frac{1}{3}x + 2$?

7

How many quadrants of the xy-plane contain solutions to the system of inequalities $y > -x + 2$ and $y \ge 3x + 4$?

8

What is the greatest value of x that satisfies the inequalities $6x + 17 \ge 5$ and $8 - 3x \ge -13$?

9

What is the least integer value of y in the ordered pair (x, y) for which the coordinates satisfy the system of inequalities $y \ge -\frac{1}{2}x + 14$ and $y \ge 3x$?

10

How many quadrants of the xy-plane contain solutions to the system of inequalities $y < -\frac{1}{2}x + 14$ and $y \le 3x$?

11

What is the greatest integer value of y in the ordered pair $(-8, y)$ for which the point lies in the solution region of the graph of the system of inequalities $y \le -9x + 58$ and $y \le \frac{7}{2}x + 178$?

12

If the system of linear inequalities $y \ge \frac{1}{2}x - 4$ and $x - 2y > k$ has no solutions, what is the least possible value for k?

13

If the linear inequality $2x - 3y > t$ has no solutions in the second quadrant of the xy-plane, what is the least possible value for t?

Name ____________________ Date ____________ Class ____________

Interpret a point in the solution set of a linear inequality or system of linear inequalities.

ANSWER SHEET

1. A B C D
○ ○ ○ ○

2. A B C D
○ ○ ○ ○

3. A B C D
○ ○ ○ ○

4. A B C D
○ ○ ○ ○

5. A B C D
○ ○ ○ ○

6.
/ ○○
. ○○○○
0 ○○○○
1 ○○○○
2 ○○○○
3 ○○○○
4 ○○○○
5 ○○○○
6 ○○○○
7 ○○○○
8 ○○○○
9 ○○○○

7.
/ ○○
. ○○○○
0 ○○○○
1 ○○○○
2 ○○○○
3 ○○○○
4 ○○○○
5 ○○○○
6 ○○○○
7 ○○○○
8 ○○○○
9 ○○○○

8.
/ ○○
. ○○○○
0 ○○○○
1 ○○○○
2 ○○○○
3 ○○○○
4 ○○○○
5 ○○○○
6 ○○○○
7 ○○○○
8 ○○○○
9 ○○○○

9.
/ ○○
. ○○○○
0 ○○○○
1 ○○○○
2 ○○○○
3 ○○○○
4 ○○○○
5 ○○○○
6 ○○○○
7 ○○○○
8 ○○○○
9 ○○○○

10.
/ ○○
. ○○○○
0 ○○○○
1 ○○○○
2 ○○○○
3 ○○○○
4 ○○○○
5 ○○○○
6 ○○○○
7 ○○○○
8 ○○○○
9 ○○○○

11.
/ ○○
. ○○○○
0 ○○○○
1 ○○○○
2 ○○○○
3 ○○○○
4 ○○○○
5 ○○○○
6 ○○○○
7 ○○○○
8 ○○○○
9 ○○○○

12.
/ ○○
. ○○○○
0 ○○○○
1 ○○○○
2 ○○○○
3 ○○○○
4 ○○○○
5 ○○○○
6 ○○○○
7 ○○○○
8 ○○○○
9 ○○○○

13.
/ ○○
. ○○○○
0 ○○○○
1 ○○○○
2 ○○○○
3 ○○○○
4 ○○○○
5 ○○○○
6 ○○○○
7 ○○○○
8 ○○○○
9 ○○○○

Name ______________________ Date ____________ Class ____________

Find and use proportional relationships, ratios, rates, and units in real-world situations.

SAMPLE MULTIPLE CHOICE

Year	Subscriptions (thousands)
2014	86
2015	107
2016	135
2017	170

The table above shows the number of subscriptions to an online magazine over a four-year period. What is the average rate of change in the number of subscriptions from 2014 to 2017?

A) 21,000 per year
B) 28,000 per year
C) 42,000 per year
D) 84,000 per year

The average rate of change in the number of subscriptions on a per-year basis is the slope of the line between the corresponding data points. Using the points (2014, 86) and (2017, 170):

$$\text{Average rate of change} = \frac{170-86}{2017-2014} = \frac{84}{3} = 28$$

Since the number of subscriptions is given in thousands, the average rate of change is 28,000 per year.

The correct answer is B.

A B C D
○ ● ○ ○

1

In a recent vote, 23 members of the Central City town council voted for a countywide proposal, while 8 members voted against it. Which of the following city's voting ratios is closest to the ratio for Central City?

A) Eastville: 10 for, 2 against
B) Westville: 7 for, 2 against
C) Northville: 9 for, 3 against
D) Southville: 8 for, 4 against

2

The table below shows the monthly rent for apartments in a large residential building. What is the average rate of change in rent per square foot from an 897-square-foot apartment to a 1,509-square-foot apartment?

Area (ft^2)	766	897	1,131	1,509
Rent ($)	825	975	1,065	1,355

A) $0.62/ft^2
B) $0.67/ft^2
C) $0.72/ft^2
D) $0.79/ft^2

3

If there are 300 threads per inch in a set of percale sheets, how many threads are there per foot?

A) 25
B) 720
C) 1,200
D) 3,600

4

A salon sees at least 22 clients on a slow day and no more than 34 clients on a busy day. Which is a possible number of clients the salon could see in 5 days?

A) 108
B) 145
C) 172
D) 198

5

A car was purchased new in 2012 for $20,000. Each year since, the value of the car dropped by 8% of the previous year's value. What is the average rate of change of the value of the car from 2012 to 2014?

A) –$1,498/year
B) –$1,536/year
C) –$1,600/year
D) –$1,624/year

Name ______________________ Date ____________ Class ____________

SAMPLE GRID-IN

You plan to have new carpet installed in a room that measures 6 yards by 3 yards. At a home improvement store, you have selected carpet priced at \$4.50 per square foot installed. What will be the cost of the new carpet?

You will need to find the area of the room as well as convert to a common unit of either yards or feet. It is easiest to convert from yards to feet in this example.

The area of the room is $6 \times 3 = 18$ square yards. Convert this to square feet, noting that the conversion factor from yards to feet must be squared:

$$(18\text{ yd}^2)\left(\frac{3\text{ ft}}{1\text{ yd}}\right)^2 = 162\text{ ft}^2$$

Now, multiply this area by the price per square foot:

$$(162\text{ ft}^2)(\$4.50/\text{ft}^2) = \$729$$

So, the cost of the carpet will be \$729.

Grid in 729.

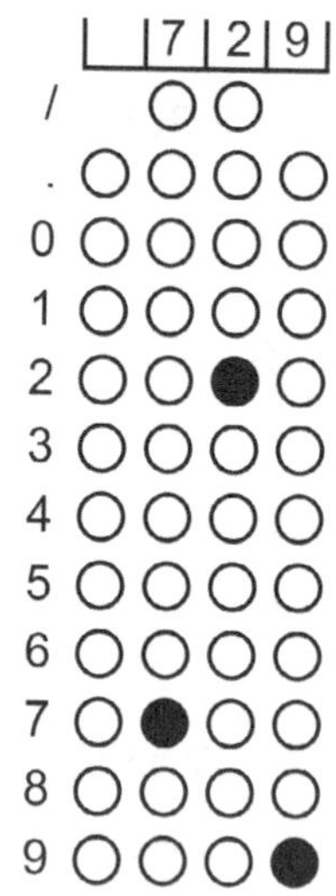

6

The Washington Monument located in Washington, DC, has a height of 555 feet $5\frac{1}{8}$ inches and a base width of 55 feet $1\frac{1}{2}$ inches. If a scale model of the monument is 12 inches tall, what is the width of the base of the model to the nearest tenth of an inch?

7

The table below gives the mountain gorilla population for selected years in Virunga National Park in Central Africa, following conservation efforts. What is the average rate of change of the gorilla population from 1981 to 2010? Round to one decimal place.

Year	1981	1989	2003	2010
Gorillas	254	320	380	480

8

During the 1989–1990 season, Larry Bird made 319 of the 343 free throws he attempted. Assuming a uniform level of consistency, how many free throws would he have made if he had attempted 400 free throws during that season?

9

The city of Champaign, Illinois, had an estimated population of 86,637 in 2016. The city has an area of 22.73 square miles. To the nearest whole number, what was the population density, in persons per square kilometer, of the city in 2016? Use the fact that 1 mile = 1.6 kilometers.

10

In 2016, the number of triplet births in the United States was 3,775, while the number of quadruplet births was 217. Using this ratio of multiple births, how many quadruplet births were there in a state with 331 triplet births?

Name ______________________ Date ______________ Class ______________

Find and use proportional relationships, ratios, rates, and units in real-world situations.

ANSWER SHEET

1. A B C D

2. A B C D

3. A B C D

4. A B C D

5. A B C D

6.
/
.
0
1
2
3
4
5
6
7
8
9

7.
/
.
0
1
2
3
4
5
6
7
8
9

8.
/
.
0
1
2
3
4
5
6
7
8
9

9.
/
.
0
1
2
3
4
5
6
7
8
9

10.
/
.
0
1
2
3
4
5
6
7
8
9

Name ______________________ Date ______________ Class______________

Solve problems involving derived units and unit conversion.

SAMPLE MULTIPLE CHOICE

5,280 feet = 1 mile
1 mile = 1.6 kilometers

A stretch of highway 15.2 kilometers in length is to be resurfaced. Using the information above, how many feet of highway will be resurfaced?

A) 48,706
B) 50,160
C) 52,390
D) 54,178

The number of kilometers must be converted to feet. There is more than one way to do this. For example, the first step can be to convert 15.2 kilometers to miles:

$$(15.2 \text{ kilometers})\left(\frac{1 \text{ mile}}{1.6 \text{ kilometers}}\right) = 9.5 \text{ miles}$$

Then convert 9.5 miles to feet:

$$(9.5 \text{ miles})\left(\frac{5{,}280 \text{ feet}}{1 \text{ mile}}\right) = 50{,}160 \text{ feet}$$

So, 15.2 kilometers is equivalent to 50,160 feet.

The correct answer is B. A ○ B ● C ○ D ○

1

As part of his exercise program, Alonso runs 3 days per week, for 1.5 hours each time. For how many minutes in total does Alonso run each week?

A) 90 C) 270
B) 160 D) 320

2

1 mile = 5,280 feet

A car is traveling at 40 miles per hour. What is its speed in feet per minute?

A) 3,520 C) 916
B) 2,794 D) 88

3

A worker-hour is the amount of work a single worker can do in one hour. It takes 5 workers 4 days to complete a project. Assuming each person works for 8 hours each day, how many worker-hours did the project take?

A) 128 C) 172
B) 160 D) 196

4

In early 2018, one U.S. dollar was approximately equivalent to 18.6 Mexican pesos. If video games were selling for $50 in the United States in 2018, how many games could be purchased with 6,000 pesos at this exchange rate?

A) 6 C) 8
B) 7 D) 9

5

1 inch = 2.54 centimeters

A desk is 4 feet long. Approximately how many centimeters long is the desk?

A) 106 C) 116
B) 112 D) 122

6

The town of Dryden, New York, has an area of 244 square kilometers. Its 2016 population was approximately 14,900. What was the population density in persons per square kilometer?

A) 47 C) 61
B) 59 D) 71

Name ______________________ Date ______________ Class ______________

SAMPLE GRID-IN

1 gallon	= 4 quarts
4 cups	= 1 quart

Using the information above, how many one-gallon jugs of milk are required for 48 one-cup servings?

The number of cups must be converted to gallons. Begin by converting 48 cups to quarts:

$$(48 \text{ cups})\left(\frac{1 \text{ quart}}{4 \text{ cups}}\right) = 12 \text{ quarts}$$

Now convert 12 quarts to gallons:

$$(12 \text{ quarts})\left(\frac{1 \text{ gallon}}{4 \text{ quarts}}\right) = 3 \text{ gallons}$$

So, 48 cups is equivalent to 3 gallons.

Grid in 3.

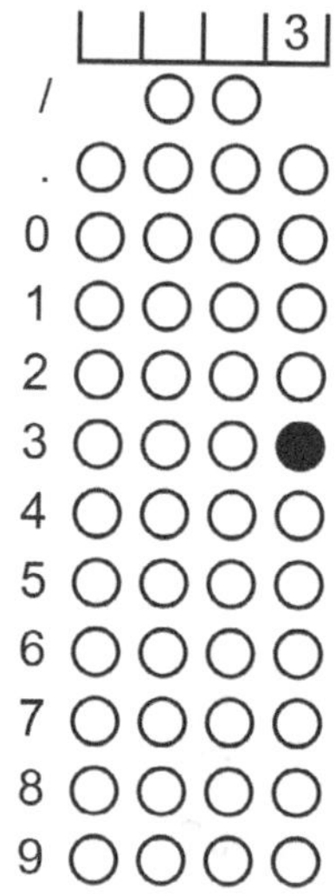

7

In early 2018, one U.S. dollar was approximately equivalent to 0.80 euros. If a plane ticket costs $560 in U.S. dollars, what is its cost in euros?

8

1 kilometer	= 1,000 meters
100 centimeters	= 1 meter

A manufacturing company uses safety wire in its products. The wire is sold in spools of 1.4 kilometers of wire, and the company uses 1,120 centimeters of wire each week. Using the information above, how many weeks does it take for the company to use an entire spool of the wire?

9

1 yard = 3 feet

A sprinter runs a 100-yard dash in 12 seconds. What is the sprinter's speed in feet per minute?

10

1 kilogram	= 2.2 pounds
16 ounces	= 1 pound

A grapefruit weighs 8.8 ounces. Using the information above, what is the mass of the grapefruit in kilograms?

11

The force exerted on an area due to pressure is commonly measured in pounds per square inch. If a 200-pound weight rests on a surface with an area of 16 square inches, what is the pressure in pounds per square inch?

12

A kilowatt-hour is a measure of electrical energy equivalent to a power consumption of 1,000 watts for 1 hour. How many kilowatt-hours are required to keep a 500-watt appliance running continuously for 1 week?

Name ______________________ Date ______________ Class______________

Solve problems involving derived units and unit conversion.

ANSWER SHEET

1. A B C D
2. A B C D
3. A B C D
4. A B C D
5. A B C D
6. A B C D

7. / . 0 1 2 3 4 5 6 7 8 9

8. / . 0 1 2 3 4 5 6 7 8 9

9. / . 0 1 2 3 4 5 6 7 8 9

10. / . 0 1 2 3 4 5 6 7 8 9

11. / . 0 1 2 3 4 5 6 7 8 9

12. / . 0 1 2 3 4 5 6 7 8 9

Name ______________________ Date ______________ Class______________

Use scale factors to compute quantities that are in a proportional relationship.

SAMPLE MULTIPLE CHOICE

A supermarket sells canned tuna at a cost of 4 cans for $5.00. How much will 7 cans of tuna cost?

A) $7.75
B) $8.75
C) $9.25
D) $9.75

The number of cans of tuna and the price are in a proportional relationship. The answer can be obtained by setting up and solving a proportion, where x is the cost for 7 cans:

$$\frac{4\text{ cans}}{5\text{ dollars}} = \frac{7\text{ cans}}{x\text{ dollars}}$$

Either cross-multiplying or multiplying each side of the equation by $5x$ yields the same result:

$$4x = 35$$

$$x = \frac{35}{4} = 8.75$$

The correct answer is B. A ○ B ● C ○ D ○

1

If 3 employees can assemble 72 circuit boards per day, how many circuit boards can be assembled each day by 11 employees?

A) 154
B) 264
C) 300
D) 432

2

Two-Wheel-Deals, a bicycle shop, rents bicycles at a rate of $14 per bicycle per day. If a tour group of 25 people rents bicycles from this shop, what will the cost be per day for the group?

A) $270
B) $280
C) $310
D) $350

3

A recipe calls for 2 cups of water for every 6 ounces of vegetables. How many cups of water will be needed for 1 pound (16 ounces) of vegetables?

A) $4\frac{1}{2}$
B) $5\frac{1}{3}$
C) $6\frac{3}{4}$
D) $7\frac{2}{3}$

4

The distance that a given bicycle moves forward for each full turn of its pedals is directly proportional to its gear ratio. A certain bicycle will move forward 163 inches when its gear ratio is $22:11$. How far, in inches, will the bike move forward when the gear ratio is $33:11$?

A) 244.5
B) 278
C) 310.5
D) 326

5

1 cubic yard = 27 cubic feet

A landscaping company sells mulch for $39 per cubic yard. What is the cost of the mulch per cubic foot, rounded to the nearest cent?

A) $1.28
B) $1.37
C) $1.44
D) $1.61

Name ______________________ Date ______________ Class______________

SAMPLE GRID-IN

If the current is constant, the voltage drop across a resistor is directly proportional to the resistance of the resistor. Assuming a constant current, if the voltage drop across a 2,400-ohm resistor is 6 volts, what will the voltage drop be across a 1,200-ohm resistor?

The resistance and the voltage drop are in a proportional relationship. Set up and solve a proportion, where x is the voltage drop across the 1,200-ohm resistor:

$$\frac{2{,}400\text{ ohms}}{6\text{ volts}} = \frac{1{,}200\text{ ohms}}{x\text{ volts}}$$

This can be solved by either cross-multiplying or multiplying both sides of the equation by $6x$:

$$6x \cdot \frac{2{,}400}{6} = 6x \cdot \frac{1{,}200}{x}$$

$$2{,}400x = 7{,}200$$

$$x = 3$$

So, the voltage drop across a 1,200-ohm resistor is 3 volts.

Grid in 3.

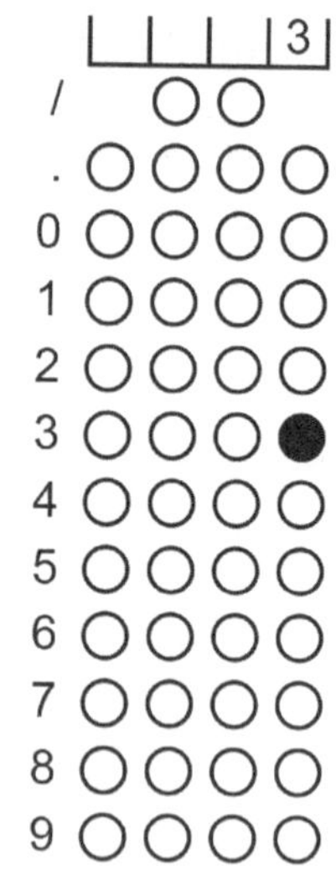

6

The speed limit on a certain highway is 60 miles per hour. If you drive at the speed limit, how many miles can you drive in 3.5 hours?

7

A blueprint for a building uses the scale $1\text{ inch} = 9\text{ feet}$. If the width of the actual building is 108 feet, what is the width of the building on the blueprint in inches?

8

A recipe calls for $1\frac{1}{3}$ cups of rice and 2 pounds of chicken. Aja is making the recipe for a dinner party and plans to use 4 cups of rice. How many pounds of chicken should Aja use if she wishes to keep the proportion of rice to chicken the same as in the recipe?

9

The cafeteria staff has determined that the students at Northern High School prefer apples to oranges by a ratio of $4:3$. The students consumed 620 apples last week. Assuming that the ratio is accurate, how many oranges did the students eat last week?

10

A baker needs to purchase 15 pounds of flour to fulfill a customer's order. If flour costs \$2.69 for a 5-pound bag, how much (in dollars) will the baker pay for the flour?

11

The fuel economy for a certain car is 35 miles per gallon of gasoline. If the cost of gasoline is \$2.75 per gallon, how many miles can the car drive on \$23.10 worth of gasoline?

Name ______________________ Date ______________ Class ______________

Use scale factors to compute quantities that are in a proportional relationship.

ANSWER SHEET

1. A B C D

2. A B C D

3. A B C D

4. A B C D

5. A B C D

6.
/
.
0
1
2
3
4
5
6
7
8
9

7.
/
.
0
1
2
3
4
5
6
7
8
9

8.
/
.
0
1
2
3
4
5
6
7
8
9

9.
/
.
0
1
2
3
4
5
6
7
8
9

10.
/
.
0
1
2
3
4
5
6
7
8
9

11.
/
.
0
1
2
3
4
5
6
7
8
9

Name ______________________ Date ______________ Class ______________

Find and use percentages to solve problems in real-world situations.

SAMPLE MULTIPLE CHOICE

Students in a biology class have been monitoring the growth of a plant. The plant grew by 14% in the first month that they monitored it and by 9% in the second month. If h represents the initial height of the plant, which expression models the plant's height after the second month in terms of the initial height h?

A) $\frac{h}{(1.09)(1.14)}$

B) $(1.09)(1.14)h$

C) $(1+(0.09+0.14))h$

D) $\frac{h}{1+(0.09+0.14)}$

Since the plant grew by 14% in the first month, then the height after one month is given by $h+0.14h=1.14h$.

The plant then grew by 9% in the second month. Its height at the start of the second month was $1.14h$, so its height at the end of the month is given by $1.14h+0.09(1.14h)=(1.14h)(1+0.09)$.

So, expressed in terms of its initial height h, the height after the second month is $(1.09)(1.14)h$.

The correct answer is B. A ○ B ● C ○ D ○

1

An investment decreased by 2.9% in its first year and then increased by 4.5% in the second year. If V represents the value of the investment after 2 years, what was the value of the original investment in terms of V?

A) $\frac{V}{1+(0.045-0.029)}$

B) $(1+(0.045-0.029))V$

C) $(0.971)(1.045)V$

D) $\frac{V}{(0.971)(1.045)}$

2

The average annual rainfall in a certain region has decreased from 24 inches per year to 18 inches per year over a 50-year period. By what percent has the annual average rainfall decreased over this time period?

A) 25% C) 37.5%

B) 33.3% D) 42.1%

3

Jaime purchased a jacket that was discounted by 25% off its original price. If he paid $51.72 for the jacket and did not pay any tax on the purchase, what was the original price of the jacket?

A) $63.75 C) $67.49

B) $64.65 D) $68.96

4

After a $20 discount was applied to a customer's bill for a restaurant meal, the final bill was $44. The customer added an 18% tip based on the cost of the meal prior to the discount. How much did the customer pay in total?

A) $51.92 C) $55.52

B) $53.90 D) $58.60

5

After receiving a 5% increase in her pay rate, Sheila earns $16.38 per hour working as a bookkeeper. What was her previous hourly rate?

A) $15.56 C) $16.10

B) $15.60 D) $16.33

Name ______________________ Date ______________ Class______________

SAMPLE GRID-IN

Tanya picked 6% more apples than Mieko picked. If Tanya picked 53 apples, how many more apples than Mieko did Tanya pick?

First, determine how many apples Mieko picked. Let t and m represent the number of apples that Tanya and Mieko picked, respectively.

The equation $1.06m = t$ models the relationship between m and t. Since Tanya picked 53 apples, substitute 53 for t and solve for m.

$$1.06m = t$$

$$1.06m = 53$$

$$m = \frac{53}{1.06} = 50$$

So Mieko picked 50 apples. Since Tanya picked 53 apples, she picked 3 more apples than Mieko picked.

Grid in 3.

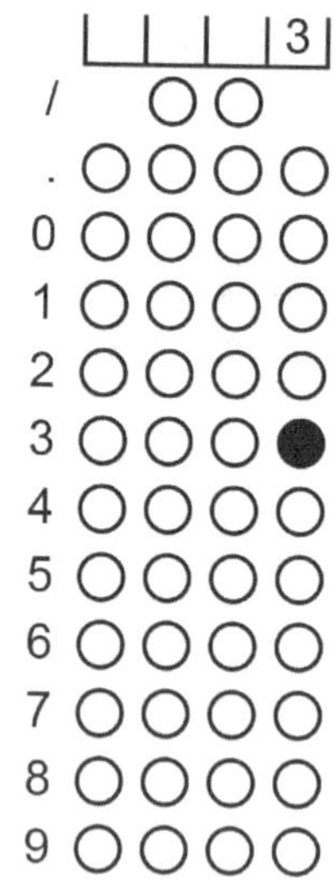

6

A real estate agent earns a commission on each house she sells. Her commission rate is 5% of the sale price. If the agent received $17,500 in commission, what was the sale price of the house in thousands of dollars? Ignore the dollar sign when gridding your answer.

7

In 2012, a company filled 42,500 orders for its product. In 2016, the company filled 70,125 orders. By what percent did the number of orders increase over that four-year period?

8

The seventh-grade class at East Middle School has 138 students. This number is 15% more than the number of students in the seventh-grade class at West Middle School. How many students are in the seventh-grade class at West Middle School?

9

The price of a stock decreased by 5.4% in the last year. If its current price is $8.76, what was the price of the stock prior to the decrease? Round to the nearest cent, and ignore the dollar sign when gridding your answer.

10

Jada purchased her textbooks for the semester at a store that gave a 30% discount. She paid a total of $308.70 for the books, including a 5% sales tax on the discounted price. What was the original price of the books before the discount? Ignore the dollar sign when gridding your answer.

11

On Thursday, 20% of the students at a school were absent. On Friday, 10% of the students who were absent on Thursday returned to school. If there are 350 students at the school, how many students were absent on Friday?

Name ____________________ Date ____________ Class ____________

Find and use percentages to solve problems in real-world situations.

ANSWER SHEET

1. A B C D
2. A B C D
3. A B C D
4. A B C D
5. A B C D

6.
/
.
0
1
2
3
4
5
6
7
8
9

7.
/
.
0
1
2
3
4
5
6
7
8
9

8.
/
.
0
1
2
3
4
5
6
7
8
9

9.
/
.
0
1
2
3
4
5
6
7
8
9

10.
/
.
0
1
2
3
4
5
6
7
8
9

11.
/
.
0
1
2
3
4
5
6
7
8
9

Name ______________________ Date ______________ Class______________

Recognize and use the relationship between growth factor and percent change.

SAMPLE MULTIPLE CHOICE

Each year, the cost of a membership at a local health club increases by 4%. By what multiplicative factor does the cost increase over two years?

A) 0.04

B) 1.04

C) 1.08

D) $(1.04)^2$

Begin by recognizing that each year the cost is 104% of the previous year's cost, or 1.04 times that cost. Letting x represent the cost in one year and letting y represent the cost the next year, then:

$$y = 1.04x$$

Now let z be the cost in the following year. Then z is given by:

$$z = 1.04y = 1.04(1.04x) = (1.04)^2 x$$

Therefore, the multiplicative factor over a two-year period is $(1.04)^2$.

The correct answer is D. A ○ B ○ C ○ D ●

1

A new car costs $24,000, and its value depreciates 8% per year. Which function models the value V, in thousands of dollars, of the car after t years?

A) $V(t) = 24(1.08)^t$

B) $V(t) = 24(0.92)^t$

C) $V(t) = 24(0.08)^t$

D) $V(t) = -24(0.08)^t$

2

The population B of a colony of bacteria in a petri dish is initially B_0 and increases by 100% every hour for t hours. Which function models the population of the bacteria?

A) $B(t) = B_0(1)^t$

B) $B(t) = B_0(1.1)^t$

C) $B(t) = B_0(1.5)^t$

D) $B(t) = B_0(2)^t$

3

On average, a company's workforce has been increasing in size at a rate of 6% per year. If the company had 100 employees in the year 2000, how many employees did it have in 2015?

A) 190

B) 216

C) 240

D) 256

4

A newspaper's circulation C is given by the function $C(t) = 12{,}329(0.89)^t$, where t is the number of years after 2012. By what percent is the circulation changing per year?

A) −89%

B) −11%

C) 89%

D) 111%

5

The population P in a certain town t years after 2010 is given by the function $P(t) = 23{,}571(1.025)^t$. By what percent is the population increasing per year?

A) 0.025%

B) 1.025%

C) 2.5%

D) 25%

Name ______________________ Date ______________ Class ______________

SAMPLE GRID-IN

$$A(t) = 2{,}000(1.03)^t$$

The function above gives the amount A, in dollars, of a bank account t years after an initial deposit of \$2,000 was made. No other deposits were made to the account. By what percent does the amount increase between $t = 2$ and $t = 3$?

A calculator can be used to find the ratio of $A(3) - A(2)$ and $A(2)$ as follows:

$$\frac{A(3) - A(2)}{A(2)} = \frac{2{,}000(1.03)^3 - 2{,}000(1.03)^2}{2{,}000(1.03)^2}$$

$$= \frac{63.654}{2{,}121.8}$$

$$= 0.03$$

So, the amount increased by 3%.

Grid in 3. (Ignore the percent sign when gridding your response.)

Time-Saving Tip: You can quickly answer this question if you recognize that the base of the exponential function, 1.03, indicates that the annual growth rate is 3%.

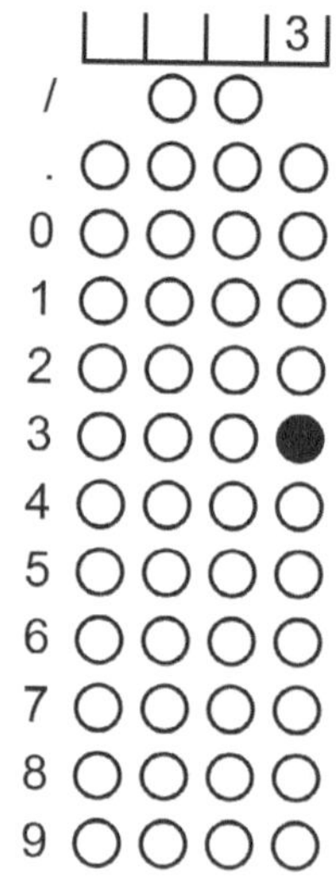

6

$$V(t) = 18(b)^t$$

Several years ago, Andrew paid \$18,000 for a new car. The function shown above models the value V of the car, in thousands of dollars, t years after he purchased it. If the car has been depreciating in value by 5% per year, what is the value of b in the function?

7

An investor deposited money into an account 12 years ago. No additional deposits have ever been made to the account. The value of the account has increased at an average annual rate of 4% per year. If its current value is \$2,801.81, what was the amount of the initial deposit? Round to the nearest dollar, and ignore the dollar sign when gridding your answer.

8

The function $R(t) = 60(2.1)^t$ models a company's total revenue R, in thousands of dollars, where t is the number of years after the company was formed. By what percent is the revenue increasing per year? Ignore the percent symbol when gridding your answer.

9

In a certain region, home values appreciate at an average of 3% per year. By what percent has the value of a home there appreciated over 20 years? Round to the nearest whole percent; ignore the percent symbol when gridding your answer.

10

Due to overfishing, the population of a certain species of fish has been decreasing at a rate of 7% per year. If the total population of the species was 86 thousand in 2005, what was the population, in thousands, in 2017? Round to the nearest thousand.

Name ______________________ Date ______________ Class ______________

Recognize and use the relationship between growth factor and percent change.

ANSWER SHEET

1. A B C D

2. A B C D

3. A B C D

4. A B C D

5. A B C D

6.

/
.
0
1
2
3
4
5
6
7
8
9

7.

/
.
0
1
2
3
4
5
6
7
8
9

8.

/
.
0
1
2
3
4
5
6
7
8
9

9.

/
.
0
1
2
3
4
5
6
7
8
9

10.

/
.
0
1
2
3
4
5
6
7
8
9

Name ______________________ Date ______________ Class ______________

Choose appropriate graphical representations for data.

SAMPLE MULTIPLE CHOICE

Several people at a mall were surveyed about how much time they spend reading each week. The results are shown below. Which type of graphical representation would best display this data?

Hours	Number of People
0–2	12
2–4	8
4–6	4
6–8	6

A) Line graph
B) Histogram
C) Circle graph
D) Bar graph

Notice that the number of hours shown in the table is given in equal intervals that touch but do not overlap. The type of display that is best for showing numerical data in equal intervals is a *histogram*. Histograms look similar to bar graphs, but bar graphs display categorical data rather than quantitative data.

The correct answer is B. A ○ B ● C ○ D ○

1

Dana periodically records the time and the total distance traveled during a bicycle trip. Which type of graphical representation would be most appropriate to display this data?

A) Histogram
B) Stem-and-leaf plot
C) Line graph
D) Box plot

2

Arturo recorded the color of the cars in a parking lot. The table below shows his data. Which type of graphical representation would be most appropriate to display this data?

Blue	𝍸
Green	II
Red	𝍸 III
White	IIII
Black	II

A) Bar graph
B) Stem-and-leaf plot
C) Histogram
D) Line graph

3

A teacher wants to compare the distribution of test scores for two of her classes. Which type of graphical representation would be most appropriate to display this data?

A) Box plot
B) Line graph
C) Bar graph
D) Circle graph

4

A school records the 100-meter dash times of students at the beginning of a physical education program. Which type of graphical representation would be most appropriate to display this data?

A) Box plot
B) Stem-and-leaf plot
C) Histogram
D) Circle graph

5

Which type of graphical representation is used to compare qualitative data?

A) Box plot
B) Stem-and-leaf plot
C) Histogram
D) Bar graph

Name ______________________ Date ____________ Class____________

6

A manager at a restaurant asks randomly selected customers how long they had to wait for their lunches and will compare these times with the wait times of customers in the evening. Which type of graphical representation would be most appropriate to display this data?

A) Bar graph
B) Box plot
C) Circle graph
D) Line graph

7

Professor Blum uses stacked box plots to compare the scores on the midterm exam for her three statistics classes. Which of the following is NOT apparent from the box plots?

A) The highest and lowest scores
B) The class with the lowest score
C) The number of students in each class
D) The class with the highest median score

8

Which type of graphical representation is best used to show the central tendency and distribution of quantitative data?

A) Line graph
B) Bar graph
C) Histogram
D) Circle graph

9

Which type of graphical representation is best used to show percentages of qualitative data?

A) Box plot
B) Bar graph
C) Histogram
D) Circle graph

10

Which type of graphical representation is NOT used to compare quantitative data?

A) Box plot
B) Bar graph
C) Stem-and-leaf plot
D) Histogram

11

A scientist compares data about the rainfall amounts for days with measurable rain from two regions. Which gives a reason the scientist might choose to use a double stem-and-leaf plot instead of stacked box plots to display the rainfall data?

A) The original data values are preserved.
B) The stem-and-leaf plot gives the interquartile range.
C) The median rainfall amounts can be immediately compared.
D) Only the stem-and-leaf plot allows you to determine the range of the data values.

12

Which type of graphical representation is used to show continuous quantitative data in equal intervals?

A) Histogram
B) Box plot
C) Dot plot
D) Circle graph

13

Which type of graphical representation does NOT give some indication of the central tendency and spread of a data set?

A) Stem-and-leaf plot
B) Circle graph
C) Dot plot
D) Box plot

Name ______________________ Date ______________ Class______________

Choose appropriate graphical representations for data.

ANSWER SHEET

1. A B C D ○ ○ ○ ○
2. A B C D ○ ○ ○ ○
3. A B C D ○ ○ ○ ○
4. A B C D ○ ○ ○ ○
5. A B C D ○ ○ ○ ○
6. A B C D ○ ○ ○ ○
7. A B C D ○ ○ ○ ○
8. A B C D ○ ○ ○ ○
9. A B C D ○ ○ ○ ○
10. A B C D ○ ○ ○ ○
11. A B C D ○ ○ ○ ○
12. A B C D ○ ○ ○ ○
13. A B C D ○ ○ ○ ○

Name ______________________ Date ____________ Class ____________

Interpret information about real-world data from a given representation.

SAMPLE MULTIPLE CHOICE

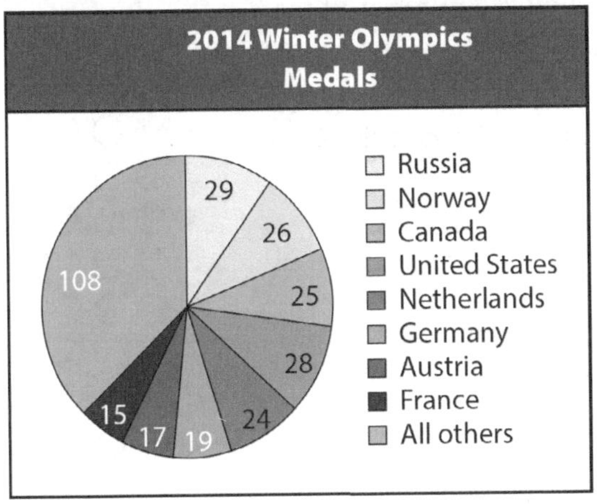

What was the mean number of medals won by the 26 countries that won medals at the 2014 Winter Olympics, rounded to the nearest whole number?

A) 10 C) 12

B) 11 D) 20

The mean is the sum of the data values (numbers of medals) divided by the number of data values (countries). Add the numbers of medals from each section of the circle graph to find the total number of medals. The number of countries is given.

Total medals: $108 + 29 + \cdots + 17 + 15 = 291$

Number of countries: 26

Calculate the mean (average).

$$\frac{291}{26} \approx 11.19$$

So, rounded to the nearest whole number, the mean number of medals won was 11 medals.

The correct answer is B. A ○ B ● C ○ D ○

Questions 1–3 refer to the following information.

The bar graph shows the number and type of medals won at the 2016 Summer Olympics by the three countries who won the most medals.

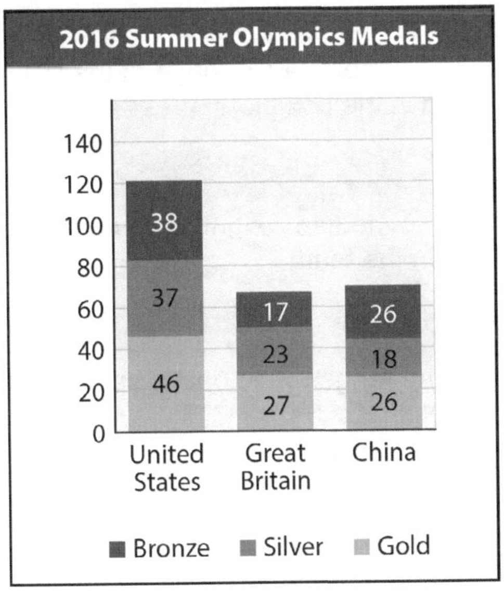

1

What is the median total number of medals won by the three countries?

A) 86 C) 33

B) 70 D) 27

2

What is the mean number of medals won by the three countries?

A) 86 C) 33

B) 70 D) 27

3

What is the mean of the differences between the number of gold medals and the number of silver medals won by the three countries?

A) 7 C) 3

B) 5 D) 1

Name ______________________ Date ______________ Class ______________

SAMPLE GRID-IN

Lily recorded the daily low temperatures shown (in degrees Fahrenheit) for a period of time. What is the mean of the low temperatures in degrees Fahrenheit?

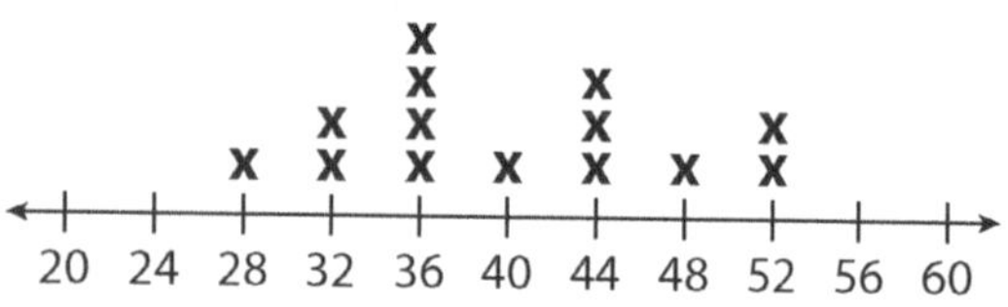

To find the mean of the temperatures, add the recorded temperatures and divide by the number of temperatures.

Counting the number of X's shows that the plot displays 14 low temperatures.

$$\frac{28+32+\cdots+52}{14}=\frac{560}{14}=40$$

So, the mean of the low temperatures is 40°F.

Grid in 40.

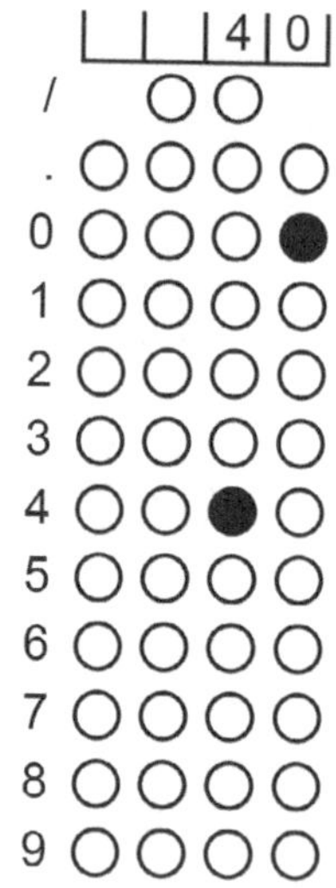

Questions 4–6 refer to the following information.

The stem-and-leaf plot shows the daily high temperatures (in °F) in a city during the month of February.

Stem	Leaves
4	6 7 7 8
5	2 3 4 4 5 6
6	2 3 6 6 6 7 8 9 9
7	3 5 5 6 7 8 8
8	2 3

Key: 4|6 means 46

4

What is the median temperature displayed in the plot? Ignore the degree symbol when gridding your answer.

5

What is the interquartile range of the data displayed in the plot?

6

What is the mode of the temperatures in the plot? Ignore the degree symbol when gridding your answer.

Questions 7–10 refer to the following information.

The box plot shows the distribution of the weights in pounds of the players on a high school football team.

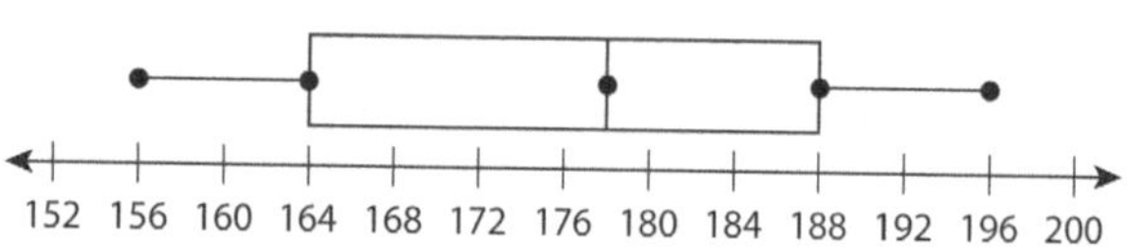

7

What percent of the team's players weigh at most 188 pounds?

8

What is the interquartile range of the data displayed in the box plot?

9

What is the median weight in pounds of the players on the team?

10

What is the range of the data displayed in the box plot?

Name ______________________ Date ______________ Class ______________

Interpret information about real-world data from a given representation.

ANSWER SHEET

1. A B C D

2. A B C D

3. A B C D

4.
/
.
0
1
2
3
4
5
6
7
8
9

5.
/
.
0
1
2
3
4
5
6
7
8
9

6.
/
.
0
1
2
3
4
5
6
7
8
9

7.
/
.
0
1
2
3
4
5
6
7
8
9

8.
/
.
0
1
2
3
4
5
6
7
8
9

9.
/
.
0
1
2
3
4
5
6
7
8
9

10.
/
.
0
1
2
3
4
5
6
7
8
9

Name ______________________ Date ______________ Class ______________

Analyze and interpret data distributions represented in tables, histograms, and plots.

SAMPLE MULTIPLE CHOICE

The scores on a recent test are displayed below. What can be concluded about the test?

Kate's class		Tom's class
4	5	6 8
8 5	6	3 4 5 6 6
8 8 6 2	7	1 4 6 7 8 8 9
8 8 6 6 2	8	2 4
2 0	9	

Key: |5|6 *means* 56 *points*
4|5| *means* 54 *points*

A) There is nothing to conclude.
B) Test scores in Kate's class were generally higher than in Tom's class.
C) Test scores in Tom's class were generally higher than in Kate's class.
D) Kate's class and Tom's class had similar test scores.

This stem-and-leaf plot shows a data distribution where the stem represents the tens place and the leaves represent the ones place of the data values.

Examine the leaves for each class. Most of the students in Kate's class scored in the 70's and 80's. Most of the students in Tom's class scored in the 60's and 70's.

So, in general, the scores in Kate's class were higher than those in Tom's class.

The correct answer is B. A ○ B ● C ○ D ○

Questions 1–3 refer to the following information.

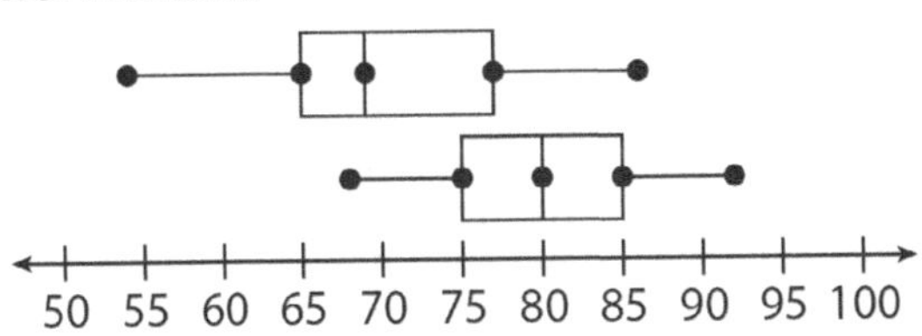

The boxplots model the test scores in Class A (top) and in Class B (bottom).

1

What can be concluded from the boxplot?

A) There is nothing to conclude.
B) Test scores in Class A were generally higher than in Class B.
C) Test scores in Class B were generally higher than in Class A.
D) Classes A and B had similar test scores.

2

What is the interquartile range of the data for Class A?

A) 10
B) 12
C) 17
D) 33

3

What percentage of students in Class A scored at or above 65?

A) 25%
B) 50%
C) 66%
D) 75%

4

The test scores on a recent test are displayed below. What can be concluded about the test?

Paul's class		Sarah's class
8 4	5	6 8
8 8 8 7 7 5	6	3 4 5
8 8 6 2	7	1 4 6 7 8 8 9
6 1	8	2 4
0	9	0

Key: |5|6 *means* 56 *points*
4|5| *means* 54 *points*

A) Scores in Paul's class were generally higher than in Sarah's class.
B) Scores in Sarah's class were generally higher than in Paul's class.
C) The two classes had similar scores.
D) Five students still need to take the test.

Name ______________________ Date ____________ Class ____________

SAMPLE GRID-IN

The bar graph below shows the student population in five small cities. If there are 2,500 students living in City B, estimate the student population of City D.

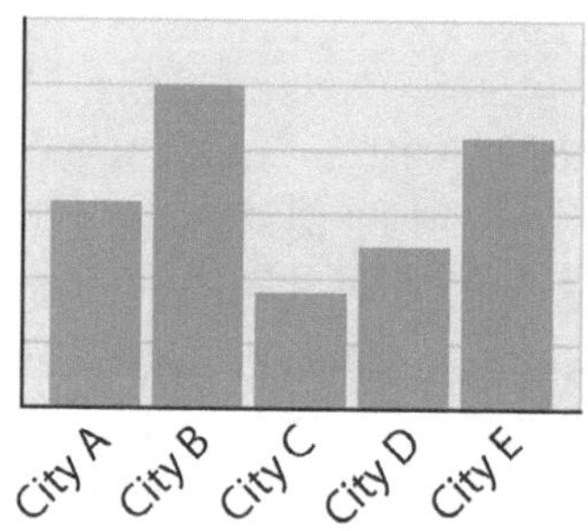

Although the vertical axis is unlabeled, you can see that the bar representing City B reaches to the fifth evenly-spaced horizontal line. Therefore, the scale for the vertical axis must be 500. The bar for City D reaches approximately halfway between the second and third horizontal lines. Thus, the student population of City D is about:

$$2.5 \times 500 = 1{,}250$$

So, the student population of City D is approximately 1,250 students.

Grid in 1250.

Time-Saving Tip: Notice that the height of the bar representing City D is half the height of the bar representing City B.

$$\frac{2{,}500}{2} = 1{,}250$$

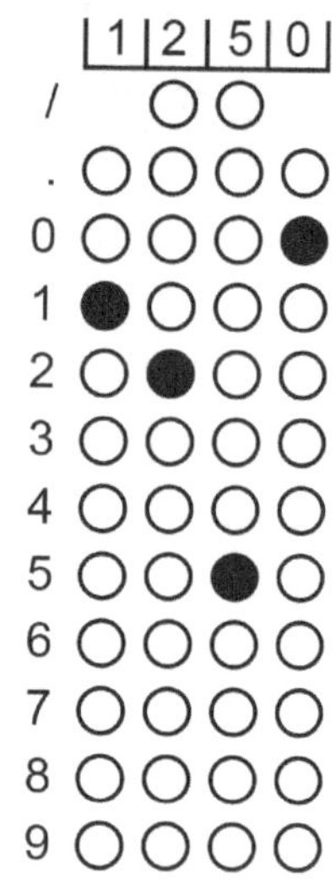

Questions 5–7 refer to the following information.

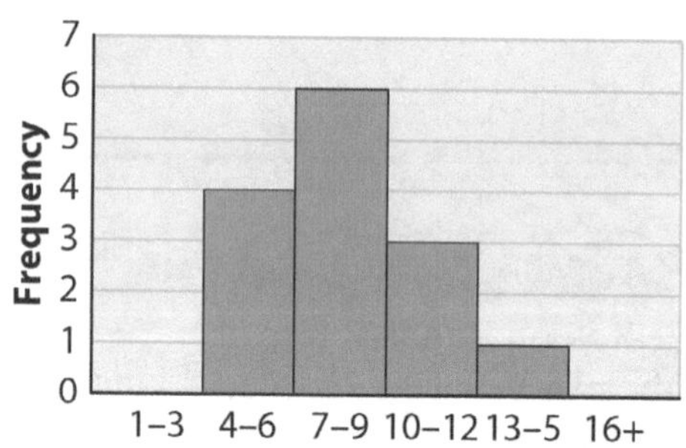

The histogram above is a record of the distances, in kilometers, that Robin ran during her training runs last month.

5

How many times did Robin go running last month?

6

How many more times did Robin go for a 7–9-km run than a 10–12-km run?

7

Give a reasonable estimate, to the nearest whole number, for Robin's average distance per run.

8

Which value appears to be an outlier?

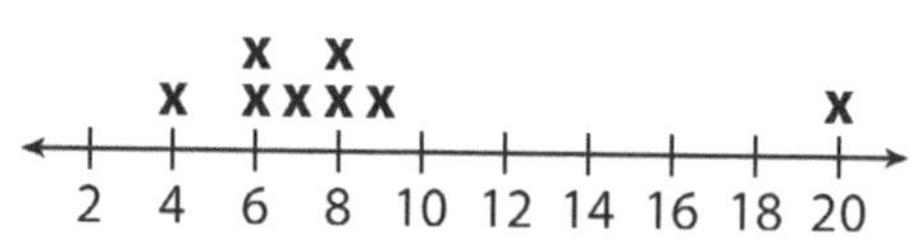

9

What is the mode in the given data set?

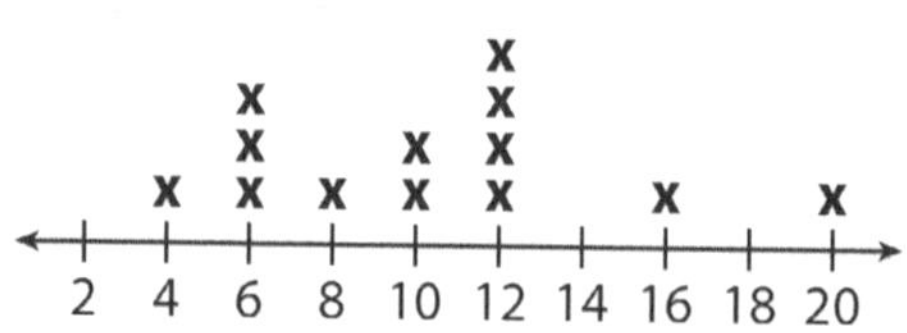

Name ________________________ Date ______________ Class ______________

Analyze and interpret data distributions represented in tables, histograms, and plots.

ANSWER SHEET

1. A B C D
○ ○ ○ ○

2. A B C D
○ ○ ○ ○

3. A B C D
○ ○ ○ ○

4. A B C D
○ ○ ○ ○

5. |_|_|_|_|
/ ○ ○
. ○ ○ ○ ○
0 ○ ○ ○ ○
1 ○ ○ ○ ○
2 ○ ○ ○ ○
3 ○ ○ ○ ○
4 ○ ○ ○ ○
5 ○ ○ ○ ○
6 ○ ○ ○ ○
7 ○ ○ ○ ○
8 ○ ○ ○ ○
9 ○ ○ ○ ○

6. |_|_|_|_|
/ ○ ○
. ○ ○ ○ ○
0 ○ ○ ○ ○
1 ○ ○ ○ ○
2 ○ ○ ○ ○
3 ○ ○ ○ ○
4 ○ ○ ○ ○
5 ○ ○ ○ ○
6 ○ ○ ○ ○
7 ○ ○ ○ ○
8 ○ ○ ○ ○
9 ○ ○ ○ ○

7. |_|_|_|_|
/ ○ ○
. ○ ○ ○ ○
0 ○ ○ ○ ○
1 ○ ○ ○ ○
2 ○ ○ ○ ○
3 ○ ○ ○ ○
4 ○ ○ ○ ○
5 ○ ○ ○ ○
6 ○ ○ ○ ○
7 ○ ○ ○ ○
8 ○ ○ ○ ○
9 ○ ○ ○ ○

8. |_|_|_|_|
/ ○ ○
. ○ ○ ○ ○
0 ○ ○ ○ ○
1 ○ ○ ○ ○
2 ○ ○ ○ ○
3 ○ ○ ○ ○
4 ○ ○ ○ ○
5 ○ ○ ○ ○
6 ○ ○ ○ ○
7 ○ ○ ○ ○
8 ○ ○ ○ ○
9 ○ ○ ○ ○

9. |_|_|_|_|
/ ○ ○
. ○ ○ ○ ○
0 ○ ○ ○ ○
1 ○ ○ ○ ○
2 ○ ○ ○ ○
3 ○ ○ ○ ○
4 ○ ○ ○ ○
5 ○ ○ ○ ○
6 ○ ○ ○ ○
7 ○ ○ ○ ○
8 ○ ○ ○ ○
9 ○ ○ ○ ○

Name ________________ Date ________ Class ________

Calculate, compare, and interpret the mean, median, and range of quantitative data. Interpret standard deviation.

SAMPLE MULTIPLE CHOICE

A data set consisting of 30 values has a median and mode of 30, a mean of 32.5, a maximum of 40, and a range of 12. Which is the most reasonable conclusion about the distribution of data?

A) The distribution is skewed left.

B) The distribution is skewed right.

C) There is not enough information.

D) The distribution is symmetric about 30.

The minimum value of the data is $40-12=28$, which is close to the median and mode, so most of the data are clustered to the left. The mean, however, is significantly greater than the median, and the maximum of 40 means that there is a long tail to the right, so the distribution is skewed right.

The correct answer is B. A B C D ○●○○

Questions 1–3 refer to the following information.

The data below represent the numbers of words per sentence in a random sample of 16 sentences from a book.

7, 7, 8, 8, 8, 8, 9, 9,
10, 10, 11, 11, 12, 12, 14, 16

1

What is the mean number of words per sentence in the sample?

A) 9 C) 10

B) 9.5 D) 10.5

2

What is the median number of words per sentence in the sample?

A) 9 C) 10

B) 9.5 D) 10.5

3

Compare the mean sentence length and the median sentence length.

A) The mean sentence length is less than the median sentence length.

B) The mean sentence length is greater than the median sentence length.

C) The mean and median sentence lengths are the same.

D) There is not enough information.

4

Random sample A has a mean of 16 and a standard deviation of 3. Random sample B has a mean of 15 and a standard deviation of 4. Assuming samples A and B were selected from the same population, what can be concluded about the samples?

A) There is more variation among the sample A data.

B) There is more variation among the sample B data.

C) Sample A better represents the population than sample B.

D) There is not enough information to compare the samples.

5

Students in a class took two exams. The mean score on the first exam was 85.75, with a standard deviation of 6.9. The mean score on the second exam was 73, with a standard deviation of 6.9. What can be concluded?

A) There is more variation in the first exam scores.

B) A score of 79 was within one standard deviation of the mean for both exams.

C) The distribution in scores was more symmetric for the second exam.

D) More students made a score of 100 on the first exam.

Name ______________________ Date ______________ Class ______________

SAMPLE GRID-IN

A science class measures the temperature (in °F) every 30 minutes one day and records the following data:

42, 44, 52, 48, 46, 42, 38,

36, 36, 35, 34, 35

What is the range of the data set?

Begin by ordering the data to identify the least and greatest values in the data set.

least: 34

greatest: 52

To find the range, subtract the least value from the greatest.

$52 - 34 = 18$

So, the range of the data set is 18.

Grid in 18.

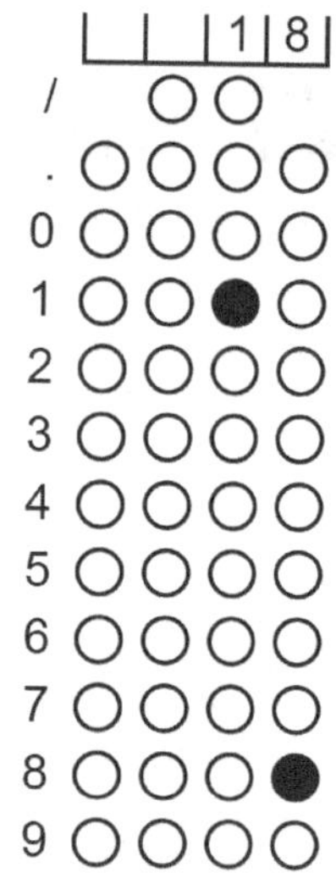

Questions 6–8 refer to the following information.

A science class measures the percent relative humidity on the school grounds every half hour one day and records the following data:

53, 52, 51, 49, 44, 53, 62, 68, 72

6

What is the range of the relative humidity data?

7

What is the median of the relative humidity data?

8

What is the mean of the relative humidity data?

9

The data values shown below represent the heights in inches of several corn stalks in an agricultural test plot 8 weeks after sprouting. What is the difference between the median and mean stalk height in inches for the data set?

64, 66, 69, 71, 71, 73, 74, 82

10

Jessie wrote down the scores of 6 out of the 7 tests she took this semester in geography class but could not remember the other score. The scores she wrote down are shown below.

86, 88, 89, 92, 93, 96

Jessie's geography teacher told her that her average test score was exactly 91. What is the score that she could not remember?

Questions 11–13 refer to the following information.

Javier counted the number of cars parked on the street on his block at 7 A.M. every morning for a week. His results are shown below.

118, 98, 102, 97, 106, 98, 123

11

What is the range of Javier's data set?

12

What is the median of Javier's data set?

13

What is the mean of Javier's data set?

Name ______________________ Date ______________ Class ______________

Calculate, compare, and interpret the mean, median, and range of quantitative data. Interpret standard deviation.

ANSWER SHEET

1. A B C D ○○○○

2. A B C D ○○○○

3. A B C D ○○○○

4. A B C D ○○○○

5. A B C D ○○○○

6. Grid-in: / ○○; . ○○○○; 0–9 ○○○○

7. Grid-in: / ○○; . ○○○○; 0–9 ○○○○

8. Grid-in: / ○○; . ○○○○; 0–9 ○○○○

9. Grid-in: / ○○; . ○○○○; 0–9 ○○○○

10. Grid-in: / ○○; . ○○○○; 0–9 ○○○○

11. Grid-in: / ○○; . ○○○○; 0–9 ○○○○

12. Grid-in: / ○○; . ○○○○; 0–9 ○○○○

13. Grid-in: / ○○; . ○○○○; 0–9 ○○○○

Name ______________________ Date ____________ Class____________

Use measures of center and spread to compare distributions.

SAMPLE MULTIPLE CHOICE

Which of the distributions described by the statistics given below is most likely to have the smallest range of values?

A) Mean: 80; Standard Deviation: 10

B) Mean: 80; Standard Deviation: 20

C) Mean: 90; Standard Deviation: 20

D) Mean: 70; Standard Deviation: 30

Standard deviation is a measure of the spread of the data values. Distributions with smaller standard deviations have less variability in the data values. Also, data values far from the mean increase the standard deviation more. So, a distribution with a smaller standard deviation will tend to have a smaller range than a distribution of similar data with a larger standard deviation.

The smallest standard deviation is 10.

So, the correct answer is A.

A ● B ○ C ○ D ○

1

Which of the distributions described by the statistics given below is most likely to have the largest range of values?

A) Mean: 70; Standard Deviation: 10

B) Mean: 70; Standard Deviation: 20

C) Mean: 80; Standard Deviation: 5

D) Mean: 80; Standard Deviation: 15

2

Which of the distributions described by the statistics given below is most likely to contain a value greater than 100?

A) Mean: 70; Standard Deviation: 25

B) Mean: 80; Standard Deviation: 15

C) Mean: 80; Standard Deviation: 20

D) Mean: 90; Standard Deviation: 5

3

A line plot of which of the distributions described by the statistics given below is most likely to exhibit a spread similar to that of a distribution with a mean of 100 and a standard deviation of 10?

A) Mean: 100; Standard Deviation: 20

B) Mean: 200; Standard Deviation: 15

C) Mean: 300; Standard Deviation: 10

D) Mean: 400; Standard Deviation: 5

4

A boxplot of which of the distributions described by the statistics given below is most likely to exhibit a spread similar to a distribution with a median of 250 and an interquartile range (IQR) of 40?

A) Median: 150; IQR: 40

B) Median: 150; IQR: 30

C) Median: 250; IQR: 20

D) Median: 250; IQR: 10

5

The following are statistics for four samples of size 100.

I. Mean: 100; Standard Deviation: 10

II. Mean: 100; Standard Deviation: 30

III. Mean: 200; Standard Deviation: 10

IV. Mean: 200; Standard Deviation: 30

If you made histograms of the four distributions using bars of equal width, which histogram(s) would most likely have the tallest bars?

A) I only

B) I and III only

C) II and IV only

D) III and IV only

Name ______________________ Date ______________ Class______________

Questions 6–13 refer to the following information.

The line plots below display four different distributions of twelve data values.

I.

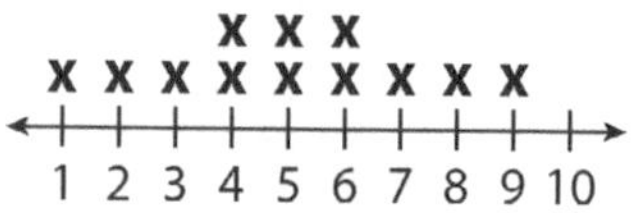

II.

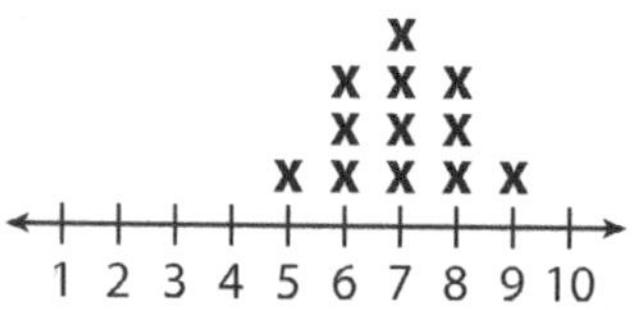

III.

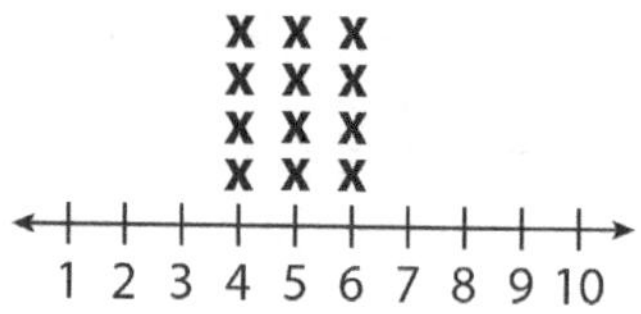

IV.

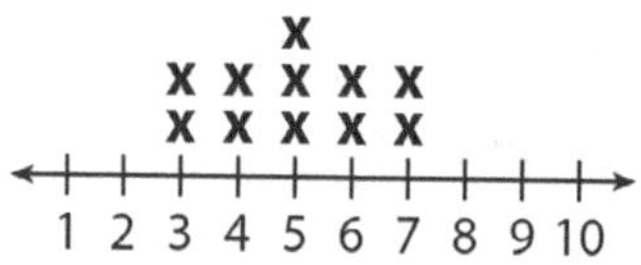

6

Which distribution has the greatest standard deviation?

A) I
B) II
C) III
D) IV

7

Which distributions have the same median?

A) I and II only
B) II and IV only
C) I, III, and IV only
D) II, III, and IV only

8

Which distribution has the greatest range?

A) I
B) II
C) III
D) IV

9

Which distributions have the same mean?

A) I and II only
B) III and IV only
C) I, III, and IV only
D) I, II, III, and IV

10

Which distribution has the greatest mean?

A) I
B) II
C) III
D) IV

11

Which distribution has the greatest median?

A) I
B) II
C) III
D) IV

12

Which distribution has the least standard deviation?

A) I
B) II
C) III
D) IV

13

Which distribution has the least range?

A) I
B) II
C) III
D) IV

Name ______________________ Date ____________ Class ____________

Use measures of center and spread to compare distributions.

ANSWER SHEET

1. A B C D ○ ○ ○ ○
2. A B C D ○ ○ ○ ○
3. A B C D ○ ○ ○ ○
4. A B C D ○ ○ ○ ○
5. A B C D ○ ○ ○ ○
6. A B C D ○ ○ ○ ○
7. A B C D ○ ○ ○ ○
8. A B C D ○ ○ ○ ○
9. A B C D ○ ○ ○ ○
10. A B C D ○ ○ ○ ○
11. A B C D ○ ○ ○ ○
12. A B C D ○ ○ ○ ○
13. A B C D ○ ○ ○ ○

Name ______________________ Date ______________ Class ______________

Determine the effect of outliers on mean and median.

SAMPLE MULTIPLE CHOICE

For which of these descriptions of data sets of 20 values will the mean be less than the median?

A) The values are evenly spread between 7 and 11.

B) Most of the values are between 5 and 7, with two values of 15.

C) Most of the values are between 9 and 11, with two values of 1.

D) Most of the values are 15, with one value of 14 and one value of 16.

The presence of outliers, or values that are substantially less than or greater than most of the data set, tends to pull the mean away from the median. Outliers that are less than the other values pull the mean below the median, and outliers that are greater than the other values pull the mean above the median.

So for the mean to be less than the median, the outliers must be less than the other values in the data set. In choice C, the two values of 1 are outliers much less than the other values.

The correct answer is C. A ○ B ○ C ● D ○

1

For which of the following descriptions of data sets of 20 values will the mean be the same as the median?

A) Twelve of the values are 8, with four values of 6 and four values of 10.

B) Most of the values are between 2 and 5, with two values of 19.

C) Most of the values are between 15 and 17, with two values of 3.

D) Most of the values are less than 5, with 8 values greater than 15.

2

For a small data set, the minimum value is 10, the median value is 18, and the maximum value is 90. Which is the most reasonable assumption about the relationship between the mean and the median of these data?

A) The mean will be less than the median.

B) The mean will be greater than the median.

C) The mean will be the same as the median.

D) No assumptions are reasonable about the relationship between the mean and the median from the information provided.

3

The following plots display four distributions of 12 data values. For which distribution is the mean less than the median?

A)

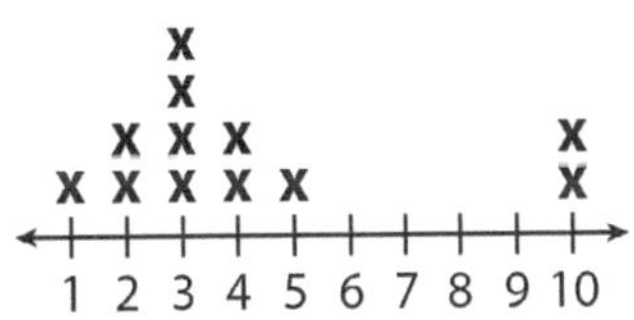

B)

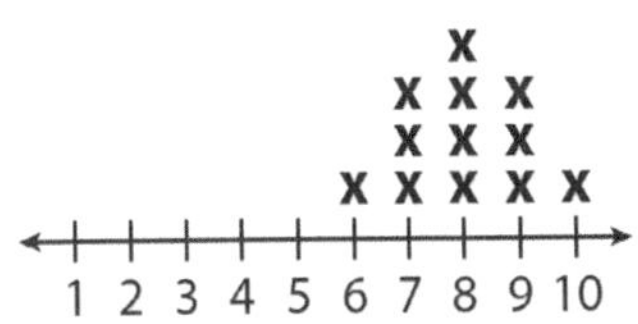

C)

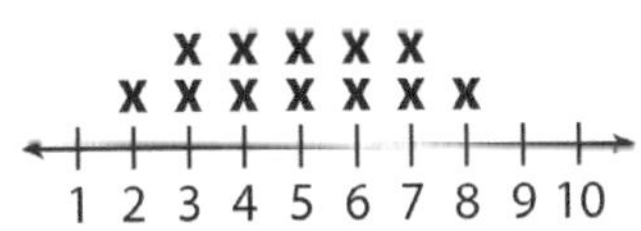

D)

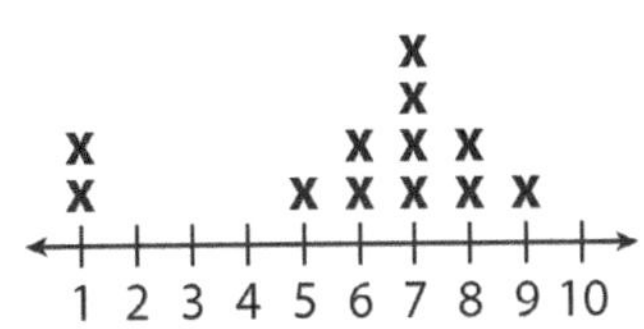

Name ____________________ Date __________ Class __________

Questions 4–6 refer to the following information.

The plots below display four distributions for 12 data values.

I.

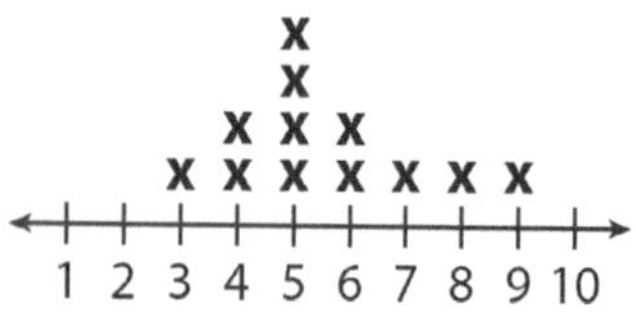

II.

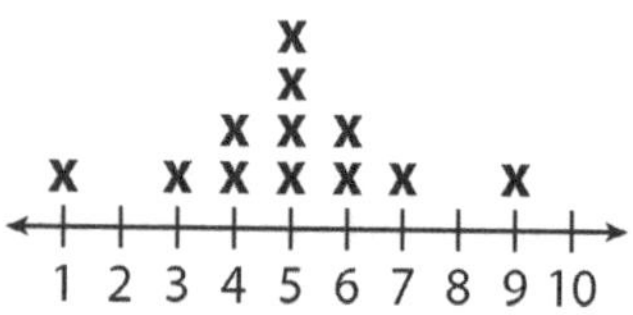

III.

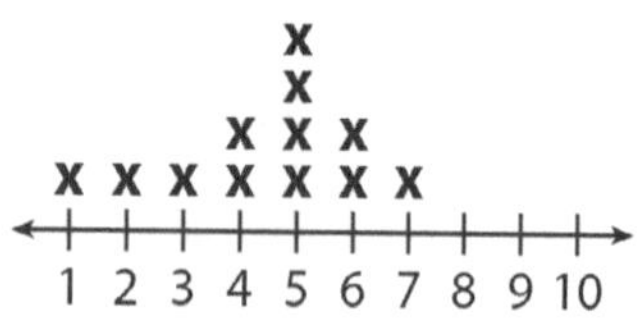

IV.

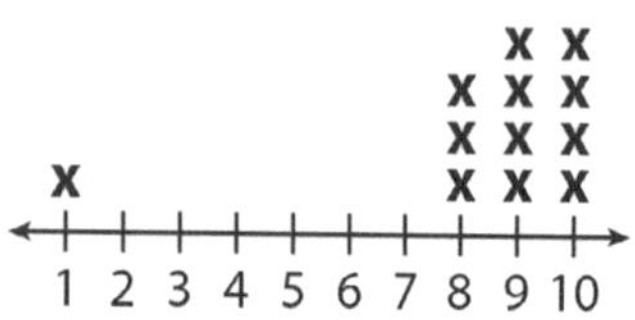

4

For which graph(s) is the mean greater than the median?

A) I only
B) III only
C) I and III only
D) I, II, and III only

5

For which graph(s) is the mean the same as the median?

A) I only
B) II only
C) I and III only
D) I, II, and III only

6

For which graph(s) is the mean less than the median?

A) I only
B) III only
C) I and II only
D) III and IV only

7

Mass of Dragonfly Nymphs (in grams)				
0.5	10.1	10.8	11.2	11.2
11.3	11.6	11.6	11.6	11.6
11.9	12.1	12.2	12.2	12.2

The table above lists the masses, to the nearest tenth of a gram, of a random sample of 15 dragonfly nymphs. The outlier mass of 0.5 gram was recorded incorrectly. The actual measurement was 10.5 grams. Which of the following will increase once this data value is corrected?

I. Mean
II. Median
III. Mode

A) I only
B) II only
C) I and III only
D) None of the values will increase.

8

The median score on a midterm exam for a biology class was 72%. All of the scores were between 60% and 85%, except one outlier of 100%. Which of the following is the most likely value of the mean score for the class?

A) 61%
B) 71%
C) 73%
D) 84%

Name ______________________________ Date ________________ Class________________

Determine the effect of outliers on mean and median.

ANSWER SHEET

1. A B C D ○ ○ ○ ○
2. A B C D ○ ○ ○ ○
3. A B C D ○ ○ ○ ○
4. A B C D ○ ○ ○ ○
5. A B C D ○ ○ ○ ○
6. A B C D ○ ○ ○ ○
7. A B C D ○ ○ ○ ○
8. A B C D ○ ○ ○ ○

Name ______________________ Date ______________ Class______________

Determine the mean of an appropriate data set.

SAMPLE MULTIPLE CHOICE

Find the mean of the following data set.

1, 16, 2, 6, 8, 9, 1, 12, 11, 4

A) 1
B) 7
C) 10
D) 70

To find the mean of a data set, divide the sum of the elements of the data set by the number of elements in the data set.

Find the sum of the given numbers.

$$1+16+2+6+8+9+1+12+11+4=70$$

There are 10 numbers in the set. Divide 70 by 10.

$$70 \div 10 = 7$$

So, the mean is 7.

The correct answer is B. A ○ B ● C ○ D ○

1

Find the mean of the following data set.

15, 3, 7, 6, 19, 17, 19, 11, 11, 14

A) 6.1
B) 11
C) 12.2
D) 122

2

In Ms. Smith's first grade class, 4 students have 1 sibling, 8 students have 2 siblings, 7 students have 3 siblings, and 2 students have 4 siblings. Which of the following is closest to the average (arithmetic mean) number of siblings per student?

A) 1 C) 3
B) 2 D) 4

3

Find the value of *x* if the mean of the following data set is 650.

918, 951, *x*, 323, 543, 428, 925, 726

A) 386
B) 650
C) 688
D) 5,200

4

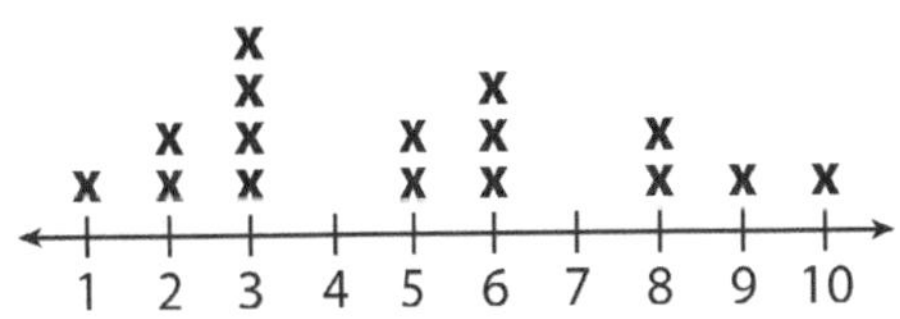

Find the mean of the data in the line plot shown above.

A) 80 C) 5.5
B) 16 D) 5

5

The table below shows Maria's scores on the exams in her biology class. The midterm counts as 2 tests, and the final exam counts as 3 tests. Calculate Maria's average for the class. Round to the nearest tenth if necessary.

Test	Score
Test 1	83
Midterm	92
Test 2	95
Final Exam	78

A) 85.1 C) 87
B) 86.3 D) 87.5

Name ______________________ Date ______________ Class ______________

SAMPLE GRID-IN

Find the mean of the data represented in the histogram shown below.

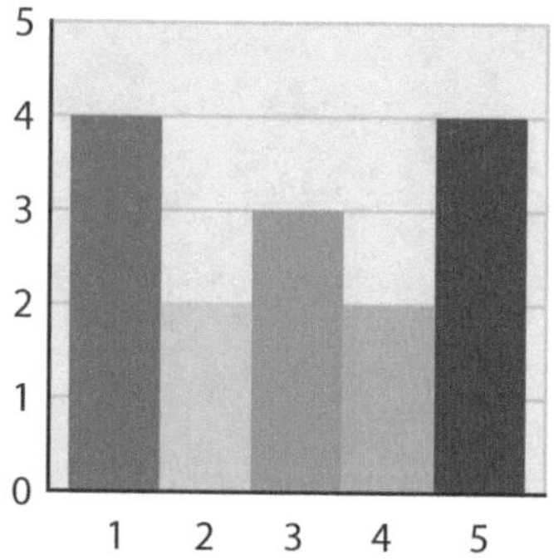

To find the mean of a data set, divide the sum of the elements of the data set by the number of elements in the data set.

Organize the information in a table, where *n* is the number of times each value *x* occurs. The total number of elements is the total of column *n*. The sum of the elements is the total of the $x \cdot n$ column.

x	*n*	$x \cdot n$
1	4	4
2	2	4
3	3	9
4	2	8
5	4	20
Total	15	45

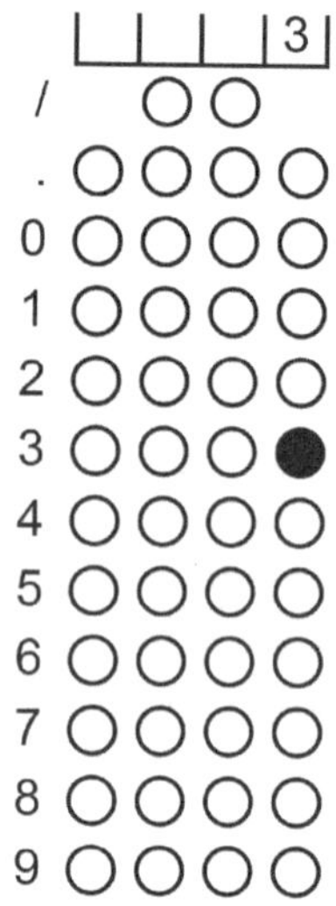

Find the mean.

$$45 \div 15 = 3$$

So, the mean is 3.

Grid in 3.

6

Find the mean of the data in the line plot.

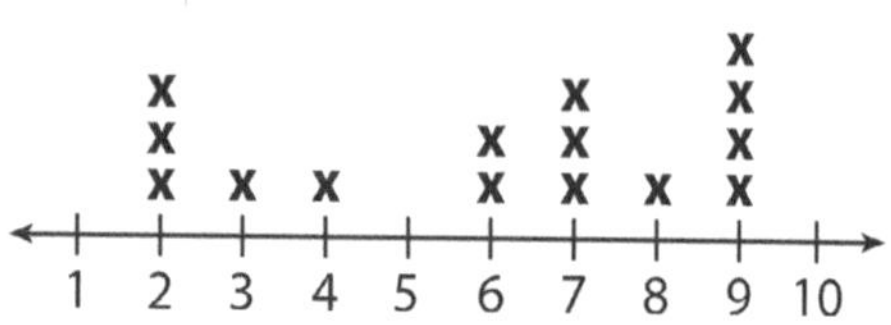

7

Find the mean of the following data set.

18, 19, 23, 27, 28, 27, 49, 33, 43, 33

8

Find the value of *x* if the mean of the following data set is 701.

639, *x*, 697, 724, 700, 713, 702

Questions 9 and 10 refer to the following histogram.

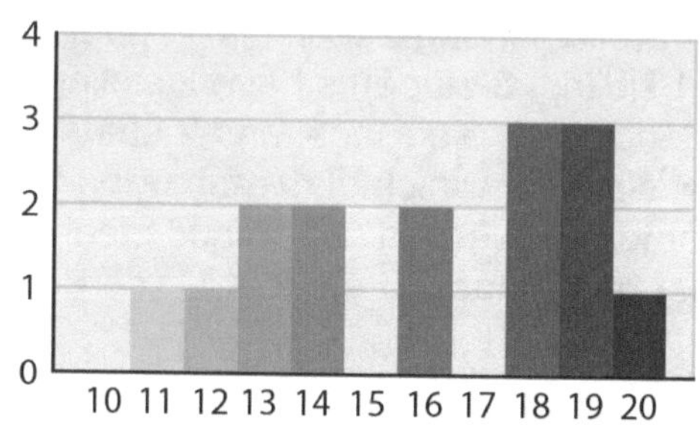

9

Find the mean of the data represented in the histogram.

10

Suppose the bars for 15 and 17 were accidentally left off the graph. If both of the missing bars has a height of 1, what is the mean of the data after the figure is corrected?

Name ______________________ Date ______________ Class ______________

Determine the mean of an appropriate data set.

ANSWER SHEET

1. A B C D

2. A B C D

3. A B C D

4. A B C D

5. A B C D

6. / . 0 1 2 3 4 5 6 7 8 9

7. / . 0 1 2 3 4 5 6 7 8 9

8. / . 0 1 2 3 4 5 6 7 8 9

9. / . 0 1 2 3 4 5 6 7 8 9

10. / . 0 1 2 3 4 5 6 7 8 9

Name ______________________ Date ____________ Class____________

Compare data values given in a scatterplot to values predicted by a model that fits the data.

SAMPLE MULTIPLE CHOICE

You are given a set of data and a linear model that represents that set of data. If the predicted value is greater than the observed value, what is the relationship between the data point and the linear model?

A) The data point is on the line.

B) The data point is above the line.

C) The data point is below the line.

D) The relationship cannot be determined.

The predicted value is the *y*-value of the linear model and the observed value is the *y*-value of the data point. Therefore, if the predicted value is greater than the observed value, then the linear model is above the data point. In other words, the data point is below the line.

The correct answer is C. A B C D ○ ○ ● ○

Questions 1–4 refer to the following information.

The scatterplot below shows commuting times and distances for 20 employees at a company and the line of best fit for the data.

Commute Time and Distance

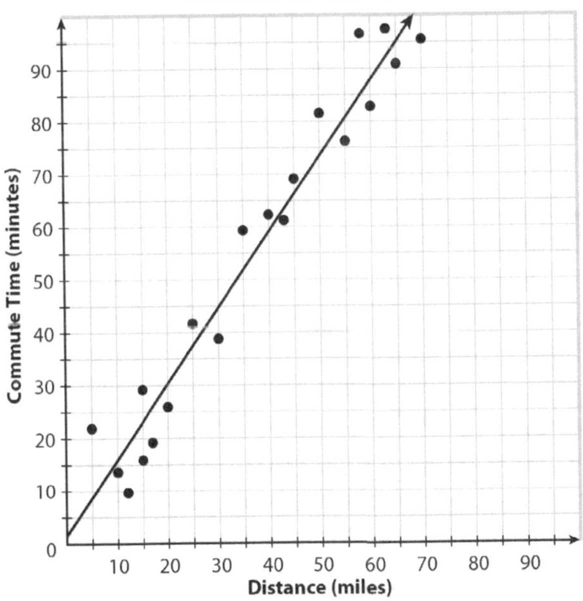

1

How many of the observed commuting times are greater than the time predicted for that distance?

A) 8 C) 10

B) 9 D) 11

2

For which distance, in miles, is the difference between the predicted and observed commute times the greatest?

A) 5 C) 35

B) 10 D) 60

3

For which distance, in miles, is the difference between the predicted and observed commute times the least?

A) 17 C) 43

B) 30 D) 58

4

How many of the observed commuting times are equal to the time predicted for that distance?

A) 0 C) 2

B) 1 D) 3

5

Suppose a set of data and its linear model are given. If the predicted value is less than the observed value, what is the relationship between the data point and the line?

A) The data point is on the line.

B) The data point is above the line.

C) The data point is below the line.

D) No determination can be made.

Name ______________________ Date ______________ Class______________

SAMPLE GRID-IN

The model that represents a set of data shown in a scatterplot is the linear equation $y = 3x - 4$. What is the absolute value of the difference between the observed y-value for the data point (10, 20) and the predicted y-value?

The observed y-value is 20. Find the predicted y-value for $x = 10$.

$$y = 3(10) - 4$$
$$= 26$$

Now find the absolute value of the difference.

$$|20 - 26| = |-6| = 6$$

Grid in 6.

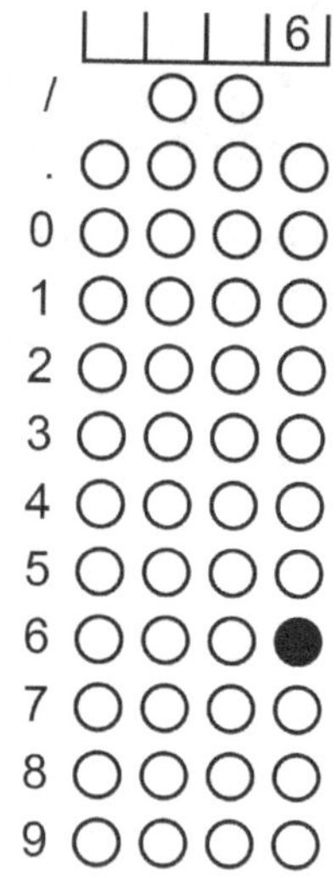

Questions 6–10 refer to the following information.

The scatterplot shows the grades and number of absences for 20 students in a class and the line of best fit for the data.

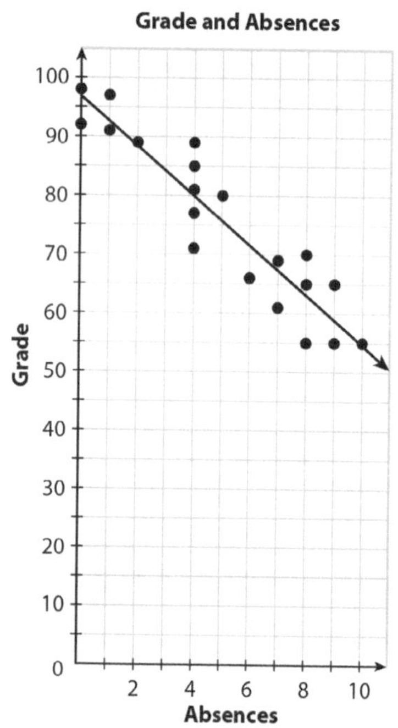

6

How many of the observed grades are less than the grade predicted for that number of absences?

7

What number of absences has at least one grade that is about 10 points greater than the predicted value?

8

What number of absences has exactly two data values greater than the predicted value and exactly one data value less than the predicted value?

9

What number of absences has only one data value and that data value is less than the predicted value?

10

What number of absences has two data values, both of which are approximately 5 points from the predicted grade?

11

The equation that models a set of data is $y = 5x + 2$. What is the absolute value of the difference between the observed y-value for the data value (7, 40) and the predicted y-value?

Name ______________________ Date ______________ Class ______________

Compare data values given in a scatterplot to values predicted by a model that fits the data.

ANSWER SHEET

1. A B C D

2. A B C D

3. A B C D

4. A B C D

5. A B C D

6. (grid-in) / . 0 1 2 3 4 5 6 7 8 9

7. (grid-in) / . 0 1 2 3 4 5 6 7 8 9

8. (grid-in) / . 0 1 2 3 4 5 6 7 8 9

9. (grid-in) / . 0 1 2 3 4 5 6 7 8 9

10. (grid-in) / . 0 1 2 3 4 5 6 7 8 9

11. (grid-in) / . 0 1 2 3 4 5 6 7 8 9

Name ________________ Date ________ Class ________

Interpret characteristics of the line of best fit in real-world situations.

SAMPLE MULTIPLE CHOICE

The equation of the line of best fit for the association between a student's grade g in a class and the student's number of absences a is $g = -4.2a + 96.8$. What does the number -4.2 in the equation represent in this context?

A) For each additional absence, the grade decreases by 4.2 points on average.

B) For each additional absence, the grade increases by 4.2 points on average.

C) For each unit increase in grade, absences decrease by 4.2 on average.

D) For each unit increase in grade, absences increase by 4.2 on average.

In the equation, -4.2 is the slope of the line of best fit. The slope of a line on a graph indicates the rate of change of the dependent variable with respect to the independent variable.

For the equation of the line given, the number of absences is the independent variable and the grade is the dependent variable. The slope is negative, so each additional absence is associated with a *decrease* in grade by 4.2 points.

The correct answer is A. A ● B ○ C ○ D ○

Questions 1 and 2 refer to the following information.

The graph below shows the flight times and distances for eight flights. The line of best fit for the association between flight time t in hours and distance d in kilometers has the equation $t = 0.0012d + 0.13$.

Flight Time Versus Distance

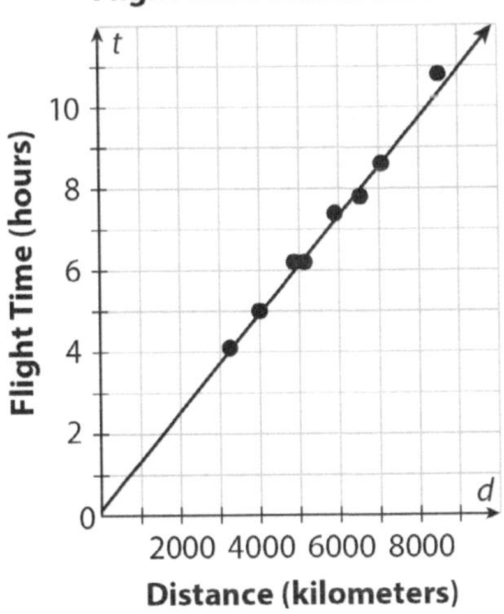

1

What does 0.0012 in the equation mean?

A) A flight's average speed increases by 0.0012 km/h for each kilometer.

B) For each hour increase in flight time, distance increases by 0.0012 kilometer on average.

C) For each kilometer increase in distance, flight time increases by 0.0012 hour on average.

D) To find the flight time, multiply the distance by 0.0012.

2

What does 0.13 in the equation mean?

A) For each 0.13 kilometer increase in distance, flight time increases by 0.0012 hour.

B) For each kilometer increase in distance, flight time increases by 0.13 hour on average.

C) You must add 0.13 hour to the flight time no matter the distance of the flight.

D) The planes taxi an average of 0.13 kilometer before takeoff.

Name ______________________ Date ______________ Class ______________

SAMPLE GRID-IN

For a company's suburban office, the line of best fit for the association between employees' commute time t in minutes and distance d in miles has the equation $t = 1.4d + 1.5$. When the distance of the commute increases from 20 to 25 miles, by how many minutes, on average, does the commute time increase?

Notice that the number 1.4 in the equation is the slope of the line of best fit. The slope indicates that for each unit of change in the value of d, the value of t is associated with a change in value of 1.4.

Because the value of d is increasing by $25 - 20 = 5$, the value of t increases by $1.4(5) = 7$.

So, the commute time increases by 7 minutes.

Grid in 7.

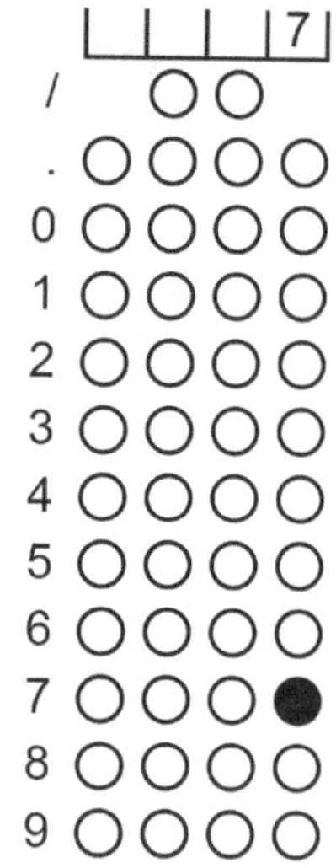

Questions 3 and 4 refer to the following information.

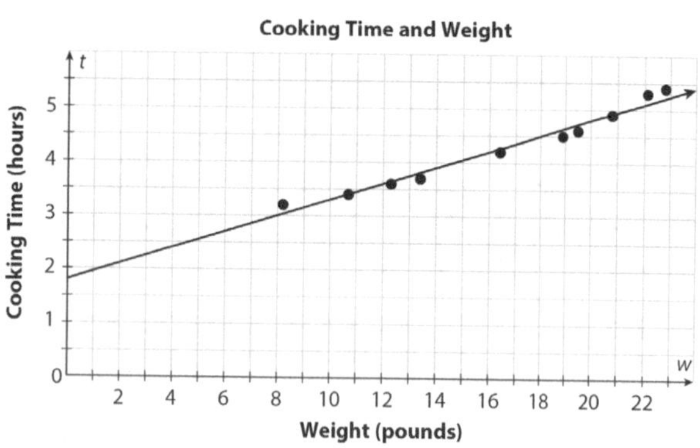

The graph above shows the cooking time t (in hours) and weight w (in pounds) for 10 turkeys plotted along with the line of best fit for the data. The equation of the line of best fit is $t = 0.15w + 1.8$.

3

By how many minutes does the average cooking time increase if the weight of the turkey increases by 1 pound?

4

What does the line of best fit predict for the weight in pounds of a turkey whose cooking time is 4 hours 15 minutes?

Questions 5 and 6 refer to the following information.

The line of best fit for data about air temperature and altitude collected by a weather balloon is $T = -0.01A + 27$, where T is the air temperature in degrees Celsius and A is the altitude in meters.

5

According to the line of best fit, at what altitude in meters is the air temperature 0°C?

6

How many meters must the balloon rise for the air temperature to decrease by 1 degree Celsius?

Name ______________________________ Date ______________ Class______________

Interpret characteristics of the line of best fit in real-world situations.

ANSWER SHEET

1. A B C D
○ ○ ○ ○

2. A B C D
○ ○ ○ ○

3. |_|_|_|_|
/ ○ ○
. ○ ○ ○ ○
0 ○ ○ ○ ○
1 ○ ○ ○ ○
2 ○ ○ ○ ○
3 ○ ○ ○ ○
4 ○ ○ ○ ○
5 ○ ○ ○ ○
6 ○ ○ ○ ○
7 ○ ○ ○ ○
8 ○ ○ ○ ○
9 ○ ○ ○ ○

4. |_|_|_|_|
/ ○ ○
. ○ ○ ○ ○
0 ○ ○ ○ ○
1 ○ ○ ○ ○
2 ○ ○ ○ ○
3 ○ ○ ○ ○
4 ○ ○ ○ ○
5 ○ ○ ○ ○
6 ○ ○ ○ ○
7 ○ ○ ○ ○
8 ○ ○ ○ ○
9 ○ ○ ○ ○

5. |_|_|_|_|
/ ○ ○
. ○ ○ ○ ○
0 ○ ○ ○ ○
1 ○ ○ ○ ○
2 ○ ○ ○ ○
3 ○ ○ ○ ○
4 ○ ○ ○ ○
5 ○ ○ ○ ○
6 ○ ○ ○ ○
7 ○ ○ ○ ○
8 ○ ○ ○ ○
9 ○ ○ ○ ○

6. |_|_|_|_|
/ ○ ○
. ○ ○ ○ ○
0 ○ ○ ○ ○
1 ○ ○ ○ ○
2 ○ ○ ○ ○
3 ○ ○ ○ ○
4 ○ ○ ○ ○
5 ○ ○ ○ ○
6 ○ ○ ○ ○
7 ○ ○ ○ ○
8 ○ ○ ○ ○
9 ○ ○ ○ ○

Name ____________ Date ____________ Class ____________

Use tables and graphs to understand relationships between two quantities.

SAMPLE MULTIPLE CHOICE

Time (h)	Odometer Reading (mi)
0	22,348
1	22,413
2	22,478

The table above shows how a car's odometer reading changed during a long trip. How many miles had the car been driven before the trip?

A) 130 C) 22,413
B) 22,348 D) 22,478

The number of miles the car had been driven before the trip started is the odometer reading at 0 hours for the trip. The table shows that the odometer reading at that point was 22,348 miles.

The correct answer is B. A B C D ○ ● ○ ○

Questions 1 and 2 refer to the following information.

Weeks Since Opening	0	1	2	3	4
Balance ($)	50	60	70	80	90

The table above shows the balance of a savings account, in dollars, each week after it was first opened. Interest is credited to the account quarterly.

1

What was the starting balance of the savings account?

A) $0
B) $10
C) $50
D) $60

2

After the account was opened, how much was deposited into it each week?

A) $0
B) $10
C) $50
D) $60

3

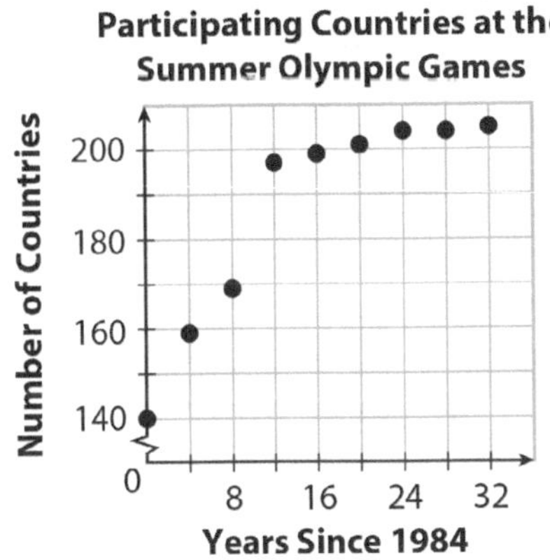

The graph above shows the number of countries that participated in each Summer Olympic Games from 1984 to 2016. Which statement is true?

A) The number of participating countries has generally been increasing.
B) The number of participating countries has both increased and decreased over time.
C) The number of participating countries has never been the same in two different years.
D) The 1988 Games saw the greatest increase in the number of participating countries from the previous Summer Olympic Games.

Name ______________________ Date ______________ Class______________

SAMPLE GRID-IN

Time (h)	0	1	2	3	4
Cost ($)	6	8	10	12	14

The table above shows how the cost for parking in a certain garage depends on the number of hours the vehicle is there. How much would it cost to park a car in this garage for 8 hours? Ignore the dollar sign when gridding your response.

The table shows that there is an initial charge of $6 and an additional charge of $2 per hour.

For a time of 8 hours, the charge would be $\$6 + 8(\$2) = \$22$.

So, the cost to park for 8 hours is $22.

Grid in 22.

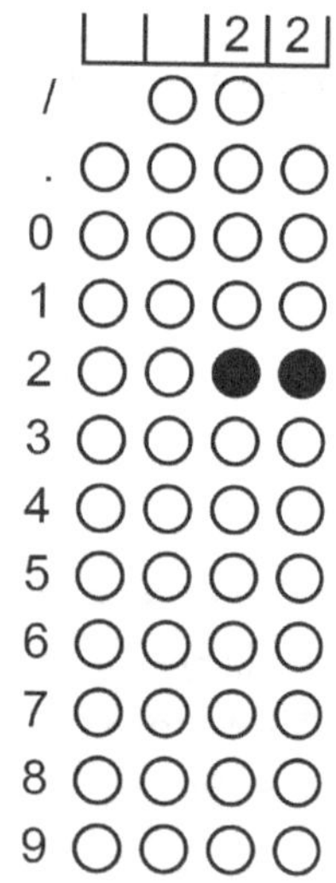

Questions 4–6 refer to the following information.

Number of Shirts	5	10	15	20
Cost ($)	45	70	95	120

The table above shows the total cost for different quantities of screen-printed shirts to be ordered for the volunteers at a charity event. The total cost includes a one-time setup charge of $20.

4

If just 1 shirt is ordered, what would be the cost? Ignore the dollar sign when gridding your response.

5

If 40 shirts were ordered, what would be the total cost of the shirts? Ignore the dollar sign when gridding your response.

6

The screen-printing company offers a discount if at least 50 shirts are ordered. With the discount, the total cost for 50 shirts is $225. What is the difference in the cost of 50 shirts with and without the discount? Ignore the dollar sign when gridding your response.

Questions 7–9 refer to the following information.

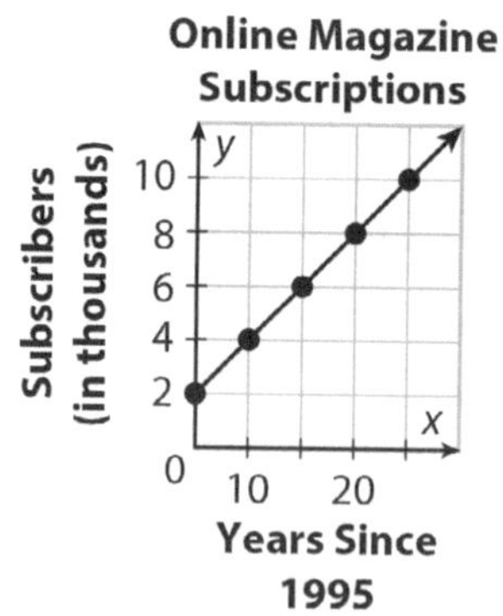

The graph above shows the number of subscriptions (in thousands) to an online magazine since 1995.

7

If the trend continues, how many thousands of subscribers will there be in the year 2020?

8

By how many thousands per year does the number of subscriptions increase? Grid your answer as a decimal.

9

How many thousands of subscribers were there in 2012? Grid your answer as a decimal.

Name ______________________ Date __________ Class ____________

Use tables and graphs to understand relationships between quantities.

ANSWER SHEET

1. A B C D
○ ○ ○ ○

2. A B C D
○ ○ ○ ○

3. A B C D
○ ○ ○ ○

4. |_|_|_|_|

/		○	○	
.	○	○	○	○
0	○	○	○	○
1	○	○	○	○
2	○	○	○	○
3	○	○	○	○
4	○	○	○	○
5	○	○	○	○
6	○	○	○	○
7	○	○	○	○
8	○	○	○	○
9	○	○	○	○

5. |_|_|_|_|

/		○	○	
.	○	○	○	○
0	○	○	○	○
1	○	○	○	○
2	○	○	○	○
3	○	○	○	○
4	○	○	○	○
5	○	○	○	○
6	○	○	○	○
7	○	○	○	○
8	○	○	○	○
9	○	○	○	○

6. |_|_|_|_|

/		○	○	
.	○	○	○	○
0	○	○	○	○
1	○	○	○	○
2	○	○	○	○
3	○	○	○	○
4	○	○	○	○
5	○	○	○	○
6	○	○	○	○
7	○	○	○	○
8	○	○	○	○
9	○	○	○	○

7. |_|_|_|_|

/		○	○	
.	○	○	○	○
0	○	○	○	○
1	○	○	○	○
2	○	○	○	○
3	○	○	○	○
4	○	○	○	○
5	○	○	○	○
6	○	○	○	○
7	○	○	○	○
8	○	○	○	○
9	○	○	○	○

8. |_|_|_|_|

/		○	○	
.	○	○	○	○
0	○	○	○	○
1	○	○	○	○
2	○	○	○	○
3	○	○	○	○
4	○	○	○	○
5	○	○	○	○
6	○	○	○	○
7	○	○	○	○
8	○	○	○	○
9	○	○	○	○

9. |_|_|_|_|

/		○	○	
.	○	○	○	○
0	○	○	○	○
1	○	○	○	○
2	○	○	○	○
3	○	○	○	○
4	○	○	○	○
5	○	○	○	○
6	○	○	○	○
7	○	○	○	○
8	○	○	○	○
9	○	○	○	○

Name ______________________ Date ______________ Class ______________

Interpret data in scatterplots and line graphs, and fit appropriate models.

SAMPLE MULTIPLE CHOICE

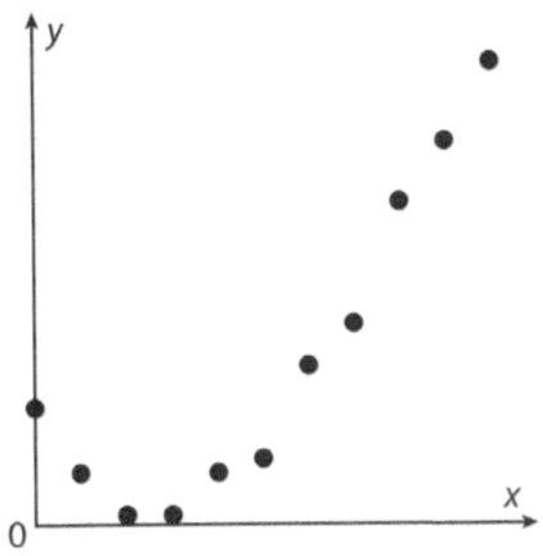

Choose the most appropriate function type to model the data in the scatterplot.

A) Linear C) Exponential
B) Quadratic D) None

To fit an appropriate function, consider whether there seems to be any relationship between the horizontal and vertical coordinates. If so, look for features of quadratic functions (the data fit a U-shaped curve), exponential functions (the data fit a curve that has an asymptote and overall only increases or only decreases), or linear functions (the data lie close to a straight line).

The graph appears to have a clear minimum with portions that curve up on either side. These are characteristics of the graph of a quadratic function.

The correct answer is B. A ○ B ● C ○ D ○

1

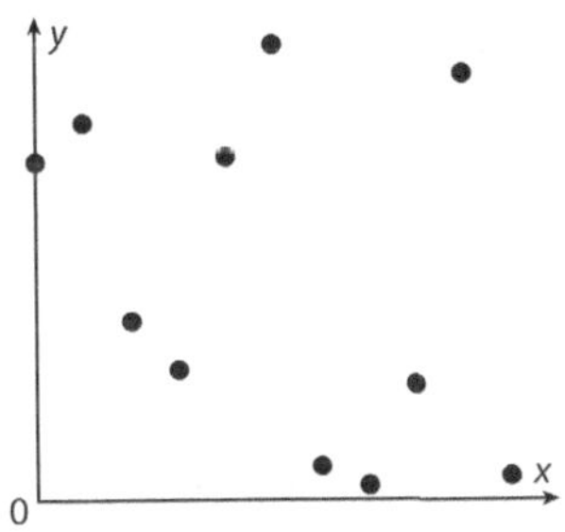

Choose the most appropriate function type to model the data in the scatterplot.

A) Linear C) Exponential
B) Quadratic D) None

2

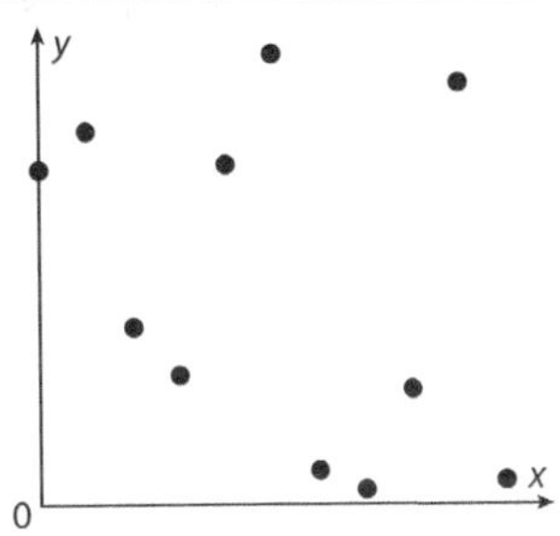

Choose the most appropriate function type to model the data in the scatterplot.

A) Linear C) Exponential decay
B) Quadratic D) Exponential growth

Questions 3 and 4 refer to the following figure.

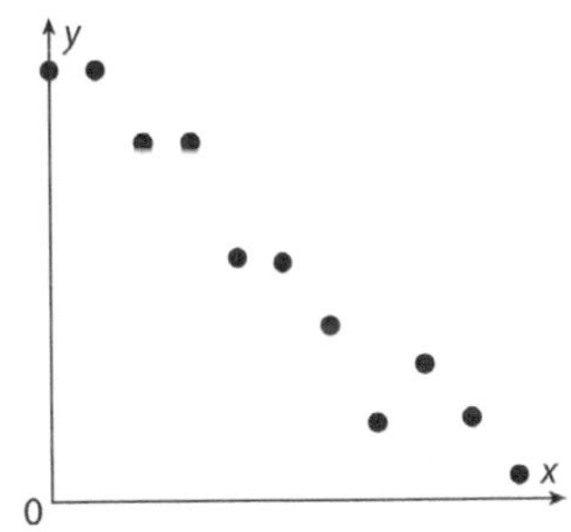

3

Choose the most appropriate function type to model the data in the scatterplot.

A) Linear C) Exponential
B) Quadratic D) None

4

Give the best description of the relationship between the variables in this data set.

A) Strong positive association
B) Weak positive association
C) Weak negative association
D) Strong negative association

Name ______________________ Date ______________ Class ______________

SAMPLE GRID-IN

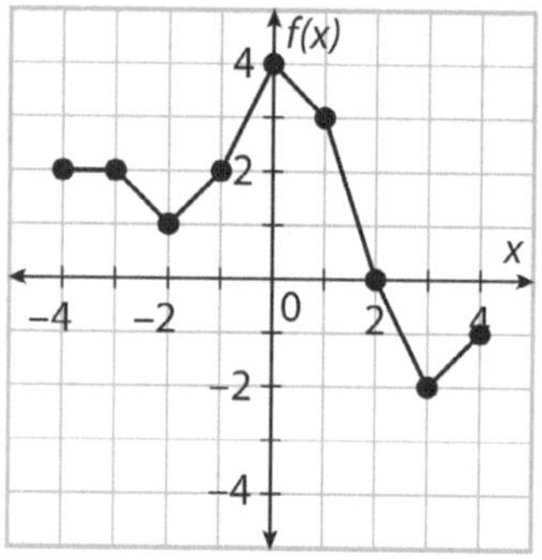

The figure above shows the graph of a piecewise-defined function *f*. Identify the value of *x* for which *f*(*x*) has a minimum value.

The minimum value of *f*(*x*) can be identified on the graph as the point with the lowest vertical position. This is the point (3, –2).

The value of *x* is the first coordinate of this ordered pair, which is 3.

Grid in 3.

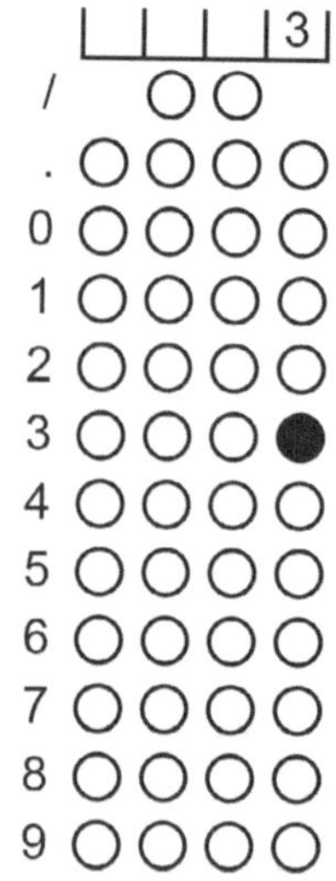

Questions 5–8 refer to the following information.

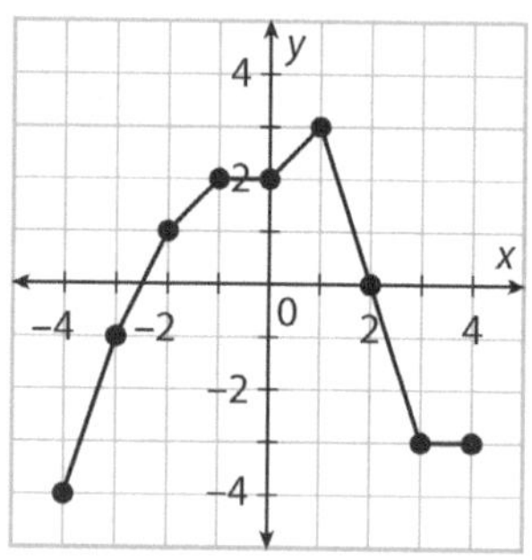

The line graph above defines a function.

5

What is the value of the *y*-intercept of this function?

6

What is the value of the positive *x*-intercept of this function?

7

What is the maximum value of *y*?

8

Find the positive difference between the *x*-values of the maximum and minimum points of the function.

Questions 9–11 refer to the following information.

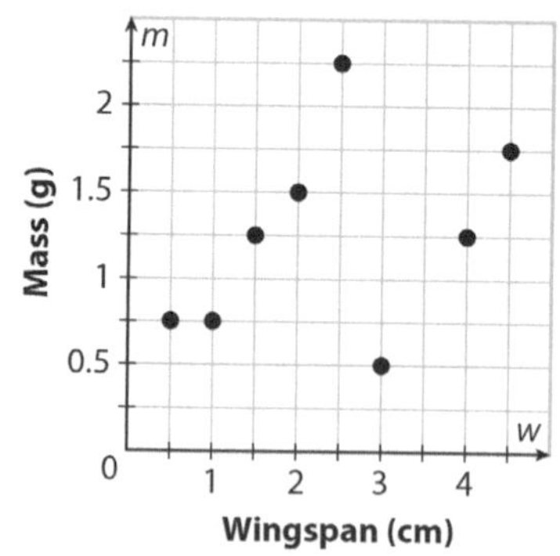

The scatterplot above shows the relationship between the wingspan (in centimeters) and mass (in grams) for eight flying insects selected at random.

9

How many of the insects sampled have masses of 1.25 grams?

10

What is the wingspan, in centimeters, of the insect with the greatest mass?

11

What is the mass, in grams, of the insect with the greatest wingspan?

Name ______________________ Date ______________ Class ______________

Interpret data in scatterplots and line graphs, and fit appropriate models.

ANSWER SHEET

1. A B C D

2. A B C D

3. A B C D

4. A B C D

5. / . 0 1 2 3 4 5 6 7 8 9

6. / . 0 1 2 3 4 5 6 7 8 9

7. / . 0 1 2 3 4 5 6 7 8 9

8. / . 0 1 2 3 4 5 6 7 8 9

9. / . 0 1 2 3 4 5 6 7 8 9

10. / . 0 1 2 3 4 5 6 7 8 9

11. / . 0 1 2 3 4 5 6 7 8 9

Name ______________________ Date ______________ Class______________

Identify appropriate graphs, and interpret graphs in real-world situations.

SAMPLE MULTIPLE CHOICE

A scientist performs an experiment measuring the average time it takes for rats to find their way through a series of mazes. The complexity of a maze is quantified by the number of forks in the maze (places where a rat must turn left or right). Which of the following would be an appropriate choice for the horizontal axis when graphing the results?

A) Average time C) Number of rats
B) Rat ID number D) Number of forks

Graphs of data show the dependent variable on the vertical axis and the independent variable on the horizontal axis. In this experiment, the scientist is studying the time needed for a rat to travel the maze as a function of the number of forks in the maze. So the number of forks is the independent variable and, therefore, the correct choice for the horizontal axis.

The correct answer is D. A B C D ○○○●

Questions 1–4 refer to the following information.

Graph I

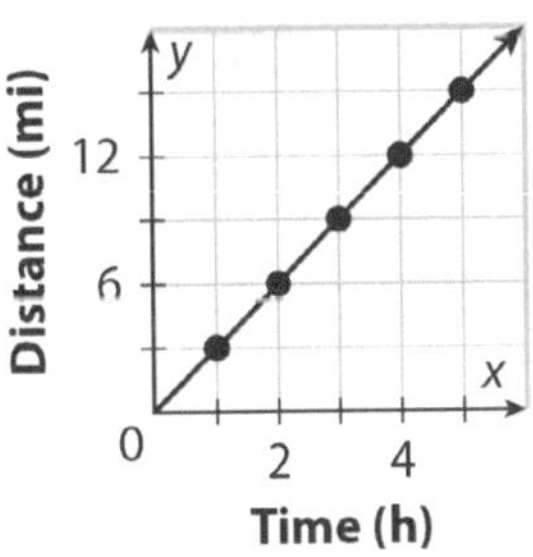

Graph II

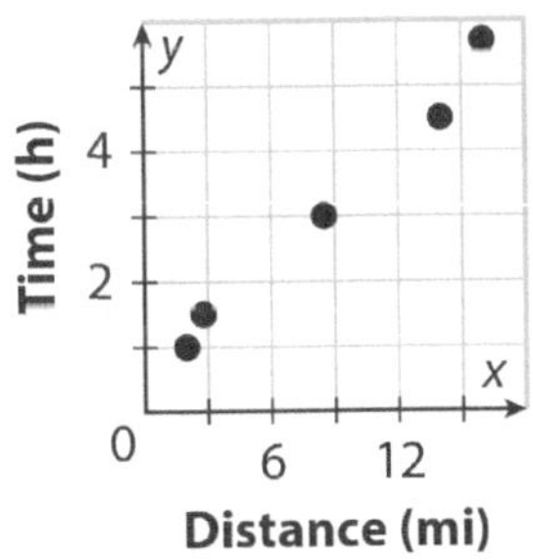

Graph III

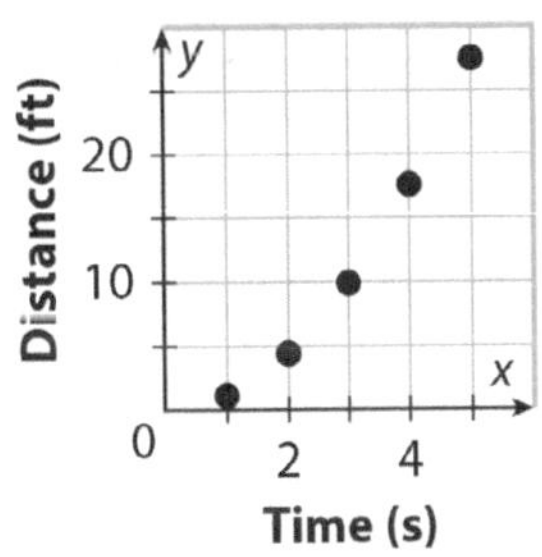

Graph IV

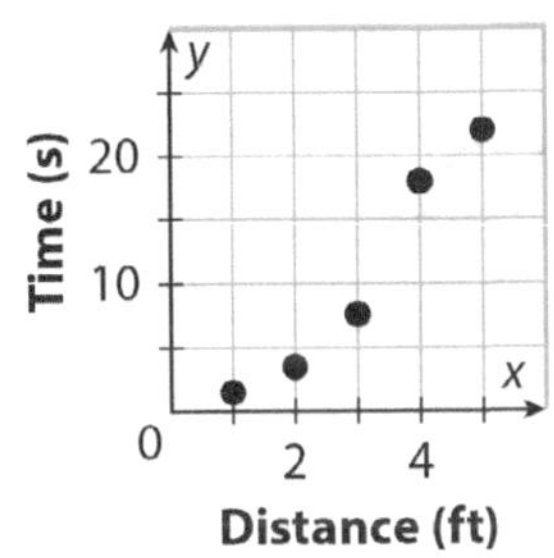

In each case, select the graph that best represents the situation described.

1

Joaquin is trying to choose a good trail for a hike with his summer camp group. He measures how long it takes him to hike each of several different nature trails.

A) Graph I C) Graph III
B) Graph II D) Graph IV

2

A scientist is studying animals' ability to smell food buried underground and measures how long it takes a dog to find the food starting from different distances.

A) Graph I C) Graph III
B) Graph II D) Graph IV

3

Guidelines for finding a missing cat suggest how far you should search based on the last time the cat was seen.

A) Graph I C) Graph III
B) Graph II D) Graph IV

4

A physics student is studying motion. She uses a rapid-firing camera to take snapshots at short time intervals to measure how far a ball has rolled down an incline.

A) Graph I C) Graph III
B) Graph II D) Graph IV

Name ______________________ Date ______________ Class ______________

SAMPLE GRID-IN

Trip to the Museum

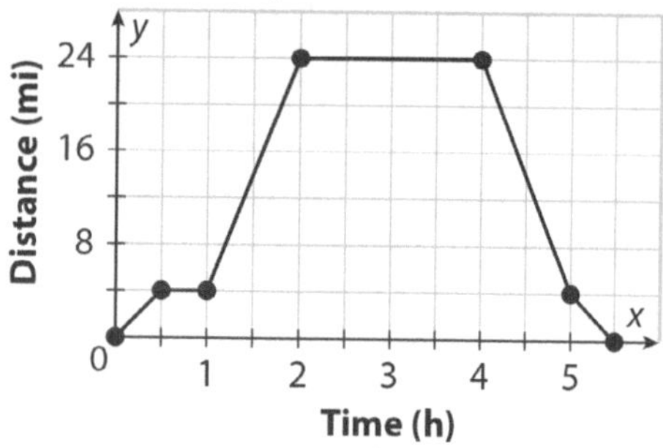

Jamie rode her bicycle to the bus stop and then rode the bus from there to the museum. After visiting the museum, she returned home the same way. The graph shows Jamie's distance along the route from home as a function of time. How many miles did Jamie travel by bus in total?

Read the description of Jamie's trip to identify the parts of the graph that correspond to bus travel.

The first leg of the trip, from 0 to 0.5 hour, corresponds to her bicycle ride to the bus stop. Then she waited 0.5 hour for the bus before riding the bus from a time of 1 hour to a time of 2 hours. The bus ride to the museum began 4 miles from her home and ended 24 miles from her home, which means she rode the bus for 20 miles. Later, Jamie rode the bus back for an additional 20 miles before bicycling home, bringing the total for her bus rides to 40 miles.

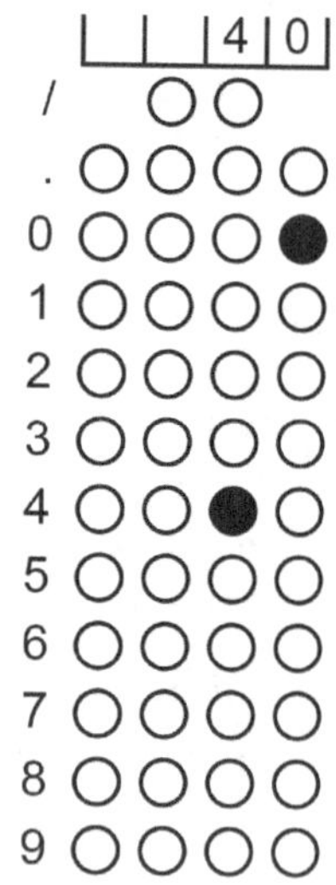

Grid in 40.

Questions 5 and 6 refer to the following information.

Company X Year-to-Year Sales

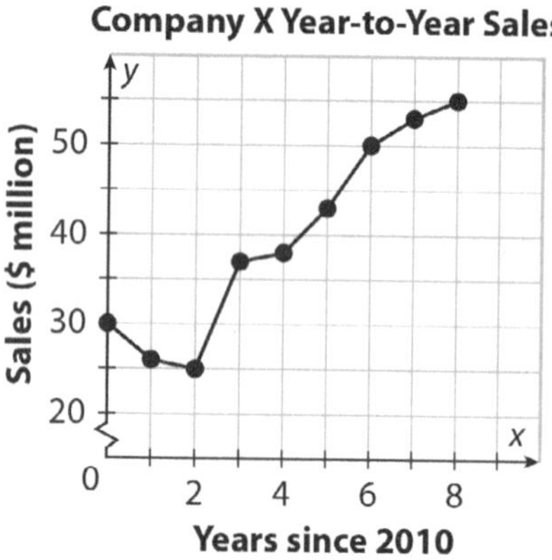

The graph shows sales for Company X.

5

How much (in millions of dollars) did sales drop from 2010 before they started increasing?

6

How many years did it take for the sales to double from their 2012 level?

Questions 7 and 8 refer to the following information.

Hours of Daylight in Boston

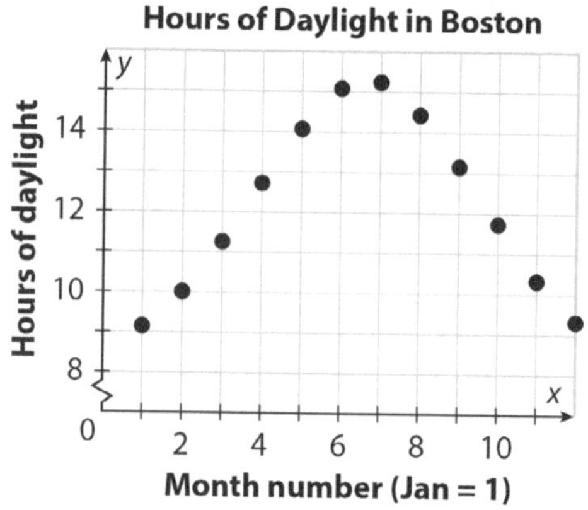

The graph shows the hours of daylight on the first day of each month in Boston.

7

How many months of the year have more than 13 hours of daylight on the first of the month?

8

How many months have more daylight on the first day than the preceding month did?

Name ________________ Date ________ Class ________

Identify appropriate graphs, and interpret graphs in real-world situations.

ANSWER SHEET

1. A B C D
○ ○ ○ ○

2. A B C D
○ ○ ○ ○

3. A B C D
○ ○ ○ ○

4. A B C D
○ ○ ○ ○

5.
/ ○ ○
. ○ ○ ○ ○
0 ○ ○ ○ ○
1 ○ ○ ○ ○
2 ○ ○ ○ ○
3 ○ ○ ○ ○
4 ○ ○ ○ ○
5 ○ ○ ○ ○
6 ○ ○ ○ ○
7 ○ ○ ○ ○
8 ○ ○ ○ ○
9 ○ ○ ○ ○

6.
/ ○ ○
. ○ ○ ○ ○
0 ○ ○ ○ ○
1 ○ ○ ○ ○
2 ○ ○ ○ ○
3 ○ ○ ○ ○
4 ○ ○ ○ ○
5 ○ ○ ○ ○
6 ○ ○ ○ ○
7 ○ ○ ○ ○
8 ○ ○ ○ ○
9 ○ ○ ○ ○

7.
/ ○ ○
. ○ ○ ○ ○
0 ○ ○ ○ ○
1 ○ ○ ○ ○
2 ○ ○ ○ ○
3 ○ ○ ○ ○
4 ○ ○ ○ ○
5 ○ ○ ○ ○
6 ○ ○ ○ ○
7 ○ ○ ○ ○
8 ○ ○ ○ ○
9 ○ ○ ○ ○

8.
/ ○ ○
. ○ ○ ○ ○
0 ○ ○ ○ ○
1 ○ ○ ○ ○
2 ○ ○ ○ ○
3 ○ ○ ○ ○
4 ○ ○ ○ ○
5 ○ ○ ○ ○
6 ○ ○ ○ ○
7 ○ ○ ○ ○
8 ○ ○ ○ ○
9 ○ ○ ○ ○

Name ______________________ Date ______________ Class ______________

Find a linear, quadratic, or exponential function that best fits a given set of data.

SAMPLE MULTIPLE CHOICE

Which quadratic function models the data in the table below?

x	0	1	2	3	4
***f*(*x*)**	–1	–3	–1	5	15

A) $f(x) = (x-1)^2 - 3$

B) $f(x) = 2(x-1)^2 - 3$

C) $f(x) = -3(x+1)^2 - 1$

D) $f(x) = (x-3)^2 - 1$

For a function written in the vertex form $f(x) = a(x-h)^2 + k$, the vertex is at (h, k). Observe that the data appear to be symmetric about $x = 1$. This means that the *x*-coordinate of the vertex is 1, so $h = 1$. The *y*-coordinate of the vertex can be read from the table as –3, so $k = -3$. Use a different point from the table, for example, $f(0) = -1$, to determine the value of *a*:

$$f(x) = a(x-h)^2 + k$$
$$f(0) = a(0-1)^2 + (-3)$$
$$-1 = a - 3$$
$$2 = a$$

The correct answer is B. A B C D ○ ● ○ ○

1

Jameis invests \$2,500 in an interest-bearing account. The value *V* of the account is \$2,550 after one year and \$2,601 after two years. Using this data and an exponential function $V = a(b)^x$ to model the value after *x* years, what is the value of *b*?

A) 0.02 C) 2

B) 1.02 D) 2,500

2

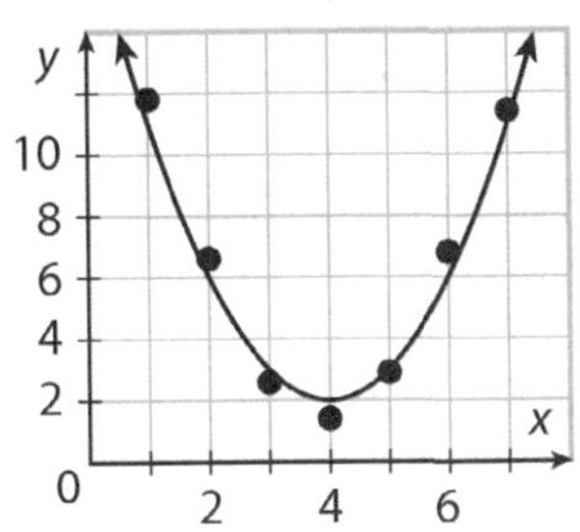

The figure shows a set of data points and the graph of quadratic function $f(x) = ax^2 + bx + c$ that best fits the data. If $a = 1$, what is the value of *b*?

A) –8 C) 4

B) –4 D) 8

3

Which function models the data in the table below?

x	0	1	2	3
***f*(*x*)**	4	6	9	13.5

A) $f(x) = 1.5(4)^x$

B) $f(x) = \frac{3}{2}x^2 - x + 4$

C) $f(x) = 1.5x + 4$

D) $f(x) = 4(1.5)^x$

4

Which function best models the data in the table below?

x	2	5	7	12
***f*(*x*)**	3.2	6.2	7.9	12.2

A) $f(x) = 1.1x + 0.9$

B) $f(x) = 0.9x + 1.5$

C) $f(x) = 1.55x$

D) $f(x) = 0.55x + 3.65$

Name ______________________ Date ______________ Class ______________

5

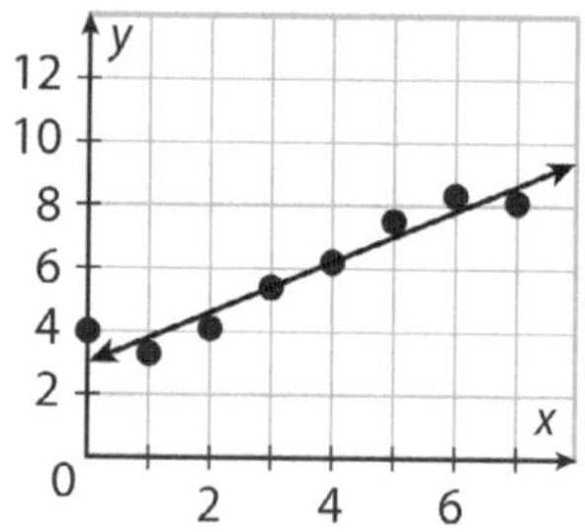

The line in the graph approximates the plotted points. Which function best matches the linear model for the data?

A) $f(x) = 1.25x + 3$

B) $f(x) = 1.25x - 3$

C) $f(x) = 0.8x + 3$

D) $f(x) = 0.8x - 3$

6

Shayla purchases a new car for \$20,000. The value *V* of the car is \$17,800 after one year. Its value is \$15,842 after two years. Which function is the best model of the value of the car *x* years after Shayla bought it?

A) $V(x) = 20{,}000(0.11)^x$

B) $V(x) = x^2 - 2{,}321x + 20{,}000$

C) $V(x) = 20{,}000 - 2{,}200x$

D) $V(x) = 20{,}000(0.89)^x$

7

Which function is the best model of the data given in the table?

x	0	1	2	3	4
f(x)	10	20	26	28	26

A) $f(x) = -2x^2 + 12x + 10$

B) $f(x) = 10(2^x)$

C) $f(x) = -2x^2 - 12x + 10$

D) $f(x) = 10(1 + x)$

8

The population of a certain town was 8,000 in the year 2000. It was 8,820 in 2002 and 9,724 in 2004. If *x* is the number of years since 2000, which function models the population of the town?

A) $P(x) = 8{,}000 + 410x$

B) $P(x) = 1.1025x^2 + 409x + 8{,}000$

C) $P(x) = 8{,}000(1.05)^x$

D) $P(x) = 8{,}000(1.1025)^x$

9

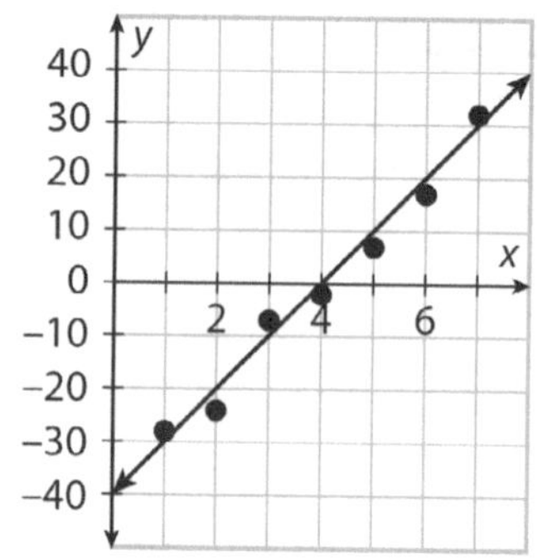

The line in the graph approximates the plotted points. Which function best matches the linear model for the data?

A) $f(x) = 10x - 30$

B) $f(x) = 10x - 40$

C) $f(x) = 15x - 30$

D) $f(x) = 15x - 40$

10

A ball is thrown straight up from an initial height of 4 feet. It reaches its greatest height of 40 feet after 1.5 seconds. It is caught at its initial height 3 seconds after it was thrown. Which function models the ball's height *h*, in feet, after *t* seconds?

A) $h(t) = -16t^2 + 48t + 4$

B) $h(t) = -16t^2 - 48t + 4$

C) $h(t) = -16t^2 + 48t$

D) $h(t) = -16t^2 - 48t$

Name ______________________ Date ______________ Class ______________

Find a linear, quadratic, or exponential function that best fits a given set of data.

ANSWER SHEET

1. A B C D ○ ○ ○ ○
2. A B C D ○ ○ ○ ○
3. A B C D ○ ○ ○ ○
4. A B C D ○ ○ ○ ○
5. A B C D ○ ○ ○ ○
6. A B C D ○ ○ ○ ○
7. A B C D ○ ○ ○ ○
8. A B C D ○ ○ ○ ○
9. A B C D ○ ○ ○ ○
10. A B C D ○ ○ ○ ○

Name ______________________ Date ______________ Class______________

Distinguish between linear and exponential growth.

SAMPLE MULTIPLE CHOICE

x	1	2	3	4
f(x)	8	32	128	512

Determine whether the growth data in the table above indicate a linear growth model or an exponential growth model. Then find the formula for the function. Select the correct choice.

A) Exponential; $f(x) = 2(4)^x$

B) Exponential; $f(x) = 8(4)^x$

C) Linear; $f(x) = 24x - 16$

D) Linear; $f(x) = 168x - 160$

To find the function type, determine whether for each unit increase in x that successive y-values are found by adding a constant or by multiplying by a constant. Since the y-values result from successive multiplication by a factor of 4, the growth is exponential. Exponential functions have the form $f(x) = a(b)^x$, where a is equal to $f(0)$ and b is the base, or multiplicative factor.

It is clear that $b = 4$. You can substitute $f(1) = 8$ in $f(x) = a(b)^x$ with $b = 4$ to solve for a. It takes less time, however, to divide $f(1)$ by 4 to obtain $f(0)$. So, $f(0) = a = 2$, and the model is $f(x) = 2(4)^x$.

The correct answer is A. A ● B ○ C ○ D ○

1

A function has the property that $f(0) = 7$, and the function values increase by 6 for each unit increase in x. Which formula represents the function?

A) $f(x) = 6x + 7$

B) $f(x) = 7x + 6$

C) $f(x) = 7(6)^x$

D) $f(x) = 6(7)^x$

2

Consider a linear function $y = \frac{9}{2}x + 3$ and an exponential function $y = 3(2)^x$. Over which interval do the linear function values exceed the exponential function values?

A) $x > 0$

B) $x > 2$

C) $0 < x < 2$

D) The linear values never exceed the exponential values.

3

A tire begins with a pressure of 32 pounds per square inch (psi) and leaks at a rate of 10% per hour. Which of the following functions models the pressure p over the time t?

A) $p(t) = -3.2t + 32$

B) $p(t) = -0.1t + 32$

C) $p(t) = 32(0.9)^t$

D) $p(t) = 32(0.1)^t$

4

The average home value in two different cities was $300,000 in 2010. In one city, the value has been rising at a rate of 6% per year. In the other city, the value has been rising at a rate of $18,000 per year. What was the difference in the average home value between the two cities in 2015, to the nearest dollar?

A) $11,468

B) $24,736

C) $366,672

D) No difference

Name ______________________ Date ______________ Class______________

SAMPLE GRID-IN

Consider a linear function $f(x) = mx + 2$ and an exponential function $g(x) = 2(b)^x$, where m and b are to be determined. The graphs of both functions contain the points (0, 2) and (2, 32). How much greater is the linear function value than the exponential function value when $x = 1$?

Determine the values of m and b. First find m using both of the given points:

$$m = \frac{32-2}{2-0} = 15$$

Now find b using the second point. Recall that $b > 0$ in an exponential function.

$$32 = 2(b^2)$$
$$16 = b^2$$
$$4 = b$$

Use the values of m and b to find the values of $f(x)$ and $g(x)$ when $x = 1$:

$$f(1) = 15(1) + 2 = 17$$
$$g(1) = 2(4^1) = 8$$

So, the linear function value is 9 greater than the exponential function value when $x = 1$.

Grid in 9.

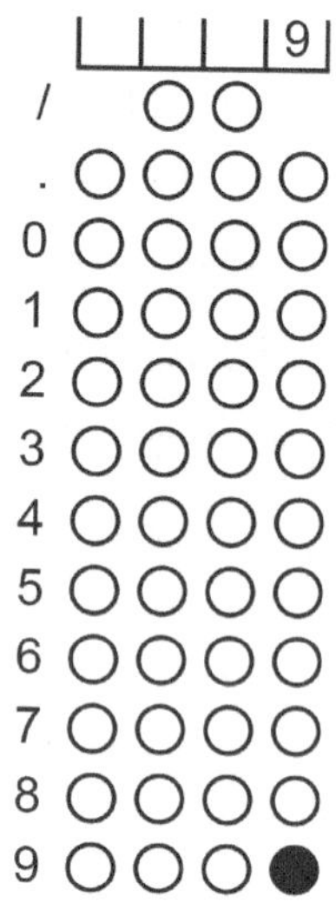

5

Consider a linear growth model $f(x) = mx + 100$ and an exponential growth model $g(x) = 100\left(b^{\frac{x}{10}}\right)$ where m and b are to be determined. The graphs of both models contain the points (0, 100) and (10, 50). By how much does $g(20)$ exceed $f(20)$?

6

Two new employees are offered jobs with a starting annual salary of $40,000. One employee chooses a guaranteed annual increase of $2,000, while the other chooses a guaranteed annual increase of 5%. What is the difference between the two employees' salaries after 12 years? Round to the nearest dollar, and do not include the dollar sign in your answer.

7

An increasing exponential function and an increasing linear function both satisfy $f(0) = 3$ and $f(2) = 12$. Determine an integer value of x in the interval $0 \le x < 4$ for which the graph of the exponential function lies above the graph of the linear function.

8

Consider the linear function $f(x) = 1.05x$ and the exponential function $g(x) = (1.05)^x$. For any function $h(x) > 0$, the percent increase in the function value from $x = a$ to $x = a + 1$ is given by $\frac{h(a+1) - h(a)}{h(a)} \cdot 100\%$. What is the least possible integer value of a for which the percent increase in the exponential function exceeds the percent increase in the linear function?

Name ______________________ Date ______________ Class ______________

Distinguish between linear and exponential growth.

ANSWER SHEET

1. A B C D
○ ○ ○ ○

2. A B C D
○ ○ ○ ○

3. A B C D
○ ○ ○ ○

4. A B C D
○ ○ ○ ○

5. Grid-in answer: / . 0 1 2 3 4 5 6 7 8 9

6. Grid-in answer: / . 0 1 2 3 4 5 6 7 8 9

7. Grid-in answer: / . 0 1 2 3 4 5 6 7 8 9

8. Grid-in answer: / . 0 1 2 3 4 5 6 7 8 9

Name ______________________ Date ______________ Class ______________

Estimate and use the line of best fit for a scatterplot.

SAMPLE MULTIPLE CHOICE

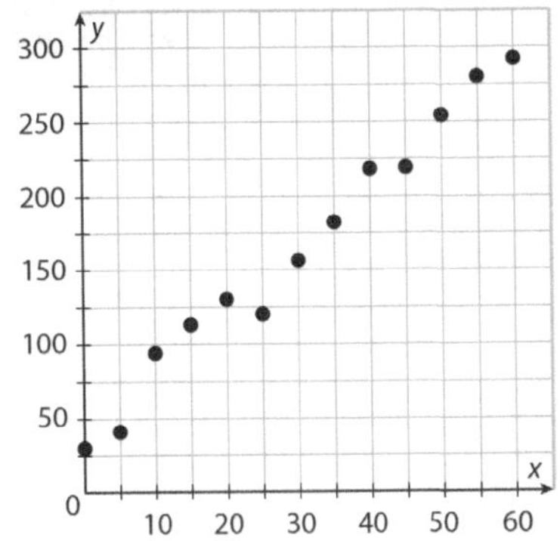

Estimate a line of best fit for the graph above. Select the best choice below.

A) $y = 4.33x + 100$

B) $y = 4.33x + 30$

C) $y = 4.33x$

D) $y = 2.33x + 30$

Select two points that would fall on a line that passes through or very close to as many of the points as possible. A reasonable choice for this scatterplot is to use the first and last points, which appear to be at about (0, 30) and (60, 290). Use these to find an equation of an estimate of the line of best fit. First, find the slope m of the line through the two points.

$$m = \frac{290 - 30}{60 - 0} = \frac{260}{60} \approx 4.33$$

You can use either point on the line to find the value of b in $y = mx + b$. Note, however, that you can see immediately that $b = 30$ because the line contains (0, 30). So, the equation of the estimated line of best fit is $y = 4.33x + 30$.

The correct answer is B. A B C D ○ ● ○ ○

1

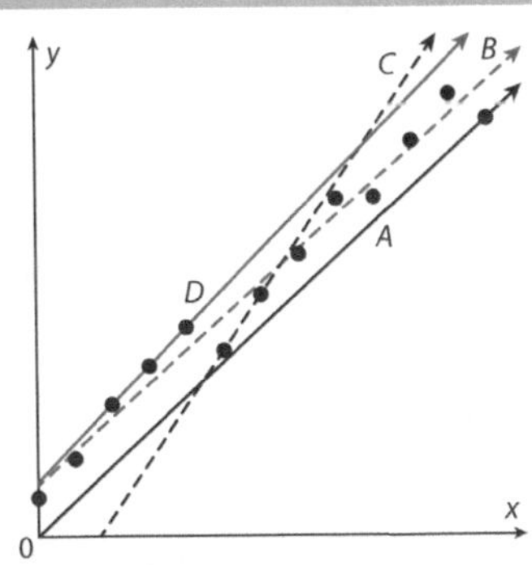

The graph above shows four lines passing through a set of plotted data. Which line appears to be closest to the line of best fit for the data?

A) Line A C) Line C

B) Line B D) Line D

2

The line $y = 4.33x + 30$ is estimated to be a line of best fit for a set of data in a scatterplot. Use this estimate to predict the value of y, to the nearest integer, when $x = 80$.

A) 340 C) 376

B) 346 D) 380

Questions 3 and 4 refer to the following figure.

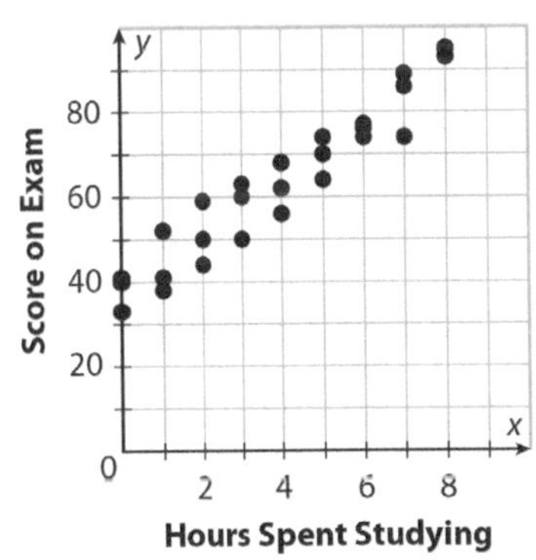

3

Which of these is the most reasonable estimate of the line of best fit for the data?

A) $y = 9x$ C) $y = 6.5x + 37$

B) $y = 6.5x + 20$ D) $y = 12x + 37$

4

Using $y = 6.8x + 34$ as the line of best fit, which would be the prediction for the exam score after studying for 9 hours?

A) 94.3 C) 95.8

B) 95.2 D) 96.7

Name ______________________ Date ______________ Class______________

SAMPLE GRID-IN

The equation $y = 2.3x + 4.5$ represents an estimated line of best fit to the data in a scatterplot. The actual data point in the scatterplot when $x = 5$ is (5, 15.5). Find the percent error in the predicted value for $x = 5$ compared to the actual value. Round to the nearest whole number. (Percent error is given by the quotient of the difference between the predicted and actual values and the actual value.) Omit the percent symbol in your answer.

Use the given equation for the line of best fit to find the predicted value when $x = 5$:

$$y = 2.3(5) + 4.5 = 16$$

Now find the percent error:

$$\% \text{ error} = \frac{\text{predicted} - \text{actual}}{\text{actual}} \cdot 100\%$$

$$= \frac{16 - 15.5}{15.5} \cdot 100\%$$

$$\approx 3\%$$

The percent error is about 3%.

Grid in 3.

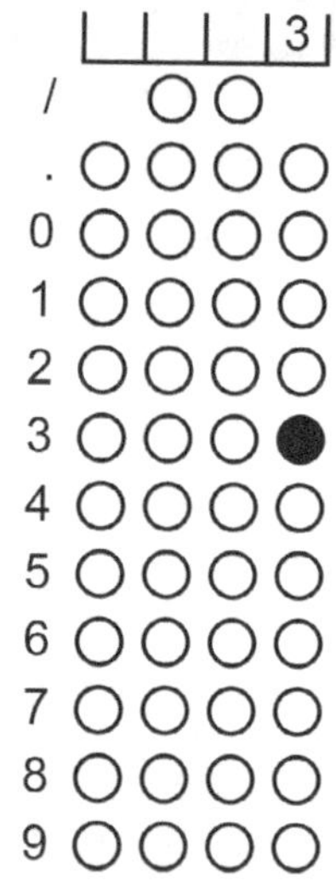

Questions 5 and 6 refer to the following information.

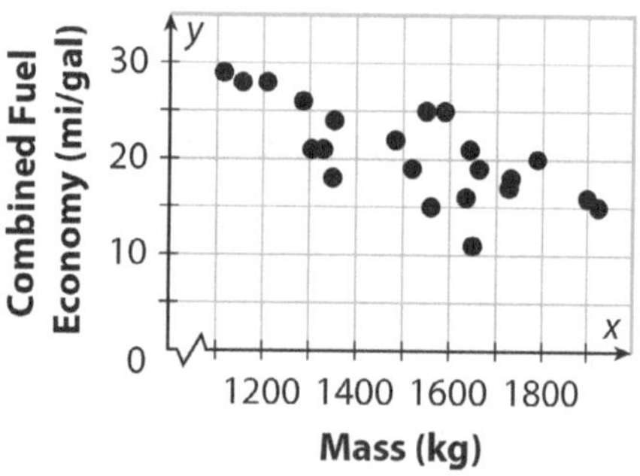

The scatterplot above displays the combined fuel economy (in miles per gallon) compared to mass for selected vehicles in 2009.

5

Two points in the scatterplot correspond to (1353, 24) and (1907, 17). If these ordered pairs are used to estimate a line of best fit, how many miles per gallon does the predicted mileage decrease per 100 additional kilograms of mass?

6

A better estimate of the line of best fit is given by $y = -0.016x + 45$. Using this model, what was the 2009 predicted combined fuel economy, in miles per gallon, for a car with a mass of 1,500 kg?

Questions 7 and 8 refer to the following figure.

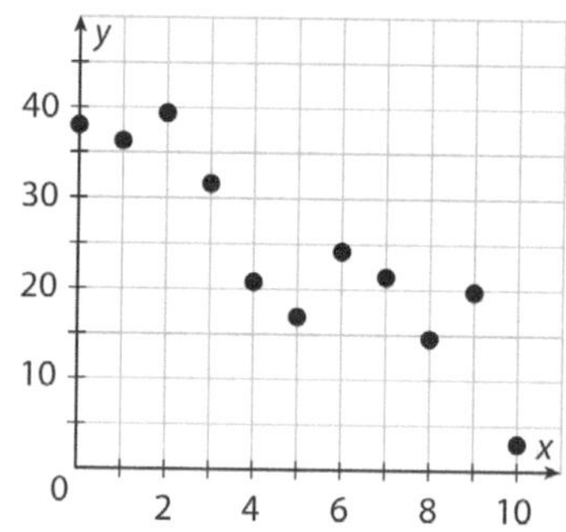

7

The points on the scatterplot for $x = 1$ and $x = 8$ have respective y-values of 36.3 and 14.4. A line through these two points appears to be a good estimate of the line of best fit. From this estimate of the line of best fit, what is the predicted y-intercept, rounded to the nearest tenth?

8

A student used two different points to estimate a line of best fit and obtained the model $y = -4.1x + 44$. Using this model, what is the percent error, to the nearest whole number, in the predicted value when $x = 5$ given that (5, 17) is the data point when $x = 5$? Ignore the percent symbol when gridding your answer.

Name ______________________ Date ____________ Class ____________

Estimate and use the line of best fit for a scatterplot.

ANSWER SHEET

1. A B C D
○ ○ ○ ○

2. A B C D
○ ○ ○ ○

3. A B C D
○ ○ ○ ○

4. A B C D
○ ○ ○ ○

5. | | | | |

/ ○ ○
. ○ ○ ○ ○
0 ○ ○ ○ ○
1 ○ ○ ○ ○
2 ○ ○ ○ ○
3 ○ ○ ○ ○
4 ○ ○ ○ ○
5 ○ ○ ○ ○
6 ○ ○ ○ ○
7 ○ ○ ○ ○
8 ○ ○ ○ ○
9 ○ ○ ○ ○

6. | | | | |

/ ○ ○
. ○ ○ ○ ○
0 ○ ○ ○ ○
1 ○ ○ ○ ○
2 ○ ○ ○ ○
3 ○ ○ ○ ○
4 ○ ○ ○ ○
5 ○ ○ ○ ○
6 ○ ○ ○ ○
7 ○ ○ ○ ○
8 ○ ○ ○ ○
9 ○ ○ ○ ○

7. | | | | |

/ ○ ○
. ○ ○ ○ ○
0 ○ ○ ○ ○
1 ○ ○ ○ ○
2 ○ ○ ○ ○
3 ○ ○ ○ ○
4 ○ ○ ○ ○
5 ○ ○ ○ ○
6 ○ ○ ○ ○
7 ○ ○ ○ ○
8 ○ ○ ○ ○
9 ○ ○ ○ ○

8. | | | | |

/ ○ ○
. ○ ○ ○ ○
0 ○ ○ ○ ○
1 ○ ○ ○ ○
2 ○ ○ ○ ○
3 ○ ○ ○ ○
4 ○ ○ ○ ○
5 ○ ○ ○ ○
6 ○ ○ ○ ○
7 ○ ○ ○ ○
8 ○ ○ ○ ○
9 ○ ○ ○ ○

Name ______________________ Date ______________ Class ______________

Determine and interpret probability and conditional probability in simple real-world situations.

SAMPLE MULTIPLE CHOICE

Each of the 100 guests attending a reception had been asked to indicate their meal choice. The table shows the choices by gender. What is the probability that a randomly selected male guest chose chicken?

	Beef	Chicken	Fish
Male	29	9	7
Female	13	20	22

A) $\frac{9}{100}$

B) $\frac{9}{45}$

C) $\frac{9}{29}$

D) $\frac{9}{20}$

Probability is the ratio of the number of occurrences of interest to the total number of possible outcomes.

The table shows that 9 male guests chose chicken. Find the total number of male guests.

$$29 + 9 + 7 = 45$$

So, the probability is $\frac{9}{45}$.

The correct answer is B. A B C D ○ ● ○ ○

1

The 100 members of a community club voted on a proposal. The table shows the votes by age. What is the probability that a randomly selected member under 50 voted for the proposal?

	For	Against	Abstain
Under 50	27	4	2
50 and Over	43	21	3

A) $\frac{27}{100}$

B) $\frac{27}{70}$

C) $\frac{27}{43}$

D) $\frac{27}{33}$

2

An aquarium at a pet store contains 40 striped fish and 10 solid-color fish. If 10 fish are randomly selected from the aquarium, which statement is true?

A) All 10 fish should be solid color.

B) You would expect 8 fish to be striped and 2 fish to be solid color.

C) Exactly 5 fish should be striped.

D) You would expect 2 fish to be striped and 8 fish to be solid color.

3

A game at a fair involves 3 boxes. Inside each box, there are 2 smaller boxes. One of the smaller boxes contains a prize, and the others are empty. The player chooses 1 of the 3 boxes. From inside that box, the player chooses 1 of the 2 smaller boxes and wins its contents. What is the probability of winning a prize?

A) $\frac{1}{9}$

B) $\frac{1}{6}$

C) $\frac{1}{3}$

D) $\frac{1}{2}$

4

A drawer contains 4 black socks, 2 blue socks, and 4 white socks. If 2 socks are selected at random at the same time, what is the probability that the socks are the same color?

A) $\frac{32}{1,000}$

B) $\frac{2}{10}$

C) $\frac{26}{90}$

D) $\frac{32}{100}$

Name ______________________ Date ______________ Class ______________

SAMPLE GRID-IN

An urn contains 12 blue marbles, 9 red marbles, and 4 yellow marbles. If a marble is selected at random from this urn, what is the probability that it is red?

Probability is the ratio of the number of occurrences of interest to the total number of possible outcomes.

There are 9 red marbles. Now find the total number of marbles in the urn.

$$12 + 9 + 4 = 25$$

So, the probability is $\frac{9}{25}$.

Grid in 9/25 or .36.

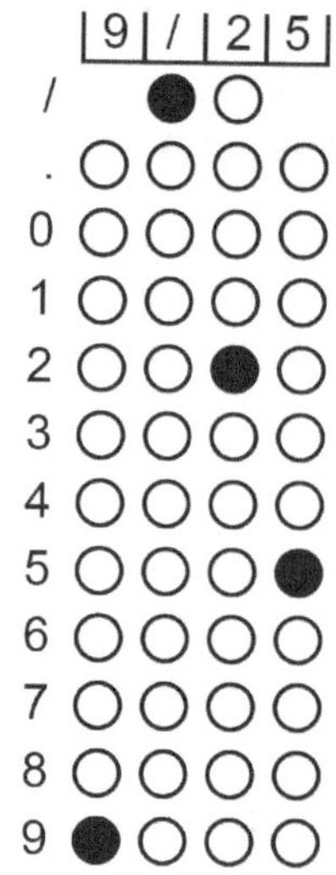

5

An urn contains 3 blue marbles, 1 red marble, and 6 yellow marbles. If a marble is selected at random from this urn, what is the probability that the marble is blue?

6

After reading a book and watching the movie adaptation of the book, the 35 students in a literature class discussed which they preferred. The table shows the preferences by grade level. What is the probability that a randomly selected freshman preferred the movie?

	Book	Movie
Freshman	12	3
Sophomore	5	4
Junior	2	5
Senior	2	2

7

A fair spinner is divided into 8 equal parts, 3 of which are green. If the spinner is spun twice and the result of the first spin is green, what is the probability that the result of the second spin is NOT green?

8

A survey of 50 college students was conducted. One of the questions asked whether or not the student was concerned about the current state of the economy. The table below shows the results by academic standing for this question. What is the probability that a randomly selected concerned student was a sophomore?

	Concerned	Not Concerned
Freshman	2	9
Sophomore	4	8
Junior	7	5
Senior	12	3

9

The only correct path through a maze passes through an intersection with 3 branches, a second intersection with 4 branches, a third intersection with 3 branches, and a final intersection with 2 branches. What is the probability of someone following the correct path on their first try?

Name ______________________ Date ______________ Class ______________

Determine and interpret probability and conditional probability in simple real-world situations.

ANSWER SHEET

1. A B C D

2. A B C D

3. A B C D

4. A B C D

5.

/ . 0 1 2 3 4 5 6 7 8 9

6.

/ . 0 1 2 3 4 5 6 7 8 9

7.

/ . 0 1 2 3 4 5 6 7 8 9

8.

/ . 0 1 2 3 4 5 6 7 8 9

9.

/ . 0 1 2 3 4 5 6 7 8 9

Name ______________________ Date ____________ Class ____________

Use formulas for probability and conditional probability.

SAMPLE MULTIPLE CHOICE

A fair spinner is divided into 10 equal parts, 3 of which are green. If the spinner is spun twice, what is the probability that the result for both spins is NOT green?

A) 6%

B) 9%

C) 14%

D) 49%

The probability that the spinner lands on green is $\frac{3}{10}$.

So the probability of landing on a section that is NOT green is:

$$1-\frac{3}{10}=\frac{7}{10}$$

The two spins are independent events. Therefore, the probability of a particular pair of results for two spins is the product of the probabilities for the particular result of each spin. So the probability of NOT green on both spins is:

$$\left(\frac{7}{10}\right)\left(\frac{7}{10}\right)=\frac{49}{100}=49\%$$

The correct answer is D. A ○ B ○ C ○ D ●

1

A fair spinner is divided into 10 equal parts, 6 of which are red. If the spinner is spun twice, what is the probability that the result for both spins is NOT red?

A) 8%

B) 12%

C) 16%

D) 36%

2

Events A and B are dependent events. The probability of event A occurring is $P(A)$. The probability of event B occurring is $P(B)$. The probability of event A occurring given that event B has already occurred is $P(A|B)$. What is the probability that both event A and event B occur?

A) $P(A)\cdot P(B)$

B) $\dfrac{P(B)}{P(A|B)}$

C) $P(A)\cdot P(A|B)$

D) $P(B)\cdot P(A|B)$

3

On average, one event occurs 3 times in 10 trials and a different event occurs 1 time in 10 trials. If, on average, both events occur together 3 times in 100 trials, what does this imply?

A) The events are complements.

B) The events are independent.

C) The events are mutually exclusive.

D) The events are dependent.

4

The probability of event A occurring is $P(A)$. The probability of event B occurring is $P(B)$. The probability of both event A and event B occurring is $P(A\cap B)$. What is the probability of either event A or event B occurring?

A) $P(A)+P(B)-P(A\cap B)$

B) $P(A)+P(B)$

C) $P(A)\cdot P(B)-P(A\cap B)$

D) $\dfrac{P(A)\cdot P(B)}{P(A\cap B)}$

Name ________________ Date ________ Class________

SAMPLE GRID-IN

In a survey, 100 randomly selected adults were asked whether they agree or disagree with two statements. The results were that 80 of the adults agreed with the first statement, 30 of them agreed with the second statement, and 10 adults agreed with both statements. What is the probability that one of the adults who agreed with the first statement also agreed with the second statement?

The probability of event A occurring given that event B has occurred is the probability of both event A and event B occurring divided by the probability of event B occurring:

$$P(A|B)=\frac{P(A\cap B)}{P(B)}.$$

In this case, event A is agreeing with the second statement and event B is agreeing with the first statement.

$$\frac{P(A\cap B)}{P(B)}=\frac{\frac{10}{100}}{\frac{80}{100}}=\frac{10}{80}=\frac{1}{8}$$

So, the probability is $\frac{1}{8}$.

Grid in 1/8 or .125.

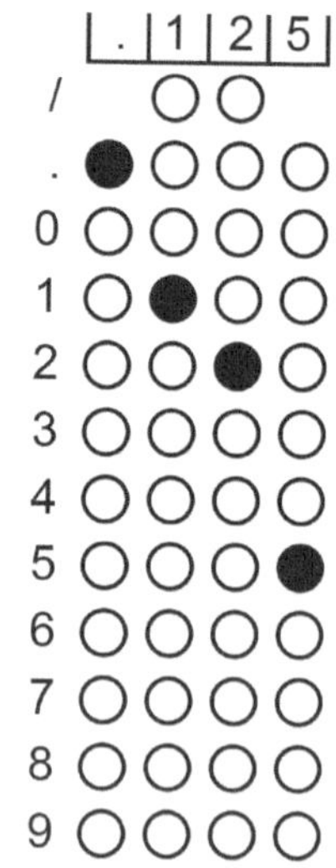

5

Events M and N are dependent events. Both event M and event N occur together 3 times in 100 trials. Whenever event M occurs, event N also occurs 4 times in 10 such trials. What is the probability that event M occurs?

6

Researchers randomly selected 100 patients with a certain condition. The patients were randomly given the traditional treatment at the normal dosage or a higher dosage. The researchers recorded which dosage the patient received and whether or not their condition improved. The results showed that 52 patients received the higher dosage and the condition improved for 49 of these patients. Overall, the condition improved for 91 of the patients. What is the probability that the condition improved given that the patient received the normal dosage?

7

In 100 trials, event A occurred 42 times and event B occurred 27 times. Both event A and event B occurred in 11 of the trials. If one of the trials is randomly selected, what is the probability that event A or event B occurred?

8

In a survey, 100 randomly selected adults were asked whether they have a pet or not, and whether they are married or not. The results were that 63 have a pet, 56 are married, and 35 have a pet and are married. What is the probability that one of the married adults also has a pet?

9

On average, event M occurs 40 times in 100 trials and both event M and event N occurred together 6 times in those 100 trials. What is the probability that event N occurs given that event M occurs?

Name ______________________ Date ____________ Class ____________

Use formulas for probability and conditional probability.

ANSWER SHEET

1. A B C D

2. A B C D

3. A B C D

4. A B C D

5. / . 0 1 2 3 4 5 6 7 8 9

6. / . 0 1 2 3 4 5 6 7 8 9

7. / . 0 1 2 3 4 5 6 7 8 9

8. / . 0 1 2 3 4 5 6 7 8 9

9. / . 0 1 2 3 4 5 6 7 8 9

Name ____________________ Date ____________ Class ____________

Estimate population parameters using sample statistics. Utilize margin of error (without calculating it).

SAMPLE MULTIPLE CHOICE

A poll of 1,000 randomly selected citizens found that 798 support a proposal to use public funds to build a new playground. What is the best estimate of the population proportion of citizens that does NOT support the proposal?

A) 8%
B) 20%
C) 50%
D) 80%

The best estimate of a population proportion is the proportion of a properly collected sample.

Find the number of citizens that do not support the proposal.

$$1,000 - 798 = 202$$

Now find the sample proportion.

$$\frac{202}{1,000} = 0.202 \approx 20\%$$

The correct answer is B. A ○ B ● C ○ D ○

1

A poll of 250 randomly selected citizens found that 205 of them do not support a proposal to build a new high school. What is the best estimate of the population proportion of citizens that does support the proposal?

A) 18%
B) 36%
C) 50%
D) 82%

2

Two samples of 100 items from the same population produce the following 95% confidence interval estimates for the population mean:

Sample 1: Between 21 and 29

Sample 2: Between 23 and 27

Which statement is true?

A) Sample 1 has the greater mean.
B) Sample 2 has the greater mean.
C) Sample 1 has the greater margin of error.
D) Sample 2 has the greater margin of error.

3

Two samples of 100 items from the same population produce the following 95% confidence interval estimates for the population proportion:

Sample 1: Between 0.5 and 0.7

Sample 2: Between 0.6 and 0.8

Which statement is true?

A) Sample 1 has the greater proportion.
B) Sample 2 has the greater proportion.
C) Sample 1 has the greater margin of error.
D) Sample 2 has the greater margin of error.

4

A quality inspector for a bagging machine weighs a random sample of 10 six-ounce bags of product. The total weight of the 10 bags is 62.4 ounces. What is the best estimate of the population mean weight, in ounces, for this product?

A) 6.00
B) 6.24
C) 60.0
D) 62.4

Name ________________________ Date ______________ Class ______________

SAMPLE GRID-IN

Volume of Oil (in liters)

1.02	1.02	1.03	1.02	0.98
1.01	0.99	1.02	0.98	1.03

The table shows the measured volumes in a random sample of 10 one-liter containers of a particular brand of olive oil. What is the best estimate of the mean volume for the population?

The best estimate of a population mean is the mean of a properly collected sample.

Note that the sum of the volumes of the 10 samples is 10.1. Find the sample mean.

$$\frac{10.1}{10} = 1.01$$

The mean volume for the population is 1.01.

Grid in 1.01.

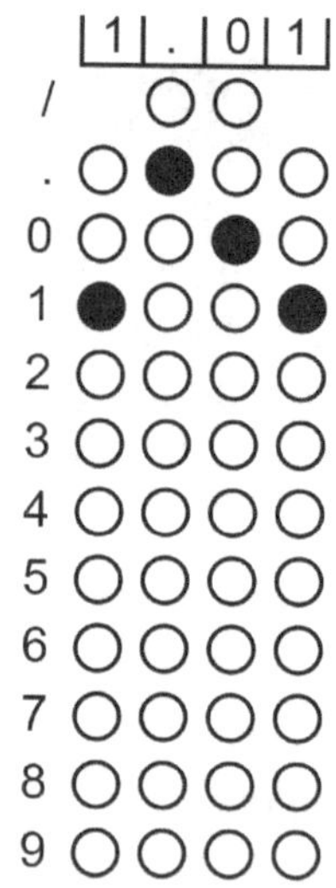

5

Force (in pounds per square inch)

354	382	350	376	381
364	367	368	391	357

Engineers tested a new latch design by applying a steadily increasing force to a door. The table above shows the force in pounds at the time of failure for a random sample of 10 test results. What is the best estimate of the mean force, in pounds per square inch, at failure for the population?

6

Spinner Outcomes

Red	Blue	Red	Red	Blue
Yellow	Blue	Yellow	Red	Red
Red	Red	Red	Blue	Yellow
Yellow	Red	Yellow	Red	Yellow

The table above shows 20 results of a fair spinner that is divided into 6 equal sections. Based on these results, what is the best estimate of how many sections of the spinner are red?

7

A random sample from a population of a particular bird produces a 95% confidence interval estimate for a population mean weight between 219 grams and 241 grams. What is the sample mean, in grams?

8

Miriam surveyed a random sample of 25 seniors at her high school to see if they planned on attending the college fair. The results showed that 64% plan to attend. There are 112 seniors at her school. To the nearest whole number, what is the best estimate for how many seniors will attend the college fair?

9

Two samples of 100 items from the same population produce 95% confidence interval estimates for the population proportion. The margins of error are equal and the lower bounds of the intervals are 0.68 and 0.52. What is the positive difference between the sample proportions?

Name ______________________ Date ____________ Class ____________

Estimate population parameters using sample statistics. Utilize margin of error (without calculating it).

ANSWER SHEET

1. A B C D
○ ○ ○ ○

2. A B C D
○ ○ ○ ○

3. A B C D
○ ○ ○ ○

4. A B C D
○ ○ ○ ○

5. | | | | |
/ ○ ○
. ○ ○ ○ ○
0 ○ ○ ○ ○
1 ○ ○ ○ ○
2 ○ ○ ○ ○
3 ○ ○ ○ ○
4 ○ ○ ○ ○
5 ○ ○ ○ ○
6 ○ ○ ○ ○
7 ○ ○ ○ ○
8 ○ ○ ○ ○
9 ○ ○ ○ ○

6. | | | | |
/ ○ ○
. ○ ○ ○ ○
0 ○ ○ ○ ○
1 ○ ○ ○ ○
2 ○ ○ ○ ○
3 ○ ○ ○ ○
4 ○ ○ ○ ○
5 ○ ○ ○ ○
6 ○ ○ ○ ○
7 ○ ○ ○ ○
8 ○ ○ ○ ○
9 ○ ○ ○ ○

7. | | | | |
/ ○ ○
. ○ ○ ○ ○
0 ○ ○ ○ ○
1 ○ ○ ○ ○
2 ○ ○ ○ ○
3 ○ ○ ○ ○
4 ○ ○ ○ ○
5 ○ ○ ○ ○
6 ○ ○ ○ ○
7 ○ ○ ○ ○
8 ○ ○ ○ ○
9 ○ ○ ○ ○

8. | | | | |
/ ○ ○
. ○ ○ ○ ○
0 ○ ○ ○ ○
1 ○ ○ ○ ○
2 ○ ○ ○ ○
3 ○ ○ ○ ○
4 ○ ○ ○ ○
5 ○ ○ ○ ○
6 ○ ○ ○ ○
7 ○ ○ ○ ○
8 ○ ○ ○ ○
9 ○ ○ ○ ○

9. | | | | |
/ ○ ○
. ○ ○ ○ ○
0 ○ ○ ○ ○
1 ○ ○ ○ ○
2 ○ ○ ○ ○
3 ○ ○ ○ ○
4 ○ ○ ○ ○
5 ○ ○ ○ ○
6 ○ ○ ○ ○
7 ○ ○ ○ ○
8 ○ ○ ○ ○
9 ○ ○ ○ ○

Name ______________________ Date ______________ Class______________

Interpret margin of error and the effects of sample size.

SAMPLE MULTIPLE CHOICE

A random sample of 500 scores on a national achievement exam has a mean of 73% with a margin of error of 2.1%. Which is the best interpretation of this information?

A) Within the sample, it is likely that a score is between 70.9% and 75.1%.

B) It is likely that the mean national score is between 70.9% and 75.1%.

C) Most of the scores nationally are between 70.9% and 75.1%.

D) The mean national score is between 70.9% and 75.1%.

The margin of error describes how close a population parameter is likely to be to an estimate of that parameter calculated using a sample. In this case, the parameter is the mean exam score. The population (national) mean exam score is likely to be within 2.1% (inclusive) of the sample mean.

So, the mean of the scores nationally on the exam is likely to be between $73 - 2.1 = 70.9\%$ and $73 + 2.1 = 75.1\%$.

The correct answer is B.

A	B	C	D
○	●	○	○

1

A random sample of 100 fish of a certain species in a lake has a mean mass of 2.37 kilograms (kg) with a margin of error of 0.25 kilogram. Which is the best interpretation of this information?

A) It is likely that the mean mass of this species of fish in the lake is between 2.12 kg and 2.62 kg.

B) The mean mass of this species of fish in the lake must be between 2.12 kg and 2.62 kg.

C) The fish caught in the sample had a mass between 2.12 kg and 2.62 kg.

D) The mean mass of the type of fish in the sample is likely between 2.12 kg and 2.62 kg.

2

In a random sample of 25 households in a city's suburbs, the mean waste recycled per day was 6.12 pounds with a margin of error of 1.6 pounds. Which of the following samples will give the most reliable estimate of the mean recycling amount in the city?

A) A random sample of 15 households in the city's suburbs

B) A random sample of 25 households throughout the city

C) A random sample of 100 households in the city's suburbs

D) A random sample of 100 households throughout the city

3

To estimate the number of potholes in a city, road crews randomly select 50 block-long stretches of street and count the potholes in each. The sample has a mean of 12 potholes with a margin of error of 4 potholes. Which is the best interpretation of this information?

A) It is likely that the number of potholes on a given city block is between 8 and 16.

B) It is likely that the mean number of potholes per block in the city is between 8 and 16.

C) The mean number of potholes per block is between 8 and 16.

D) The number of potholes per block in the sample is between 8 and 16.

4

A consumer advocacy group wants to find the mean repair cost of a clothes dryer in the region. A random sample of 50 repair costs at different shops has a mean of $127 with a margin of error of $17.50. The group wants a smaller margin of error. Which of the following random samples will most likely result in the smallest margin of error?

A) 10 dryers in a particular repair shop

B) 25 dryers in a particular repair shop

C) 25 dryers at different repair shops

D) 100 dryers at different repair shops

Name ______________________ Date ______________ Class______________

5

A news outlet randomly selected 250 registered vehicle owners in a city and asked them whether they would be willing to pay higher prices for fuel if the extra cost were applied toward reducing carbon emissions. The result was that 52% were willing to pay higher prices with a margin of error of 8%. The news outlet decides to do a second survey to determine whether it can conclude with a higher degree of certainty that a majority is willing to pay higher prices if the increase is used to reduce carbon emissions. Which of the following samples will most likely result in a smaller margin of error for the proportion of drivers willing to pay the higher prices?

A) 100 randomly selected residents of the city

B) 100 randomly selected residents of the city with a registered vehicle

C) 500 randomly selected residents of the city

D) 500 randomly selected residents of the city with a registered vehicle

6

A food processing plant fills jars with pickles. A random sample of 50 medium jars of pickles has a mean weight of 22.1 ounces with a margin of error of 0.025 ounce. Which is the best interpretation of this information?

A) The mean weight of the medium jars of pickles in the sample is between 22.075 ounces and 22.125 ounces.

B) The medium jars of pickles filled at the plant weigh between 22.075 ounces and 22.125 ounces.

C) It is likely that the mean weight of the medium jars of pickles packed at the plant is between 22.075 ounces and 22.125 ounces.

D) Within the sample, the weight of a jar is between 22.075 ounces and 22.125 ounces.

7

The mean of a random sample of 50 airfares for a roundtrip flight between two cities is $360 with a margin of error of $45. Which is the best interpretation of this information?

A) The mean airfare for a roundtrip flight between these cities is between $315 and $405.

B) It is likely that the mean airfare for a roundtrip flight between these cities is between $315 and $405.

C) The airfare for a roundtrip flight between these cities is between $315 and $405.

D) The airfares in the sample range from $315 to $405.

8

A random sample is taken from a population, and its mean for a given measure is used to predict the mean of the population for that measure. For which sample will you be able to estimate the likely population mean most closely?

A) A large sample with high variability

B) A large sample with low variability

C) A small sample with high variability

D) A small sample with low variability

9

A random sample of the wingspans of a species of moth in a preserve has a mean of 8.5 centimeters with a margin of error of 0.3 centimeter. Which conclusion about the wingspan of an individual moth can be drawn from this information?

A) No conclusion can be drawn about the wingspan of an individual moth.

B) The wingspan of the moth is between 8.2 centimeters and 8.8 centimeters.

C) It is likely that the wingspan of the moth is 8.5 centimeters.

D) There is a 50% chance that the wingspan of the moth is over 8.5 centimeters.

Name ______________________ Date ______________ Class______________

Interpret margin of error and the effects of sample size.

ANSWER SHEET

1. A B C D
○ ○ ○ ○

2. A B C D
○ ○ ○ ○

3. A B C D
○ ○ ○ ○

4. A B C D
○ ○ ○ ○

5. A B C D
○ ○ ○ ○

6. A B C D
○ ○ ○ ○

7. A B C D
○ ○ ○ ○

8. A B C D
○ ○ ○ ○

9. A B C D
○ ○ ○ ○

Name ______________________ Date ______________ Class ______________

Determine to which population the results of a random sample can be extended.

SAMPLE MULTIPLE CHOICE

A survey of randomly selected adult residents of a city found that 72.8% support a proposal to use public funds to replace pavement in playgrounds with softer surfaces. Which of the following is supported by this result?

A) About 72.8% of adult residents of the city support the proposal.

B) About 72.8% of adult residents of cities support the proposal.

C) About 72.8% of adult residents of that city make use of playgrounds.

D) About 72.8% of adults support the proposal.

If the subjects in the sample of a study are selected at random from a specified population, the results can be generalized to that specified population.

In this case, the population specified and sampled is the adult residents of a particular city. Therefore, the results can be extended only to adult residents of that city.

The correct answer is A. A ● B ○ C ○ D ○

1

A survey of randomly selected freshmen college students in a particular country found that 87% use a laptop to take notes for classes. Which of the following is supported by this result?

A) About 87% of college students use a laptop to take notes for classes.

B) About 87% of college freshmen in that country use a laptop to take notes for classes.

C) About 87% of college students in that country use a laptop to take notes for classes.

D) About 87% of college freshmen use a laptop to take notes for classes.

2

A team of researchers randomly selects 10,000 people and tests them for a certain trait. The team finds that 17% of those tested have the trait. Which is the largest group to which this result can be extended?

A) All people in the population from which the 10,000 people were selected

B) All people with the trait

C) All people in the sample

D) All people in the study who received the treatment

3

Each day, a quality manager at a flour mill randomly selects 100 bags packaged by one randomly selected filling machine and then finds the mean weight of the 100 bags. What does this mean estimate?

A) The mean weight of all bags filled that day

B) The mean weight of all samples of 100 bags

C) The mean weight of all bags filled by that machine

D) The mean weight of all bags filled by that machine that day

4

A random sample consists of 100 adults with a certain medical condition who are randomly assigned either an experimental treatment or a placebo. The symptoms of their condition are then monitored. What is the largest group to which these results can be extended?

A) All adults

B) All adults in the sample

C) All adults with this medical condition

D) All adults in the study who received the treatment

Name ______________________ Date ____________ Class ____________

5

A survey asked a random sample of employees at a large office building whether they drive to work in their personal vehicle, and, if so, whether finding parking is an issue for them. About 65% of those who responded that they drive to work reported that parking was an issue. Which of the following is supported by this result?

A) About 65% of office workers drive to work in their personal vehicle.

B) About 65% of employees at that large office building drive to work in their personal vehicle.

C) About 65% of office workers who drive to work in their personal vehicle find that parking is an issue.

D) About 65% of employees at that office building who drive to work in their personal vehicle find that parking is an issue.

6

Monthly random samples of sales prices for single-family homes in a region show that the median price has been increasing over the past year. Which of the following conclusions is best supported by this result?

A) The sales price of single-family homes has been increasing over the past year.

B) The median sales price of single-family homes has been increasing over the past year.

C) The mean sales price of single-family homes in the region has been increasing over the past year.

D) The median sales price of single-family homes in the region has been increasing over the past year.

7

A poll asked 1,000 randomly selected workers employed by companies in a country whether they felt they were better off this year than they were last year. To which population can the results most justifiably be extended?

A) Workers employed by companies in that country

B) Residents in the country with ages similar to those in the sample

C) Workers in the country

D) All residents of the country who were better off this year

8

An industry-wide survey of randomly selected people employed in that industry found that 34% of those sampled considered their jobs to be dangerous. To which group can the results of the survey be extended?

A) People in the specified industry with dangerous jobs

B) All employees working in the specified industry

C) All employees in the survey

D) All employees in the country where the survey was conducted

9

A factory manufactures wooden dowels. The mean diameter of a random sample of "15 millimeter" dowels produced in the factory today was 15.01 millimeters (mm). Which of the following statements is supported by this result?

A) The diameter of each 15 mm dowel produced today was 15.01 mm.

B) The mean diameter of 15 mm dowels that the factory produces is 15.01 mm.

C) Most of the 15 mm dowels produced today had diameters that were larger than 15 mm.

D) The mean diameter of the 15 mm dowels the factory produced today was 15.01 mm.

Name ______________________________ Date ______________ Class ______________

Determine to which population the results of a random sample can be extended.

ANSWER SHEET

1. A B C D ○ ○ ○ ○
2. A B C D ○ ○ ○ ○
3. A B C D ○ ○ ○ ○
4. A B C D ○ ○ ○ ○
5. A B C D ○ ○ ○ ○
6. A B C D ○ ○ ○ ○
7. A B C D ○ ○ ○ ○
8. A B C D ○ ○ ○ ○
9. A B C D ○ ○ ○ ○

Name ______________________ Date ______________ Class ______________

Determine if a study with random or non-random assignment provides evidence for a causal relationship.

SAMPLE MULTIPLE CHOICE

A random sample is taken from 200 people with a certain medical condition who are then randomly assigned an experimental treatment or a placebo. The symptoms of their condition are monitored. The condition improved in 92% of the 80 people who received the treatment and completed the study and in 12% of the 80 people who received the placebo and completed the study. Which is the most appropriate conclusion?

A) The treatment improves the symptoms in 92% of people with the condition.

B) There is evidence that the treatment improves the symptoms in the large majority of people with the condition.

C) There is evidence that the treatment improves the health of 92% of people.

D) The treatment is only one of many variables that can influence the condition. No conclusion is appropriate.

The sample subjects were selected at random from the population, so the results can be generalized to the entire population (those with the condition). The subjects were also randomly assigned to receive the treatment or a placebo, so it may be appropriate to make conclusions about cause and effect.

The experimental treatment had a strong rate of positive outcomes among those treated, even if those not completing the study are counted. It is unlikely that the people who received treatment and improved were influenced by other variables, since those who received the placebo had a low rate of improvement. So, there is evidence that the treatment improves the symptoms in the large majority of people with the condition.

The correct answer is B. A ○ B ● C ○ D ○

1

In a random sample of 1,000 people with arthritis in their hands, half were randomly assigned a medicated ointment and half were assigned the ointment without its active ingredient. One measure that was monitored was grip strength. Grip strength improved in 61% of those who received the medicated ointment and in 27% of those who received the non-medicated ointment. What conclusion is most appropriate?

A) There is evidence that the medicine heals arthritis in those with arthritis in their hands.

B) There is evidence that the medicine improves grip strength in those with arthritis in their hands.

C) There is evidence that the medicine improves grip strength in all who use it.

D) The medicine is only one of many variables that influence grip strength. No conclusion is appropriate.

2

To test the claim that a new dietary supplement increases egg production in hens, two poultry farmers design an experiment. One continues to feed her hens standard feed, while the other adds the supplement to her hens' standard feed. The farmers compare daily egg production for the next three months and find that the hens that receive the supplement consistently produce 20% more eggs. Which of the following is an appropriate conclusion?

A) The dietary supplement increases egg production.

B) The dietary supplement increases egg production in hens by 20%.

C) The dietary supplement increases egg production in hens at this particular farm.

D) Because the hens are from different populations and this is not a randomized, controlled study, no conclusion is possible.

Name ______________________ Date ____________ Class ____________

3

Researchers randomly select 50 people who eat fish at least once per week and 50 people who rarely, if ever, eat fish. After receiving physical exams, the subjects who eat fish at least once per week are found to be in better overall health. Which is the most appropriate conclusion?

A) There is evidence that eating fish makes people healthier.

B) There is evidence that healthy people prefer eating fish to eating other types of meat.

C) There is evidence that the higher a person's fish consumption is, the better the person's overall health will be.

D) Eating fish is only one of many variables that can influence health. Because this study looks only at associations and is not randomized, no conclusion is appropriate from the results.

4

To test which of two vaccines is more effective against avian influenza, researchers randomly select 5,000 chickens from farms in a region. The chickens are then randomly assigned to receive either vaccine A or vaccine B. After an outbreak of avian influenza, 72% of the chickens that received vaccine A survived and 90% of the chickens that received vaccine B survived. Which conclusion has the best evidence?

A) Vaccine B is more effective at preventing mortality from avian influenza for chickens in this region.

B) Vaccine B is more effective at preventing avian influenza among chickens in the region.

C) Chickens should be given vaccine A.

D) The difference in survival rate is only 18%, so no conclusion can be drawn.

5

To decide whether Brand A or Brand B exterior house paint is more durable in the local climate, a contractor tosses a fair coin to decide which brand to use for the fiber cement siding on 50 new houses in the area. The contractor has an assistant check each house twice per year, without telling the assistant which houses were painted with which paint. After 5 years, 48% of the houses painted with Brand A paint are judged as needed repainting, while 20% of those painted with Brand B are judged as needing repainting. Which conclusion is most appropriate?

A) Brand B paint is the preferred paint in the local climate.

B) There is evidence that Brand B paint is the more durable paint for fiber cement siding in the local climate.

C) There is evidence that Brand B paint lasts 2.4 times longer on houses in the local climate.

D) Too little time has passed for any conclusions to be drawn.

6

An online advertisement offers free samples of a vitamin supplement that the manufacturer claims boosts a person's energy level. To receive the sample, a person completes an online health survey. The person is asked to return to the website after three months to complete another survey. The results show that all of those who responded both times reported more energy. Which is an appropriate conclusion?

A) Because 100% of responders claimed a benefit, the supplement can be concluded to boost energy.

B) There is evidence that the supplement boosts energy level.

C) The effect from the supplement is not a placebo effect.

D) The people who filled out the surveys were not selected randomly, so no conclusion can be drawn.

Name ______________________ Date ______________ Class______________

Determine if a study with random or non-random assignment provides evidence for a causal relationship.

ANSWER SHEET

1. A B C D
○ ○ ○ ○

2. A B C D
○ ○ ○ ○

3. A B C D
○ ○ ○ ○

4. A B C D
○ ○ ○ ○

5. A B C D
○ ○ ○ ○

6. A B C D
○ ○ ○ ○

Name ______________________ Date ______________ Class______________

Explain why there is evidence for a causal relationship.

SAMPLE MULTIPLE CHOICE

A random sample of 250 people with a degenerative eye disease was selected. Each person was randomly assigned the traditional treatment or an experimental treatment in addition to the traditional treatment. The progress of the disease was monitored, and it was measurably slower in the people who received the experimental treatment. Why is this evidence that the treatment slows the progress of the disease?

A) The people were randomly assigned to a treatment group.

B) Only people who already had the disease were selected.

C) The persons were randomly selected from the population of people who have the disease.

D) The people did not know whether they were given only the traditional treatment or the experimental treatment as well.

When people are randomly assigned to treatment and control groups, the two groups are assumed to be roughly equivalent at the beginning of an experiment. This similarity of the groups makes it possible to conclude that any differences in the groups after treatment is the result of the difference in the treatment received.

In this case, the people were randomly assigned to receive just the traditional treatment or to receive the traditional treatment plus the experimental treatment. Therefore, the result of the study is evidence that the experimental treatment slows the progression of the degenerative eye disease.

The correct answer is A. A ● B ○ C ○ D ○

1

A random sample of 100 people with a certain medical condition is selected. Each person is randomly assigned an experimental treatment or a placebo. The symptoms of the condition are monitored. The condition improves for 92% of those who receive the treatment and for 12% of those who receive the placebo. Which reason correctly explains why a causal relationship exists between the experimental treatment and improvement in the medical condition?

A) The people did not know whether they were given the treatment or the placebo.

B) The persons were randomly selected from the population of people with the medical condition.

C) The people were randomly assigned to a treatment group.

D) The difference between the percentages of persons who improved is over 50%.

2

The manufacturers of a new sleep aid claim that people who use the product fall asleep in half the time. To test this claim, researchers had 50 volunteers come to a research clinic for one week while their sleep patterns were monitored. Before each sleep cycle, each volunteer was randomly selected to take the new sleep aid or a placebo. The results showed that there is no significant difference in the time needed to fall asleep when using the sleep aid versus taking the placebo. Why does this experiment show that the product does not help people fall asleep?

A) The people were volunteers.

B) The people were randomly assigned daily to a treatment group.

C) The people lived in a controlled environment and were monitored.

D) The people were randomly assigned to a treatment group for the entire one-week period.

Name ______________________ Date ______________ Class ______________

3

To compare the effectiveness of two fertilizers, brand A and brand B, a potato grower divided her fields into 40 plots with approximately equal area. For each plot, the grower tossed a coin to determine which brand of fertilizer would be used. The grower then randomly mixed the varieties of seed potatoes together and planted an equal number in each plot. The harvest of potatoes from each plot is recorded. The average weight of the potatoes harvested from plots fertilized with brand B was 22% greater than the average weight of potatoes harvested from plots fertilized with brand A. Why can the grower conclude that the harvest from her fields is greater with brand B?

A) The plots had approximately equal area.

B) The varieties of potato were randomly assigned to each plot.

C) All of the plots fertilized with brand B produced greater harvests.

D) The brand of fertilizer to use was randomly assigned to each plot.

4

To decide whether brand A or brand B house paint on cedar clapboards is more durable in the local climate, a contractor uses a coin toss to decide which brand to use for each of the next 50 houses in the area with cedar clapboard siding. After 10 years, 68% of the houses painted with brand A paint needed repainting while only 22% of those painted with brand B needed repainting. Why is this evidence that brand B house paint is more durable on cedar clapboards in the local climate?

A) The sample size is sufficiently large.

B) The difference in the percentages is so great.

C) The houses were randomly assigned a brand of paint.

D) The houses were randomly selected from the population.

5

To test whether an approved anti-viral drug is effective against a certain illness, researchers at a large hospital randomly selected 250 patients being treated for the illness. The patients were randomly assigned an injection of either the drug or vitamins. On average, the patients who received the drug recovered two days sooner than those who received the vitamins. Why is this evidence that the drug is effective against the illness?

A) The difference in the recovery time is so great.

B) The results are quantitative because time can be measured.

C) The patients had the illness before the experiment began.

D) The patients were randomly assigned to receive the drug or the vitamins.

6

One group of researchers randomly selects 100 juvenile mice from a recent shipment. Each morning, each mouse is randomly assigned to be fed one of two food supplements, A or B. Later that day, a different group of researchers has each mouse complete a maze and records the time needed. A different maze is used each day. After six months, the collected data shows that mice who received supplement B on average use 10% less time to complete the maze than mice who received supplement A. Why can the researchers conclude that the type of food supplement caused the difference in performance on the mazes?

A) The mice completed the mazes in random order.

B) The mice were randomly selected from the shipment.

C) The mice were randomly assigned the food supplement.

D) There are two groups of researchers.

Name ______________________ Date ____________ Class____________

Explain why there is evidence for a causal relationship.

ANSWER SHEET

1. A B C D ○ ○ ○ ○
2. A B C D ○ ○ ○ ○
3. A B C D ○ ○ ○ ○
4. A B C D ○ ○ ○ ○
5. A B C D ○ ○ ○ ○
6. A B C D ○ ○ ○ ○

Name ______________________ Date ______________ Class ______________

Explain why a result can be extended to a population.

SAMPLE MULTIPLE CHOICE

A polling firm selected a large sample of a city's residents at random from the city's voter registration records and found that 61% of those surveyed supported a proposal that the city issue a bond that would help to pay for improvements and a stadium to attract a professional sports team to the city. Can the results of the survey be applied to all of the residents of the city?

A) Yes, because the survey used a large sample and the registered voters were selected at random from voters throughout the city.

B) Yes, because voters are the most likely to be affected by the proposal.

C) No, because the survey did not focus specifically on fans of professional sports.

D) No, because the sample did not include an equal chance for residents who are not registered voters to be selected.

With random sampling, each individual in a specified population has the same chance to be selected for the sample, so the results can be applied to that specified population.

In this case, the subjects were randomly selected *voters*, not randomly selected *residents* in general. While the large sample and random selection do mean the results apply to the population of registered voters in the city, other residents were not included in the survey. So, the results do not apply to the larger population of city residents.

The correct answer is D.

A	B	C	D
○	○	○	●

1

A survey of 100 randomly selected freshmen at a private university found that 64% were members of intramural sports teams at the university. Can this result be applied to all freshmen at private universities?

A) Yes, because the random selection means that the chance for each freshman at the university to be selected for the survey is the same.

B) No, because the chance for a student to be selected for the survey is greater for those freshmen who are most interested in sports.

C) Yes, because the survey was conducted only among freshmen at a private university.

D) No, because the sample came from only one private university. Private universities vary in size, region, and focus, so it is not reasonable to extend the results to freshmen at all private universities.

2

A survey asks a random sample chosen from all off-campus students if they bicycle to the campus, and, if they do, if there are enough bike racks available on the campus. Of those who said that they bicycle to campus, 40% said there were not enough bike racks. Can the 40% result be applied to all students who bicycle on the campus?

A) Yes, because the chance to be selected is the same for each off-campus student.

B) Yes, because the issue of whether there are enough bike racks applies only to bicycle riders.

C) No, because the opinions of those who do not bicycle on campus were not considered.

D) No, because the survey does not include students who live on campus, who may also bicycle on campus and be affected by the issue.

Name ______________________ Date ______________ Class______________

3

A national medical screening laboratory randomly selects 6,000 blood samples. The number of samples from each region of the country is proportional to the region's population. The lab then tests the samples for a particular chemical factor. The lab finds that 18% contain the factor. Which is a reason NOT to extend the results to the national population?

A) The sample size is too small for a country.

B) The blood samples are not randomly selected from the national population. If the samples were sent in for a particular reason or reasons, the samples may not be representative of the general population.

C) Different regions of the country may have different populations of people.

D) All medical results must be obtained from randomized controlled studies.

4

A survey asks 1,250 randomly selected residents of a U.S. state, taken from among those with driver's licenses in that state, whether they had at any time in the past year considered moving to another state. Can the survey results be applied to all residents of the state who are of driving age?

A) Yes, because the chance to be selected is the same for everyone in the state with a driver's license.

B) Yes, because the population of all those who have a driver's license should be representative of state residents who are of driving age.

C) No, because those who do not have a driver's license did not have a chance to be selected, and they cannot be assumed to respond in the same way.

D) No, the sample, although random, is not large enough to draw any kind of conclusion about the residents of a state.

5

A large distributor bags oranges in 5-pound bags to ship around the country. The facility has 20 different machines filling and sealing bags of oranges. Each day, a bagging machine is chosen at random, and bags that it produces are chosen at random throughout the day and weighed to find the mean weight and the distribution of weights. Can these results be applied to all of the 5-pound bags of oranges produced at the facility that day?

A) Yes, because the chance to be selected is the same for each bag from the machine, and bags are chosen throughout the day.

B) Yes, because the machine chosen for the sampling is selected at random.

C) No, because the sample is chosen only from those bags produced from one machine. Although the results apply to that machine that day, the results cannot be assumed to apply to the other machines that day, even though the single machine was chosen at random.

D) No, because the chance for a bag to be selected depends on the number of bags filled that day.

6

A survey of 100 randomly selected students at a high school, all from different households, are asked if they have a dog at home. Which is the best reason NOT to extend the results to all households in town?

A) Not all households have children in the high school, or even of any age.

B) The sample is too small.

C) The type of dwelling is not specified.

D) Because this is an observational study, no conclusion is possible.

Name ______________________ Date ______________ Class ______________

Explain why a result can be extended to a population.

ANSWER SHEET

1. A B C D ◯ ◯ ◯ ◯

2. A B C D ◯ ◯ ◯ ◯

3. A B C D ◯ ◯ ◯ ◯

4. A B C D ◯ ◯ ◯ ◯

5. A B C D ◯ ◯ ◯ ◯

6. A B C D ◯ ◯ ◯ ◯

Name ______________________ Date ____________ Class ____________

Use algebraic structure and the properties of operations to write and identify equivalent expressions.

SAMPLE MULTIPLE CHOICE

If $4a - 3b = 2$, what is the value of $\frac{81^a}{27^b}$?

A) 3^2
B) 3^4
C) 9^3
D) The value cannot be determined from the information given.

Notice that $81 = 3^4$ and $27 = 3^3$. So,

$$\frac{81^a}{27^b} = \frac{(3^4)^a}{(3^3)^b} = \frac{3^{4a}}{3^{3b}}.$$

Use the Quotient Rule to rewrite the last expression above.

$$\frac{3^{4a}}{3^{3b}} = 3^{4a-3b}$$

It was given that $4a - 3b = 2$. Substituting in the previous expression gives $3^{4a-3b} = 3^2$.

Therefore, $\frac{81^a}{27^b} = 3^2$.

The correct answer is A. A ● B ○ C ○ D ○

1

$$\frac{2}{\frac{1}{2x+1} + \frac{1}{x-3}}$$

Which of the following is equivalent to the expression shown above?

A) $\frac{4x^2 - 10x - 6}{3x - 2}$
B) $\frac{3x - 2}{4x^2 - 10x - 6}$
C) $4x^2 - 10x - 6$
D) $3x - 2$

2

Which of the following is equivalent to $m^{\frac{3}{5}}$ for all values of m?

A) $\sqrt[3]{m^5}$
B) $\sqrt{m^{\frac{1}{5}}}$
C) $\sqrt{m^{\frac{1}{3}}}$
D) $\sqrt[5]{m^3}$

3

$$\frac{7x+5}{(x-3)^2} - \frac{2}{x-3}$$

The expression above is equivalent to $\frac{5x+a}{(x-3)^2}$. What is the value of a?

A) 7
B) 9
C) 11
D) 12

4

The expression $\frac{1}{8}x^2 - 3$ can be rewritten in the form $\frac{1}{8}(x+k)(x-k)$, where k is a positive constant. What is the value of k?

A) $2\sqrt{3}$
B) $2\sqrt{6}$
C) $3\sqrt{3}$
D) $3\sqrt{6}$

Name ______________________ Date ______________ Class ______________

SAMPLE GRID-IN

The expression $4x^2 - 35x + 49$ can be rewritten as $(4x - k)(x - k)$, where k is a positive constant. What is the value of k?

Notice that 35 and 49 share a common factor of 7 and that 49 is a square number. Identifying common factors can help you solve by factoring.

$4x^2 - 35x + 49 = (4x - 7)(x - 7)$

So, $k = 7$.

Grid in 7.

Time Saving Tip: Look at the structure of the factored expression $(4x - k)(x - k)$. Since no common factor appears, then k^2 must equal 49. So k must be 7.

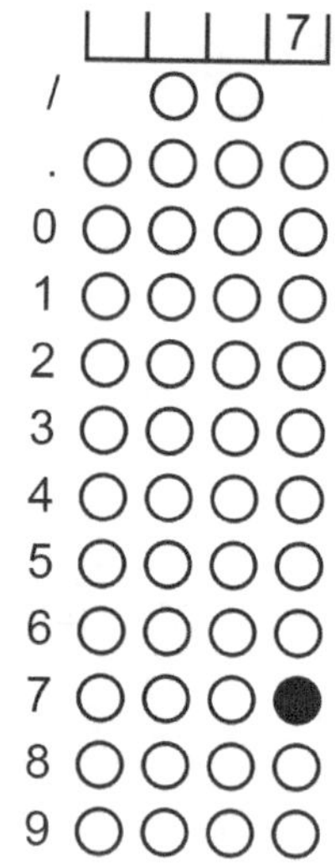

5

The expression $x^2 + 6x + 9$ can be rewritten in the form $(x + k)(x + k)$, where k is a positive constant. What is the value of k?

6

The expression $2x^2 - 3x - 9$ can be rewritten in the form $(Ax + 3)(x - 3)$, where A is a positive constant. What is the value of A?

7

The expression $3x^2 - 12$ can be rewritten in the form $A(x + 2)(x - 2)$, where A is a positive constant. What is the value of A?

8

$$\frac{x^2 + 4x + 4}{x + 2} - \frac{\sqrt{x^6}}{x^2}$$

Simplify the expression shown above.

9

Evaluate the expression $8^{\frac{2}{3}}$.

10

Simplify the following expression.

$$\frac{a^2 b}{4ab^3} \cdot \frac{\sqrt{9b^4}}{a}$$

11

$$\sqrt{\frac{x^3 y^{-4}}{x^{-3} y^2}} \cdot \frac{x^2 y}{x^5 y^{-2}}$$

Simplify the expression shown above.

12

The expression $6x^2 + 15x - 75$ can be rewritten as $3(x + k)(2x - k)$, where k is a positive constant. What is the value of k?

Name ______________________ Date ______________ Class ______________

Use algebraic structure and the properties of operations to write and identify equivalent expressions.

ANSWER SHEET

1. A ○ B ○ C ○ D ○

2. A ○ B ○ C ○ D ○

3. A ○ B ○ C ○ D ○

4. A ○ B ○ C ○ D ○

5. |__|__|__|__|

/ ○○
. ○○○○
0 ○○○○
1 ○○○○
2 ○○○○
3 ○○○○
4 ○○○○
5 ○○○○
6 ○○○○
7 ○○○○
8 ○○○○
9 ○○○○

6. |__|__|__|__|

/ ○○
. ○○○○
0 ○○○○
1 ○○○○
2 ○○○○
3 ○○○○
4 ○○○○
5 ○○○○
6 ○○○○
7 ○○○○
8 ○○○○
9 ○○○○

7. |__|__|__|__|

/ ○○
. ○○○○
0 ○○○○
1 ○○○○
2 ○○○○
3 ○○○○
4 ○○○○
5 ○○○○
6 ○○○○
7 ○○○○
8 ○○○○
9 ○○○○

8. |__|__|__|__|

/ ○○
. ○○○○
0 ○○○○
1 ○○○○
2 ○○○○
3 ○○○○
4 ○○○○
5 ○○○○
6 ○○○○
7 ○○○○
8 ○○○○
9 ○○○○

9. |__|__|__|__|

/ ○○
. ○○○○
0 ○○○○
1 ○○○○
2 ○○○○
3 ○○○○
4 ○○○○
5 ○○○○
6 ○○○○
7 ○○○○
8 ○○○○
9 ○○○○

10. |__|__|__|__|

/ ○○
. ○○○○
0 ○○○○
1 ○○○○
2 ○○○○
3 ○○○○
4 ○○○○
5 ○○○○
6 ○○○○
7 ○○○○
8 ○○○○
9 ○○○○

11. |__|__|__|__|

/ ○○
. ○○○○
0 ○○○○
1 ○○○○
2 ○○○○
3 ○○○○
4 ○○○○
5 ○○○○
6 ○○○○
7 ○○○○
8 ○○○○
9 ○○○○

12. |__|__|__|__|

/ ○○
. ○○○○
0 ○○○○
1 ○○○○
2 ○○○○
3 ○○○○
4 ○○○○
5 ○○○○
6 ○○○○
7 ○○○○
8 ○○○○
9 ○○○○

Name ______________________ Date ______________ Class ______________

Add, subtract, and multiply polynomials proficiently.

SAMPLE MULTIPLE CHOICE

$$(7n-5n^4+6n^3)-(3n^3-2n^4+8n)$$

Which of the following polynomials is equivalent to the expression above?

A) $-8n^4+8n^3-n$

B) $-8n^4+3n^3-8n$

C) $-3n^4+5n^3-15n$

D) $-3n^4+3n^3-n$

First, rewrite the expression without the parentheses. Then, combine like terms.

$$(7n-5n^4+6n^3)-(3n^3-2n^4+8n)$$
$$=7n-5n^4+6n^3-3n^3+2n^4-8n$$
$$=-5n^4+2n^4+6n^3-3n^3+7n-8n$$
$$=-3n^4+3n^3-n$$

The correct answer is D. A ○ B ○ C ○ D ●

1

$$f(x)=5x-4$$
$$g(x)=8x^2+3$$

Which of the following polynomials is equivalent to $2f(x)-5g(x)$?

A) $-16x^2+25x-26$

B) $-40x^2+10x-23$

C) $-40x^2+25x-26$

D) $-19x^2-10x-23$

2

$$(6x^2-9xy+5y^2)-(7x^2-3xy+4y^2)$$

Which of the following is equivalent to the expression above?

A) $-13x^2-6xy+2y^2$

B) $-x^2-12xy+9y^2$

C) $-x^2-6xy+y^2$

D) $-x^2-6xy+9y^2$

3

Which is equivalent to $35p^2+2p-24$?

A) $(7p-4)(5p+6)$

B) $(5p-4)(7p+6)$

C) $(7p-6)(5p+4)$

D) $(5p-7)(4p+6)$

4

Which polynomial is equivalent to $(3m-4)(2m^2+7m-9)$?

A) $2m^3+6m^2-28m-36$

B) $6m^3+13m^2\quad 23m-36$

C) $3m^3+32m^2-19m-36$

D) $6m^3+13m^2-55m+36$

Questions 5 and 6 refer to the following information.

$$f(x)=3x+2$$
$$g(x)=x^2-1$$

5

Which of the following polynomials is equivalent to $3f(x)+2g(x)$?

A) $2x^2+9x+4$

B) $3x^2+6x-4$

C) $6x^2-9x-1$

D) x^2+3x-1

6

Which of the following is equivalent to $f(x)^2+x\cdot f(x)-2g(x)-2$?

A) $(10x+1)(x+4)$

B) $2(x+1)(5x+2)$

C) $2x(5x+7)$

D) $(x+2)(x+1)$

Name ______________________ Date __________ Class __________

SAMPLE GRID-IN

If $(ax+4)(7x+6)=21x^2+46x+24$ for all values of x, what is the value of a?	Expand the expression on the left side of the equation. $(ax+4)(7x+6)$ $=(7a)x^2+(6a+28)x+24$ Therefore, $7a$ must equal 21. $7a=21$ $a=3$ So, the value of a is 3. Grid in 3.	3

7

Find the coefficient of the linear term after simplifying the expression $(6k-3k^2)-(3k^2+k-9)$.

8

$$f(x)=2x+5$$
$$g(x)=3x^2-1$$

Find $2f(x)-3g(x)$. What is the constant term of the polynomial?

9

$$(5x^3+7x^2-8)-(3x^2-2x+6)$$

What is the coefficient of the quadratic term in the simplified form of the expression shown above?

10

The product of $(4p-2)$ and $(6p+1)$ is equivalent to $24p^2-mp-2$. What is the value of m?

11

$$f(x)=8x-3$$
$$g(x)=2x^2+7$$

Find $5f(x)+2g(x)$. What is the coefficient of the linear term of the polynomial?

12

Find the coefficient of the ab-term in the product $(2a+6b)(7a-3b)$.

13

$$f(x)=(x+1)(8x+3)$$
$$g(x)=x^2-7x-4$$

Find $4f(x)+3g(x)$. What is the constant term of the polynomial?

14

$$(4x^3-x^2+9)-(3-2x^2+x^3)+3(2x^3+1)$$

What is the coefficient of the cubic term in the simplified form of the expression shown above?

Name ______________________ Date ______________ Class ______________

Add, subtract, and multiply polynomials proficiently.

ANSWER SHEET

1. A B C D
2. A B C D
3. A B C D
4. A B C D
5. A B C D
6. A B C D
7. / . 0 1 2 3 4 5 6 7 8 9
8. / . 0 1 2 3 4 5 6 7 8 9
9. / . 0 1 2 3 4 5 6 7 8 9
10. / . 0 1 2 3 4 5 6 7 8 9
11. / . 0 1 2 3 4 5 6 7 8 9
12. / . 0 1 2 3 4 5 6 7 8 9
13. / . 0 1 2 3 4 5 6 7 8 9
14. / . 0 1 2 3 4 5 6 7 8 9

Name ______________________ Date ______________ Class______________

Solve a variety of nonlinear equations and systems of equations in two variables; recognize valid solutions.

SAMPLE MULTIPLE CHOICE

$$x^2 + 3y^2 = 52$$
$$x - y = 2$$

Find all real solutions (x, y) of the system of equations shown above.

A) $(5, 3)$ and $(-2, -4)$

B) $(6, 4)$

C) $(4, 2)$

D) No real solutions

Solve this system of equations by substitution. Rewrite the second equation as $y = x - 2$, and then substitute $x - 2$ for y in the first equation.

$$x^2 + 3y^2 = 52$$
$$x^2 + 3(x-2)^2 = 52$$
$$4x^2 - 12x + 12 = 52$$
$$x^2 - 3x + 3 = 13$$
$$x^2 - 3x - 10 = 0$$
$$(x-5)(x+2) = 0$$

Setting each factor equal to 0 gives $x = 5$ and $x = -2$. To find the corresponding y-values, substitute these x-values into the equation $y = x - 2$. So, the solutions are $(5, 3)$ and $(-2, -4)$.

The correct answer is A. A ● B ○ C ○ D ○

Questions 1 and 2 refer to the following figure.

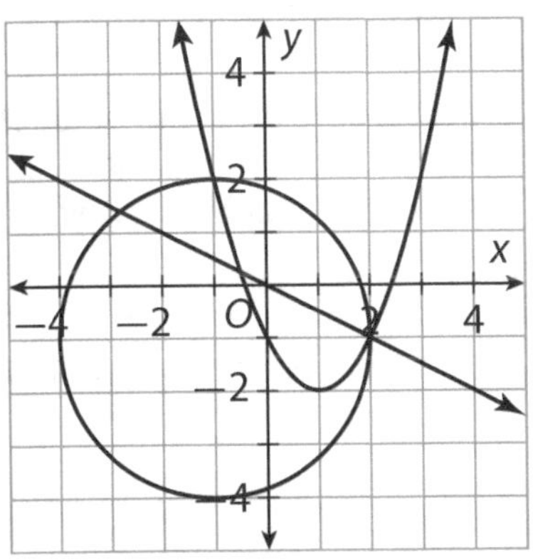

1

How many real solutions are there for the system of three equations graphed in the figure?

A) 0

B) 1

C) 4

D) 5

2

$$(x+1)^2 + (y+1)^2 = 9$$
$$x^2 - 2x - y = 1$$

Two of the equations whose graphs are shown in the figure appear above. Find all real solutions (x, y) to this system of two equations.

A) $(2, -1)$ and $(-1, 2)$

B) $(-2, 1)$ and $(1, -2)$

C) $(-1, 2)$

D) No real solutions

3

$$2x^2 + bx + 8 = 0$$

Which values of b in the equation above result in no real solution?

A) $b > 8$

B) $b < 8$

C) $-8 < b < 8$

D) $b < -8$ or $b > 8$

Name ______________________ Date ______________ Class______________

SAMPLE GRID-IN

$$\frac{x}{x-7}-\frac{2}{x-6}=\frac{2}{x^2-13x+42}$$

Find the product of all the real solutions of the equation shown above. If there is only one solution, then enter it as the answer.

Notice that $x^2-13x+42=(x-7)(x-6)$. So multiply both sides of the equation by $(x-6)(x-7)$. Then, solve the resulting equation for x.

$$\frac{x}{x-7}-\frac{2}{x-6}=\frac{2}{x^2-13x+42}$$

$$x(x-6)-2(x-7)=2$$

$$x^2-8x+12=0$$

$$(x-2)(x-6)=0$$

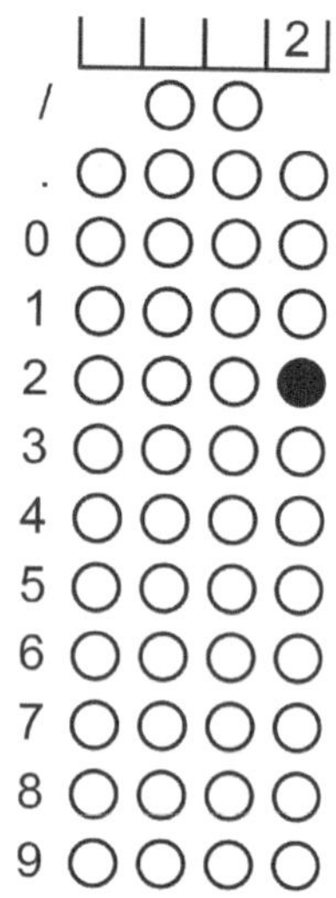

Setting each factor equal to 0 gives the solutions $x=2$ and $x=6$. Checking $x=6$ in the original equation leads to division by 0, which is undefined. So $x=6$ is an extraneous solution.

Therefore, the only solution is $x=2$.

So, the correct answer is 2.

Grid in 2.

4

$$(x-4)(2x+1)(5x+3)=0$$

Find the product of all the real solutions of the equation. If there is only one real solution, then enter it as the answer.

5

$$\frac{1}{3}|x-2|=2$$

Find the sum of all the real solutions of the equation above. If there is only one real solution, then enter it as the answer.

6

Find the product of all the real solutions of $\sqrt{x-2}=4-2x$. If there is only one real solution, then enter it as the answer.

7

What is the positive real solution of the equation $x+x^2=12$?

8

$$\frac{1}{x-2}-\frac{3x}{x+3}=\frac{5}{x^2+x-6}$$

Find the product of all the real solutions of the equation. If there is only one real solution, then enter it as the answer.

9

What is the positive real solution of the equation $x^2-4x-7=0$?

10

Find the sum of all the real solutions of $(x-3)^2+6=10$. If there is only one real solution, then enter it as the answer.

11

Find the product of all the real solutions of $\sqrt{5x-6}=x$. If there is only one real solution, then enter it as the answer.

Name ________________________ Date ______________ Class ______________

Solve a variety of nonlinear equations and systems of equations in two variables; recognize valid solutions.

ANSWER SHEET

1. A B C D

2. A B C D

3. A B C D

4. / . 0 1 2 3 4 5 6 7 8 9

5. / . 0 1 2 3 4 5 6 7 8 9

6. / . 0 1 2 3 4 5 6 7 8 9

7. / . 0 1 2 3 4 5 6 7 8 9

8. / . 0 1 2 3 4 5 6 7 8 9

9. / . 0 1 2 3 4 5 6 7 8 9

10. / . 0 1 2 3 4 5 6 7 8 9

11. / . 0 1 2 3 4 5 6 7 8 9

Name ____________________ Date ____________ Class ____________

Given a single-variable, nonlinear equation, interpret its parts or the solution based on the context.

SAMPLE MULTIPLE CHOICE

$$-16t^2 + 32t = 0$$

The equation above can be solved to find the time t, in seconds, that an object spends in the air after it is launched from the ground with an initial velocity of 32 feet per second. Why does the equation have two solutions?

A) The object could be in the air for either 0 or 2 seconds. More information is needed to decide which is correct.

B) The speed of the object when it is launched is 0 feet per second, and its speed when it lands is 2 feet per second.

C) The time 0 seconds represents when the object was launched, and the time 2 seconds represents when it lands.

D) Only 2 seconds solves the given equation. The solution, 0 seconds, can be ruled out by checking it in the original equation.

Consider what the equation represents in the context of this situation. An object launched into the air from the ground has a height that can be modeled by the quadratic function $h = -16t^2 + 32t$. The object will have a height of 0 when it is on the ground, so the given equation models the time t when $h = 0$. The solutions of the equation give the times when the height is 0, including when the object is first launched at $t = 0$. So, $t = 0$ represents the time when the object was launched, and $t = 2$ represents the time when it lands.

The correct answer is C. A B C D ○ ○ ● ○

Questions 1 and 2 refer to the following information.

$$\frac{8}{x+2} + \frac{8}{x-2} = 6$$

The equation models the following scenario. A boat travels a distance downriver and then back to its starting point. The boat travels at a constant speed of x miles per hour. (Ignore the time it takes to turn the boat back upstream.) The current in the river is moving at a speed of 2 miles per hour.

1

What does the 8 in the numerators of the rational expressions represent?

A) The distance traveled each way

B) The time the boat took to travel to the turnaround point on the river

C) The total distance traveled over the round-trip

D) The total time for the entire trip

2

What does the 6 on the right side of the equation represent?

A) The distance traveled each way

B) The time the boat took to travel to the turnaround point on the river

C) The total distance traveled over the round-trip

D) The total time for the entire trip

3

$$400x = \sqrt{200^2 + 500^2}$$

An airplane travels in a straight line with an average speed of 400 miles per hour. It lands 200 miles north and 500 miles east of its starting point. What does x represent in the equation above?

A) The one-way distance

B) The time spent flying

C) The average speed of the flight

D) The round-trip distance

Name ______________________ Date ____________ Class ____________

SAMPLE GRID-IN

The dimensions of a rectangle with a width of x units and an area of 10 square units can be found by solving the equation $x(x + 3) = 10$. What is the perimeter of the rectangle?

Both sides of the equation represent the area of the rectangle. The left side is a product of the unknown width and another factor, which must represent the length of the rectangle. Solve for x to find the width.

$$x(x+3)=10$$
$$x^2+3x=10$$
$$x^2+3x-10=0$$
$$(x+5)(x-2)=0$$

Setting both factors equal to 0 and solving for x gives $x=-5$ or $x=2$. Since x represents a dimension of a figure, it must be positive. So the width is 2 units.

The length of the rectangle is given as $x+3$, so the length is $2+3=5$ units.

Now use the length and width to determine the perimeter.

$$\begin{aligned}\text{perimeter} &= 2(\text{length})+2(\text{width})\\ &= 2(2)+2(5)\\ &= 14\end{aligned}$$

So, the perimeter of the rectangle is 14.

Grid in 14.

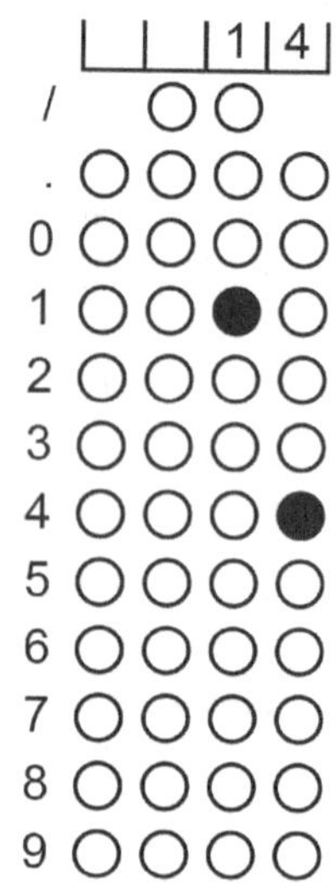

4

The unknown length x of one leg of a right triangle can be found by solving the equation $x^2+24^2=25^2$. What is the length of the hypotenuse?

5

A rotating sprinkler sprays water in a circular pattern. It is placed in a rectangular community garden 35 feet from the east side and 10 feet from the north side. A sidewalk runs along the north side of the garden. The equation $(x-35)^2+(-10)^2=26^2$ can be solved to determine where water from the sprinkler begins to reach the edge of the sidewalk. What length of the sidewalk, in feet, is hit by water from the sprinkler?

6

A football kicked from the 35-yard line lands a distance downfield that can be found by solving $(x - 35)(x - 95) = 0$, where x is the distance from the goal line behind the kicker. At what horizontal distance x, in yards, does the football reach its maximum height?

7

A rectangular garden is surrounded by a walkway with a uniform width of x yards. The area of the garden is 240 square yards. The dimensions of the garden and the walkway together are 14 yards by 28 yards. This situation is represented by the equation $(14-2x)(28-2x)=240$. What is the width of the walkway in yards?

Name ______________________ Date ______________ Class ______________

Given a single-variable, nonlinear equation, interpret its parts or the solution based on the context.

ANSWER SHEET

1. A B C D
○ ○ ○ ○

2. A B C D
○ ○ ○ ○

3. A B C D
○ ○ ○ ○

4.

/		○	○	
.	○	○	○	○
0	○	○	○	○
1	○	○	○	○
2	○	○	○	○
3	○	○	○	○
4	○	○	○	○
5	○	○	○	○
6	○	○	○	○
7	○	○	○	○
8	○	○	○	○
9	○	○	○	○

5.

/		○	○	
.	○	○	○	○
0	○	○	○	○
1	○	○	○	○
2	○	○	○	○
3	○	○	○	○
4	○	○	○	○
5	○	○	○	○
6	○	○	○	○
7	○	○	○	○
8	○	○	○	○
9	○	○	○	○

6.

/		○	○	
.	○	○	○	○
0	○	○	○	○
1	○	○	○	○
2	○	○	○	○
3	○	○	○	○
4	○	○	○	○
5	○	○	○	○
6	○	○	○	○
7	○	○	○	○
8	○	○	○	○
9	○	○	○	○

7.

/		○	○	
.	○	○	○	○
0	○	○	○	○
1	○	○	○	○
2	○	○	○	○
3	○	○	○	○
4	○	○	○	○
5	○	○	○	○
6	○	○	○	○
7	○	○	○	○
8	○	○	○	○
9	○	○	○	○

Name ______________________ Date ______________ Class______________

Solve an equation or formula in two or more variables for a variable of interest.

SAMPLE MULTIPLE CHOICE

Coulomb's law expresses the force F acting on a particle with a charge of q_1 by a second particle with a charge of q_2 when the particles are at a distance r from each other. The formula, shown below, includes a constant factor k.

$$F = \frac{kq_1q_2}{r^2}$$

Which is the formula solved for the distance in terms of the charges, the force, and k?

A) $r = \frac{Fq_1}{kq_2}$ C) $r = \sqrt{\frac{F}{kq_1q_2}}$

B) $r = \frac{kq_1q_2}{F}$ D) $r = \sqrt{\frac{kq_1q_2}{F}}$

Isolate r by applying inverse operations, starting with multiplying both sides of the equation by r^2.

$$F = \frac{kq_1q_2}{r^2}$$

$$Fr^2 = kq_1q_2$$

$$r^2 = \frac{kq_1q_2}{F}$$

$$r = \sqrt{\frac{kq_1q_2}{F}}$$

Since r represents a distance, do not include the negative root.

The correct answer is D. A ○ B ○ C ○ D ●

1

The amount A that an initial deposit P is worth t months after being placed in an account earning interest at an annual rate r that is compounded monthly can be calculated using the following formula.

$$A = P\left(1 + \frac{r}{12}\right)^t$$

Rewrite the formula so that it expresses the interest rate necessary for the account to reach a balance of A in a given time t.

A) $r = 12\left(\sqrt[t]{\frac{A}{P}} + 1\right)$

B) $r = 12\left(\frac{A}{Pt} - 1\right)$

C) $r = 12\left(\sqrt[t]{\frac{A}{P}} - 1\right)$

D) $r = 12\left(\frac{A}{Pt} + 1\right)$

2

The ideal gas law $PV = nRT$ relates the product of the pressure P and volume V of a gas to the product of the number of moles n and the temperature T of the gas, where R is the ideal gas constant. Solve the ideal gas law for n in terms of P, V, R, and T.

A) $n = \frac{PV}{RT}$ C) $n = \frac{RT}{PV}$

B) $n = PVRT$ D) $n = \frac{PT}{RV}$

3

The volume V of a cone with radius r and height h is given by this formula:

$$V = \frac{1}{3}\pi r^2 h$$

Which equation can be used as a formula to find the radius of a cone given its height and volume?

A) $r = \sqrt{\frac{\pi h}{3V}}$ C) $r = \left(\frac{\pi h}{3V}\right)^2$

B) $r = 3\sqrt{\frac{V}{\pi h}}$ D) $r = \sqrt{\frac{3V}{\pi h}}$

Name ______________________ Date ____________ Class ____________

4

The Pythagorean theorem states that if a right triangle has legs whose lengths are *a* and *b* and a hypotenuse whose length is *c*, then the following relationship between the side lengths is true.

$$a^2 + b^2 = c^2$$

Solve this equation for *b*. The result allows the length of the remaining leg to be found when the lengths of one leg and the hypotenuse are known.

A) $b = (c^2 - a^2)^2$

B) $b = \sqrt{c^2 + a^2}$

C) $b = \sqrt{a^2 - c^2}$

D) $b = \sqrt{c^2 - a^2}$

5

The surface area *A* of a cylinder with a radius of *r* and a height of *h* is given by the formula below.

$$A = 2\pi r^2 + 2\pi rh$$

Solve the formula for the height of a cylinder in terms of its area and radius.

A) $h = \sqrt{A - \pi r}$

B) $h = \dfrac{2\pi r}{A - 2\pi r^2}$

C) $h = \dfrac{A}{2\pi r} - r$

D) $h = \sqrt{\dfrac{2\pi r^2}{A}} - 2\pi r$

6

One way a company can determine its financial structure is by using the debt-to-capital ratio given by the formula below, where *R* represents the debt-to-capital ratio, *D* is the company's debt, and *E* is the company's equity.

$$R = \frac{D}{D + E}$$

Solve the formula for the equity *E* in terms of *R* and *D*.

A) $E = \dfrac{D + RD}{R}$

B) $E = \dfrac{R}{D + RD}$

C) $E = \dfrac{D - RD}{R}$

D) $E = (D + RD)R$

7

The potential energy *E* stored in a spring that is stretched or compressed to a length of *x* from a resting length of x_0 is described by Hooke's Law:

$$E = \frac{1}{2}k(x - x_0)^2$$

In the formula, *k* is a constant that is related to the stiffness of a particular spring. Solve Hooke's law for the length *x* of the spring in terms of *E*, *k*, and x_0.

A) $x = x_0 \pm \sqrt{\dfrac{2E}{k}}$

B) $x = \pm\sqrt{x_0 - \dfrac{2E}{k}}$

C) $x = \pm\sqrt{E + \dfrac{1}{2}kx_0}$

D) $x = \left(E - \dfrac{1}{2}kx_0\right)^2$

8

The height *h* of an object *t* seconds after it begins to free fall is given by the formula below.

$$h = \frac{1}{2}gt^2 + h_0$$

In the formula, h_0 is the initial height of the object, and *g* is a constant that expresses the acceleration due to the force of gravity. Solve this equation for *t*. Assume that $t > 0$.

A) $t = \sqrt{\dfrac{h - h_0}{2g}}$

B) $t = \sqrt{\dfrac{2(h - h_0)}{g}}$

C) $t = \dfrac{2(h - h_0)}{g}$

D) $t = \sqrt{\dfrac{g}{2(h - h_0)}}$

Name ______________________ Date ______________ Class______________

Solve an equation or formula in two or more variables for a variable of interest.

ANSWER SHEET

1. A B C D
   ◯ ◯ ◯ ◯

2. A B C D
   ◯ ◯ ◯ ◯

3. A B C D
   ◯ ◯ ◯ ◯

4. A B C D
   ◯ ◯ ◯ ◯

5. A B C D
   ◯ ◯ ◯ ◯

6. A B C D
   ◯ ◯ ◯ ◯

7. A B C D
   ◯ ◯ ◯ ◯

8. A B C D
   ◯ ◯ ◯ ◯

Name ______________________ Date ______________ Class______________

Complete the square or use the quadratic formula to solve quadratic equations in standard form.

SAMPLE MULTIPLE CHOICE

What values of x are the solutions of the equation $x^2 - 4x - 2 = 0$?

A) $4 \pm \sqrt{6}$

B) $2 \pm 3\sqrt{2}$

C) $2 \pm \sqrt{6}$

D) $4 \pm 3\sqrt{2}$

This is a non-factorable quadratic equation in the standard form $ax^2 + bx + c = 0$, where $a = 1$, $b = -4$, and $c = -2$. To solve by completing the square, move the constant term to the right side of the equation. Then add the constant $\left(\frac{b}{2}\right)^2 = \left(\frac{-4}{2}\right)^2 = 4$ to both sides of the equation.

$$x^2 - 4x = 2$$
$$x^2 - 4x + 4 = 2 + 4$$
$$x^2 - 4x + 4 = 6$$

The quadratic expression on the left can be factored as a perfect square binomial. Solve for x.

$$(x-2)^2 = 6$$
$$x - 2 = \pm\sqrt{6}$$
$$x = 2 \pm \sqrt{6}$$

The correct answer is C. A ○ B ○ C ● D ○

1

What are the values of x that solve the equation $12x^2 + 15x + 1 = 0$?

A) $-\frac{5}{8} \pm \frac{\sqrt{177}}{24}$

B) $-\frac{5}{8} \pm \frac{\sqrt{273}}{24}$

C) $\frac{5}{8} \pm \frac{\sqrt{177}}{24}$

D) $\frac{5}{8} \pm \frac{\sqrt{273}}{24}$

2

What are the values of x for which $x^2 + 2x - 4 = 0$?

A) $1 + \sqrt{3}$ and $1 - \sqrt{3}$

B) $-1 + \sqrt{5}$ and $1 - \sqrt{5}$

C) $-1 + \sqrt{3}$ and $1 - \sqrt{3}$

D) $-1 + \sqrt{5}$ and $-1 - \sqrt{5}$

3

What values of x are solutions of the equation $x^2 + \frac{2}{3}x - \frac{2}{3} = 0$?

A) $-1 \pm \sqrt{7}$

B) $-\frac{1}{3} \pm \frac{\sqrt{7}}{3}$

C) $\frac{1}{3} \pm \frac{\sqrt{7}}{3}$

D) $\frac{1}{9} \pm \frac{\sqrt{7}}{9}$

4

For what values of x is $x^2 - 6x + 7 = 0$?

A) 7 and -1

B) -7 and 1

C) $3 + \sqrt{2}$ and $3 - \sqrt{2}$

D) $-3 + \sqrt{2}$ and $-3 - \sqrt{2}$

Name ______________________ Date ______________ Class ______________

SAMPLE GRID-IN

Find the positive value of x that satisfies the equation $3x^2 - 4x - 2 = 0$.

This is a non-factorable quadratic equation in the standard form $ax^2 + bx + c = 0$, where $a = 3$, $b = -4$, and $c = -2$. To solve using the quadratic formula, substitute the values for a, b, and c into the quadratic formula and simplify.

$$x = \frac{-b \pm \sqrt{b^2 - 4ac}}{2a}$$

$$x = \frac{-(-4) \pm \sqrt{(-4)^2 - 4(3)(-2)}}{2(3)}$$

$$x = \frac{4 \pm \sqrt{40}}{6}$$

$$x = \frac{2}{3} \pm \frac{\sqrt{10}}{3}$$

Using a calculator to estimate the solutions gives $x \approx 1.72$ or $x \approx -0.39$. Use the positive solution.

Grid in 1.72.

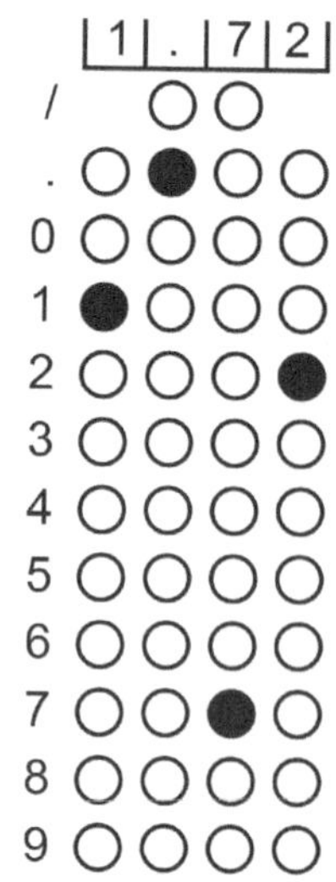

5

There are two values of x that satisfy the equation $5x^2 + 8x + 2 = 0$. What is the product of those values?

6

Of the two values of x that satisfy the equation $3x^2 + 8x - 5 = 0$, which value of x is greater?

7

The equation $\frac{2}{3}x^2 - \frac{7}{4}x + \frac{1}{2} = 0$ has two solutions. What is the greater of these two solutions?

8

The equation $\frac{1}{10}x^2 - \frac{4}{5}x + 1 = 0$ has two positive solutions. What is the value of the lesser of the solutions?

9

Let t_1 and t_2 be the two distinct solutions of the quadratic equation $-4.9t^2 + 27.3t - 23.2 = 0$. What is the value of the lesser of t_1 and t_2?

10

The equation $x^2 + 6.73x - 3.35 = 0$ has two solutions. One of the solutions is positive and the other is negative. What is the value of the positive solution?

11

What is the positive value of x that satisfies the quadratic equation $x^2 - 7x - 3 = 0$?

12

There are two values of x that satisfy the equation $x^2 - 5x + 1 = 0$. What is the lesser of these values?

Name ______________________ Date ______________ Class ______________

Complete the square or use the quadratic formula to solve quadratic equations in standard form.

ANSWER SHEET

1. A B C D ○ ○ ○ ○

2. A B C D ○ ○ ○ ○

3. A B C D ○ ○ ○ ○

4. A B C D ○ ○ ○ ○

5. Grid-in: / ○○; . ○○○○; 0–9 ○○○○

6. Grid-in: / ○○; . ○○○○; 0–9 ○○○○

7. Grid-in: / ○○; . ○○○○; 0–9 ○○○○

8. Grid-in: / ○○; . ○○○○; 0–9 ○○○○

9. Grid-in: / ○○; . ○○○○; 0–9 ○○○○

10. Grid-in: / ○○; . ○○○○; 0–9 ○○○○

11. Grid-in: / ○○; . ○○○○; 0–9 ○○○○

12. Grid-in: / ○○; . ○○○○; 0–9 ○○○○

Name ______________________ Date ______________ Class ______________

Use quadratic or exponential functions to solve real-world problems.

SAMPLE MULTIPLE CHOICE

$$h(t) = 1,250 - 16t^2$$

The function above models the height h in feet of an object t seconds after starting to fall from a height equal to that of the roof of the Empire State Building. To the nearest tenth of a second, how long will it take the object to reach the ground?

A) 6.3
B) 7.5
C) 8.8
D) 10.1

You can use the fact that $h(t) = 0$ when the object reaches the ground:

$$h(t) = 0$$
$$1,250 - 16t^2 = 0$$
$$-16t^2 = -1,250$$
$$t^2 = 78.125$$
$$t = \pm\sqrt{78.125}$$
$$t \approx \pm 8.8$$

Only the positive answer makes sense, so it takes the object about 8.8 seconds to reach the ground.

The correct answer is C. A ○ B ○ C ● D ○

1

$$h(t) = 519 - 16t^2$$

The function above models the height h in feet of an object t seconds after it is dropped from a height equal to that of the observation deck of the Space Needle in Seattle, Washington. To the nearest tenth of a second, how long will it take the object to reach the ground?

A) 4.0
B) 5.7
C) 7.4
D) 9.0

2

At the start of an experiment, there are 5,000 bacteria in a culture. The bacteria count doubles every hour. Which function models the bacteria count N when the experiment has been running for t hours?

A) $N(t) = t^2 + 5,000$
B) $N(t) = 5,000t^2$
C) $N(t) = 5,000(0.5)^t$
D) $N(t) = 5,000(2)^t$

3

$$G(n) = \frac{1}{2}(n^2 - n)$$

The function above gives the number of games G that can be played in a tournament with n teams when all of the teams play each other once. How many games can be played in a tournament with 10 teams?

A) 5
B) 45
C) 55
D) 90

4

$$B(t) = 200(1.02)^t$$

The function above gives the balance B, in dollars, in a bank account earning 2% interest compounded annually at a time of t years after the account is opened. Assume that no additional deposits were made after the initial deposit. How much was initially deposited in the account?

A) \$100
B) \$102
C) \$200
D) \$204

Name ______________________ Date ______________ Class ______________

SAMPLE GRID-IN

$$B(t) = 750(1.03)^t$$

The function above gives the balance B, in dollars, in a bank account earning 3% interest compounded annually after t years. No additional deposits were made after the initial deposit. To the nearest dollar, how much interest does the account earn in the first 9 years? (Ignore the dollar sign when gridding your response.)

A calculator can be used to find the initial and final balances of the account as follows:

$$B(0) = 750(1.03)^0 = 750$$

$$B(9) = 750(1.03)^9 \approx 979$$

Subtract to find the interest:

$$979 - 750 = 229$$

So, the account earns about \$229 in interest.

Grid in 229.

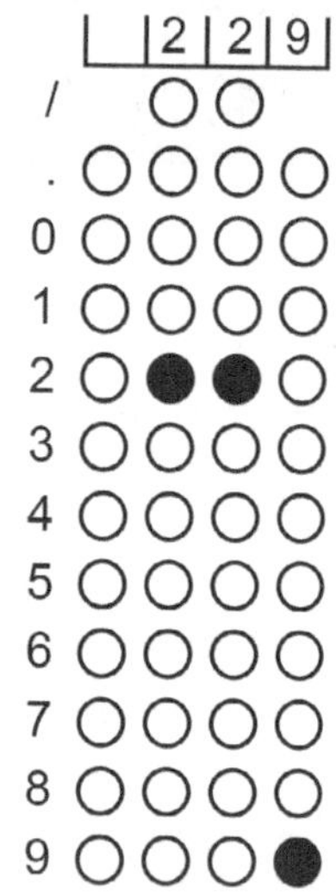

5

$$P(t) = 2{,}400(2)^{0.0462t}$$

The function above models the population P of a city t years after it is incorporated. To the nearest whole number, by how many people does the model predict the city's population increases in the first 6 years after incorporation?

6

$$h(x) = -0.015x^2 + 1.5x + 4.5$$

A football player punts the ball down the field. The function above gives the height h of the ball in feet after it has traveled x feet horizontally. What is the maximum height, in feet, that the ball reaches?

7

$$T(m) = 23 + 71(0.5)^{0.4184m}$$

The function above gives the temperature T (in °C) of a cup of water m minutes after it is removed from a microwave oven. To the nearest tenth of a degree, what is the temperature of the water after 10 minutes?

8

$$d(x) = -0.00635x^2 + 4x$$

The function above approximates the shape of the Gateway Arch in St. Louis, Missouri, where d is the distance in feet from the ground up to the arch at a point x feet horizontally from one of the bases. To the nearest foot, what is the width of the arch at the base?

9

$$N(d) = -0.3d^2 + 7.8d + 12$$

The function above models the number of tickets N that were sold each day for a show after it had been advertised for d days. After how many days of advertising were the most tickets sold in a single day?

10

$$A(t) = 100(0.5)^{0.125t}$$

Iodine-131 is a radioactive element often used in medical diagnoses. The function above gives the amount A, in grams, of 100 grams of iodine-131 remaining in a storage container t days after it is produced. To the nearest tenth of a gram, how much will remain after 1 week?

Name ______________________ Date ______________ Class ______________

Use quadratic or exponential functions to solve real-world problems.

ANSWER SHEET

1. A B C D

2. A B C D

3. A B C D

4. A B C D

5. / . 0 1 2 3 4 5 6 7 8 9

6. / . 0 1 2 3 4 5 6 7 8 9

7. / . 0 1 2 3 4 5 6 7 8 9

8. / . 0 1 2 3 4 5 6 7 8 9

9. / . 0 1 2 3 4 5 6 7 8 9

10. / . 0 1 2 3 4 5 6 7 8 9

Name ______________________ Date ______________ Class______________

Create, use, and make connections between different representations of quadratic or exponential functions.

SAMPLE MULTIPLE CHOICE

The graph of $y = 2(x-5)(x-3)$ is a parabola in the xy-plane. In which of the following equivalent equations do the coordinates of the vertex appear as constants or coefficients?

A) $y = 2(x-4)^2 + (-2)$

B) $y = 2x(x-8) + 30$

C) $y = (x-5)(2x-6)$

D) $y = 2x^2 - 16x + 30$

You can rewrite the equation in vertex form, $y = a(x-h)^2 + k$, to display the vertex (h, k):

$$y = 2(x-5)(x-3)$$
$$y = 2x^2 - 16x + 30$$
$$y = 2(x^2 - 8x) + 30$$
$$y = 2(x^2 - 8x + 16) + 30 - 32$$
$$y = 2(x-4)^2 + (-2)$$

Time-Saving Tip: Since it was stated that all of the equations are equivalent to the given equation, the question can be answered quickly by recognizing that the equation in choice A is in vertex form.

The correct answer is A. A ● B ○ C ○ D ○

1

The graph of $y = 2x^2 - 8x + 6$ is a parabola in the xy-plane. In which of the following equivalent equations do the x-coordinates of the zeros appear as constants or coefficients?

A) $y = (x-1)(2x-6)$

B) $y = 2(x-2)^2 + (-2)$

C) $y = 2x(x-4) + 6$

D) $y = 2(x-1)(x-3)$

2

$$P(t) = 25{,}000 - 20{,}000(0.5)^{0.0577t}$$

The function above models the monthly profit P, in dollars, a store can expect from a certain product t months after the product is introduced. What monthly profit does the prediction made by the model begin to approach after a period of several years has passed?

A) \$5,000

B) \$20,000

C) \$25,000

D) \$45,000

3

$$h(t) = -16t^2 + 64t + 336$$

The function above models the height h of an object t seconds after it is launched from the top of a cliff. What is the ordered pair that represents the highest point of the object's trajectory?

A) (7, 0)

B) (2, 400)

C) (0, 336)

D) (–3, 0)

4

The graph of $y = x^2$ is a parabola in the xy-plane. The graph of $y = (x+2)^2$ is the image of the graph of $y = x^2$ after which of the following translations?

A) 2 units left

B) 2 units right

C) 2 units up

D) 2 units down

Name ______________________ Date ______________ Class ______________

SAMPLE GRID-IN

$$N(t) = 250(2)^{\frac{t}{34}}$$

The function above gives the number N of bacteria in a culture after t days. What is the doubling time of the number of bacteria, in days?

Find the initial number of bacteria:

$$N(0) = 250(2)^{\frac{0}{34}} = 250$$

Find the time t for which the number of bacteria is double this number, or 500:

$$250(2)^{\frac{t}{34}} = 500$$

$$2^{\frac{t}{34}} = 2$$

$$\frac{t}{34} = 1$$

$$t = 34$$

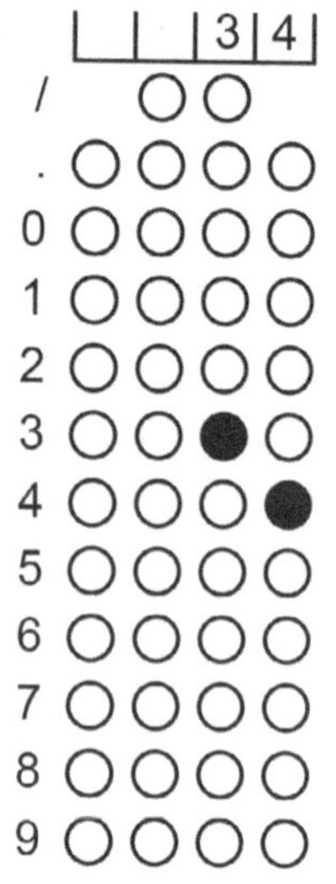

Time-Saving Tip: Less time is needed to answer the question if you understand that for $N(t) = N_0(2)^{\frac{t}{d}}$, the doubling time is $t = d$. So, the doubling time is 34 days.

Grid in 34.

5

$$Q(t) = 25\left(\frac{1}{2}\right)^{\frac{t}{5,730}}$$

The function above models the quantity Q of carbon-14 remaining in a sample after t years. After how many years is the quantity of carbon-14 in a sample one half of the quantity present at the beginning of the time period?

6

Simon deposits $500 into a savings account. He does not plan to deposit any additional money into the account. Simon wants to use a function of the form $B(t) = 500(k)^t$ to describe the balance B of the account in dollars after t years. The account earns 2% interest compounded annually. What number should Simon use in place of k?

7

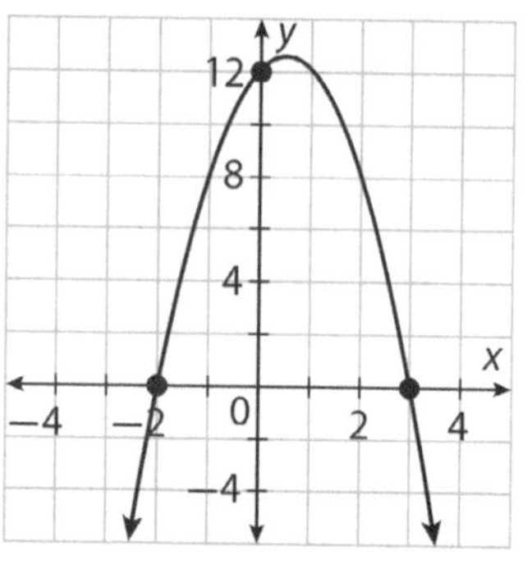

If the parabola graphed above is modeled by the equation $y = ax^2 + bx + c$, what is the value of c?

Name ______________________ Date ______________ Class______________

Create, use, and make connections between different representations of quadratic or exponential functions.

ANSWER SHEET

1. A B C D
○ ○ ○ ○

2. A B C D
○ ○ ○ ○

3. A B C D
○ ○ ○ ○

4. A B C D
○ ○ ○ ○

5.

/		○	○	
.	○	○	○	○
0	○	○	○	○
1	○	○	○	○
2	○	○	○	○
3	○	○	○	○
4	○	○	○	○
5	○	○	○	○
6	○	○	○	○
7	○	○	○	○
8	○	○	○	○
9	○	○	○	○

6.

/		○	○	
.	○	○	○	○
0	○	○	○	○
1	○	○	○	○
2	○	○	○	○
3	○	○	○	○
4	○	○	○	○
5	○	○	○	○
6	○	○	○	○
7	○	○	○	○
8	○	○	○	○
9	○	○	○	○

7.

/		○	○	
.	○	○	○	○
0	○	○	○	○
1	○	○	○	○
2	○	○	○	○
3	○	○	○	○
4	○	○	○	○
5	○	○	○	○
6	○	○	○	○
7	○	○	○	○
8	○	○	○	○
9	○	○	○	○

Name ______________________ Date ______________ Class______________

Work with factorable polynomial functions and simple rational functions, and their graphs.

SAMPLE MULTIPLE CHOICE

$$V(x) = 4x^3 - 100x^2 + 600x$$

A rectangular piece of cardboard measures 20 centimeters by 30 centimeters. A square x centimeters long is removed from each corner. The remaining piece of cardboard is folded up to make an open box. The function above gives the volume V, in cubic centimeters, of the box. Which of the following describes the volume of the box when the squares have 3-centimeter sides?

A) $V(3) = 336$

B) $V(3) = 408$

C) $V(3) = 956$

D) $V(3) = 1{,}008$

You can use the given formula for $V(x)$ to evaluate $V(3)$.

$$\begin{aligned} V(x) &= 4x^3 - 100x^2 + 600x \\ V(3) &= 4(3)^3 - 100(3)^2 + 600(3) \\ &= 4(27) - 100(9) + 600(3) \\ &= 108 - 900 + 1{,}800 \\ &= 1{,}008 \end{aligned}$$

So, the volume of the box if the sides of the square are 3 centimeters long is 1,008 square centimeters.

The correct answer is D. A ○ B ○ C ○ D ●

1

$$D(x) = 0.72x^2 - 0.12x^3,\ 0 < x \le 4$$

A gymnast is doing a routine on the high bar. The function above gives the deflection D, in inches, at a point x feet from one end of the bar. Which of the following describes the deflection at a point 3 feet from one end of the bar?

A) $D(3) = 0.6$

B) $D(3) = 3.24$

C) $D(3) = 5.28$

D) $D(3) = 9.72$

2

The graph of a polynomial function crosses the x-axis at -3, -1, 2, and 4. Which of the following could be the equation of the function?

A) $y = (x-1)(x-2)(x-3)(x-4)$

B) $y = (x-1)(x+2)(x-3)(x+4)$

C) $y = (x+1)(x+2)(x+3)(x+4)$

D) $y = (x+1)(x-2)(x+3)(x-4)$

3

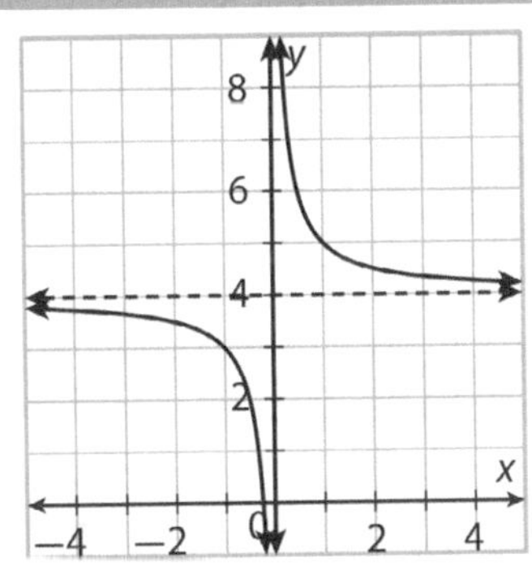

What is the equation of the rational function graphed above?

A) $f(x) = \dfrac{1}{x} + 4$

B) $f(x) = \dfrac{1}{x} - 4$

C) $f(x) = \dfrac{1}{x+4}$

D) $f(x) = \dfrac{1}{x-4}$

4

The function $E(t) = -t^3 + 6t^2 + 16t$ models the efficiency E of a worker when she has been working for t hours. Which of the following represents her efficiency after 5 hours?

A) $E(105) = 5$

B) $E(355) = 5$

C) $E(5) = 105$

D) $E(5) = 355$

Name ______________________ Date ______________ Class ______________

SAMPLE GRID-IN

The graph of the rational function $g(x)=\frac{1}{x+7}-2$ has two asymptotes, one horizontal and one vertical. If the asymptotes intersect at the point (a, b), what is the value of $\frac{a}{b}$?

Begin by visualizing the graph of $g(x)$. The graph of $g(x)$ is the graph of $f(x)=\frac{1}{x}$ after it has been translated 7 units left and 2 units down.

This means the asymptotes of $g(x)$ are $x=-7$ and $y=-2$. The asymptotes intersect at $(-7, -2)$, so $a=-7$ and $b=-2$.

$$\frac{a}{b}=\frac{-7}{-2}=\frac{7}{2}$$

So, the answer is $\frac{7}{2}$.

Grid in 7/2 or 3.5.

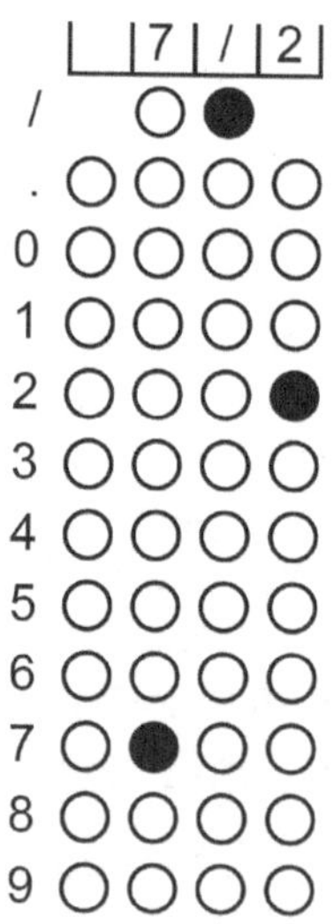

5

The graph of $g(x)=\frac{1}{x-3}+5$ has two asymptotes, one horizontal and one vertical. If the asymptotes intersect at the point (a, b), what is the value of $a+b$?

6

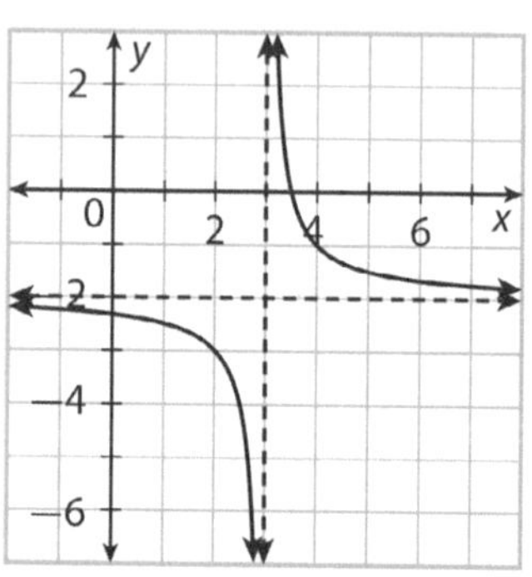

The rational function graphed above can be written in the form $h(x)=\frac{1}{x+a}-b$. What is the value of b?

7

The graph of a polynomial function passes through the points $(-2, 0)$, $(1, 0)$, and $(7, 0)$. What is the minimum number of distinct factors that could appear in the factored form of the function?

8

$$p(x)=(x-4)(x-1)(x+1)(x+3)$$

What is the y-intercept of the graph of the function shown above?

9

$$R(t)=\frac{7}{t+1}+1$$

The function above describes the rate R of a chemical reaction t minutes after an experiment begins. What is the value of $R(4)$?

Name ______________________ Date ______________ Class ______________

Work with factorable polynomial functions and simple rational functions, and their graphs.

ANSWER SHEET

1. A B C D

2. A B C D

3. A B C D

4. A B C D

5.

/ . 0 1 2 3 4 5 6 7 8 9

6.

/ . 0 1 2 3 4 5 6 7 8 9

7.

/ . 0 1 2 3 4 5 6 7 8 9

8.

/ . 0 1 2 3 4 5 6 7 8 9

9.

/ . 0 1 2 3 4 5 6 7 8 9

Name ______________________ Date ____________ Class ____________

Solve problems about geometric figures using information such as length, surface area, or volume.

SAMPLE MULTIPLE CHOICE

A pyramid has a rectangular base with a length of 20 feet and a width of 15 feet. How tall, in feet, is the pyramid if it has a volume of 600 cubic feet?

A) 6
B) 8
C) 10
D) 12

The height can be found by using the volume formula of a pyramid. The base is a rectangle, so use $B = \ell \cdot w$.

$$V = \frac{1}{3} \cdot B \cdot h$$

$$V = \frac{1}{3} \cdot \ell \cdot w \cdot h$$

$$600 = \frac{1}{3} \cdot 20 \cdot 15 \cdot h$$

$$600 = 100 \cdot h$$

$$6 = h$$

So, the height of the pyramid is 6 feet.

The correct answer is A. A ● B ○ C ○ D ○

1

Tom just bought a new fish tank that is 40 centimeters long, 22 centimeters wide, and 28 centimeters tall. He puts an even layer of sand in the bottom of the tank to a height of 3 centimeters. Tom then fills the tank until the water level is 1 centimeter below the top of the tank. How much water, in cubic centimeters, is in the tank? Assume that no water is absorbed into the sand.

A) 21,120 C) 24,000
B) 23,760 D) 24,640

2

Tyra is making a cylindrical golf ball container to hold 6 golf balls stacked in a single column. The lid of the container will just touch the top of the stack. The diameter of a golf ball is 1.68 inches. What is the volume, in cubic inches, of the cylindrical container? Round to the nearest hundredth.

A) 14.90 C) 89.38
B) 22.34 D) 119.17

3

Pang wants to make a spherical lantern for Chinese New Year. He starts by making a ball with a volume of $\frac{32\pi}{3}$ cubic inches out of newspaper. The next step is to cover the ball with red paper. How many square inches of red paper does Pang need? Assume that there will be no wasted paper.

A) 8π C) 16π
B) 12π D) 32π

4

When fully sharpened, the end of a round pencil has the shape of a cone. A pencil has a diameter of 8 millimeters and the sharpened portion of the pencil has a height of 21 millimeters. What is the volume, in cubic millimeters, of the sharpened portion of the pencil? Round to the nearest whole number.

A) 318 C) 1,056
B) 352 D) 1,407

Name ______________________ Date ______________ Class ______________

SAMPLE GRID-IN

The base of a cone has a radius of 4 units. How tall is the cone if it has a volume of 240π cubic units?

The volume of the cone and the radius of its base are given. The height can be found by substituting these values into the formula for the volume of a cone and then solving for *h*.

$$V = \frac{1}{3}\pi r^2 h$$

$$240\pi = \frac{1}{3}\pi(4)^2 h$$

$$\frac{240\pi \cdot 3}{16\pi} = h$$

$$45 = h$$

So, the height is 45 units.

Grid in 45.

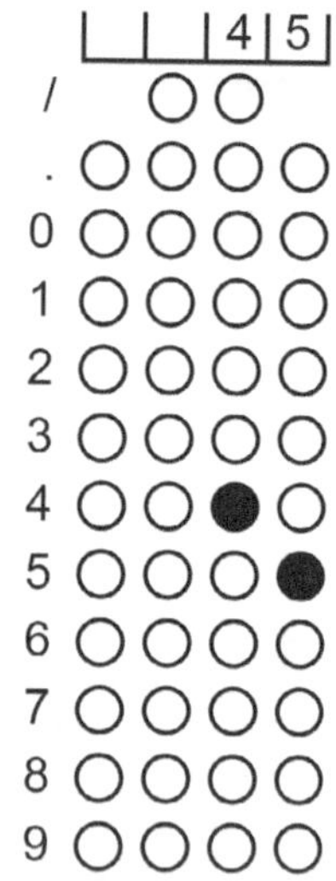

Questions 5 and 6 refer to the following information.

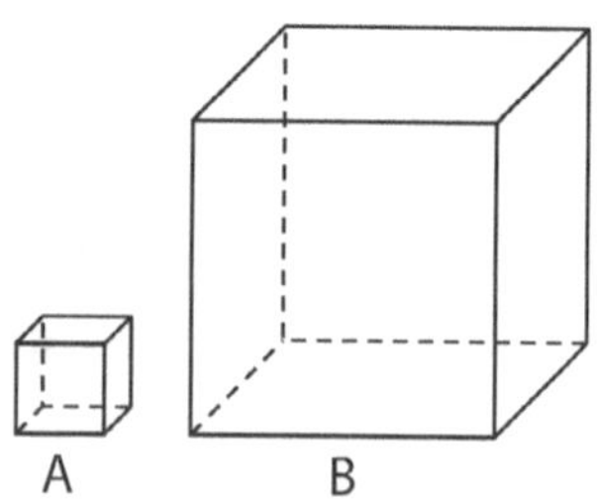

Figures A and B are cubes.

5

Suppose the edges of cube B are each 3 times the length of each edge of cube A. How many times greater is the volume of cube B than that of cube A?

6

Suppose the surface area of cube B is 25 times the surface area of cube A. How many times longer are the edges of cube B than the edges of cube A?

7

Tomas wants to build a wooden ramp to practice some skateboarding tricks. The ramp is a right triangular prism with a height of 6 feet. The legs of the base are 4 feet and 3.5 feet long. Find the volume of the wooden ramp, in cubic feet.

8

Liz is designing a cylindrical lipstick tube for her marketing class. The lipstick tube is 2.5 inches tall and has a diameter of 1 inch. She is only going to draw on the curved surface of the tube. Find the area, in square inches, that Liz will be drawing on. Use 3.14 for π.

9

Elena bought a new jewelry box that is smaller than her current jewelry box. She wants to put a coat of sealer on the new box. Both jewelry boxes are rectangular prisms, but each dimension of the new jewelry box is half that of her current jewelry box. If that box has a surface area of 720 square centimeters, what is the surface area of her new jewelry box, in square centimeters?

Name ______________________ Date ______________ Class ______________

Solve problems about geometric figures using information such as length, surface area, or volume.

ANSWER SHEET

1. A B C D
○ ○ ○ ○

2. A B C D
○ ○ ○ ○

3. A B C D
○ ○ ○ ○

4. A B C D
○ ○ ○ ○

5. | | | | |
/ ○ ○
. ○ ○ ○ ○
0 ○ ○ ○ ○
1 ○ ○ ○ ○
2 ○ ○ ○ ○
3 ○ ○ ○ ○
4 ○ ○ ○ ○
5 ○ ○ ○ ○
6 ○ ○ ○ ○
7 ○ ○ ○ ○
8 ○ ○ ○ ○
9 ○ ○ ○ ○

6. | | | | |
/ ○ ○
. ○ ○ ○ ○
0 ○ ○ ○ ○
1 ○ ○ ○ ○
2 ○ ○ ○ ○
3 ○ ○ ○ ○
4 ○ ○ ○ ○
5 ○ ○ ○ ○
6 ○ ○ ○ ○
7 ○ ○ ○ ○
8 ○ ○ ○ ○
9 ○ ○ ○ ○

7. | | | | |
/ ○ ○
. ○ ○ ○ ○
0 ○ ○ ○ ○
1 ○ ○ ○ ○
2 ○ ○ ○ ○
3 ○ ○ ○ ○
4 ○ ○ ○ ○
5 ○ ○ ○ ○
6 ○ ○ ○ ○
7 ○ ○ ○ ○
8 ○ ○ ○ ○
9 ○ ○ ○ ○

8. | | | | |
/ ○ ○
. ○ ○ ○ ○
0 ○ ○ ○ ○
1 ○ ○ ○ ○
2 ○ ○ ○ ○
3 ○ ○ ○ ○
4 ○ ○ ○ ○
5 ○ ○ ○ ○
6 ○ ○ ○ ○
7 ○ ○ ○ ○
8 ○ ○ ○ ○
9 ○ ○ ○ ○

9. | | | | |
/ ○ ○
. ○ ○ ○ ○
0 ○ ○ ○ ○
1 ○ ○ ○ ○
2 ○ ○ ○ ○
3 ○ ○ ○ ○
4 ○ ○ ○ ○
5 ○ ○ ○ ○
6 ○ ○ ○ ○
7 ○ ○ ○ ○
8 ○ ○ ○ ○
9 ○ ○ ○ ○

Name ______________________ Date ______________ Class ______________

Solve problems involving congruent and similar triangles using appropriate concepts and theorems.

SAMPLE MULTIPLE CHOICE

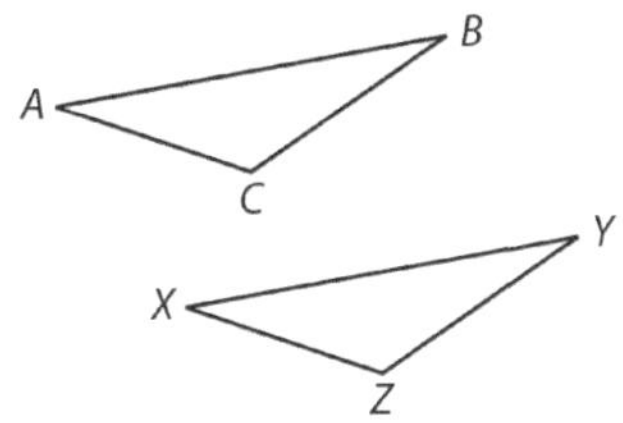

In the figure above, triangles *ABC* and *XYZ* are congruent. If $\angle ABC \cong \angle XYZ$, $\angle BCA \cong \angle YZX$, and $\angle CAB \cong \angle ZXY$, which side must be congruent to $\overline{AB}$?

A) $\overline{XZ}$ C) $\overline{YZ}$

B) $\overline{XY}$ D) $\overline{BC}$

The corresponding parts of congruent triangles are congruent. Identify the points in $\triangle XYZ$ that correspond to the endpoints of $\overline{AB}$ in $\triangle ABC$. Those points are the endpoints of the side of $\triangle XYZ$ that is congruent to $\overline{AB}$.

Since $\angle CAB \cong \angle ZXY$, point *A* corresponds to point *X*. Since $\angle ABC \cong \angle XYZ$, point *B* corresponds to point *Y*. Therefore, it must be that $\overline{XY} \cong \overline{AB}$.

The correct answer is B. A ○ B ● C ○ D ○

Questions 1–3 refer to the following information.

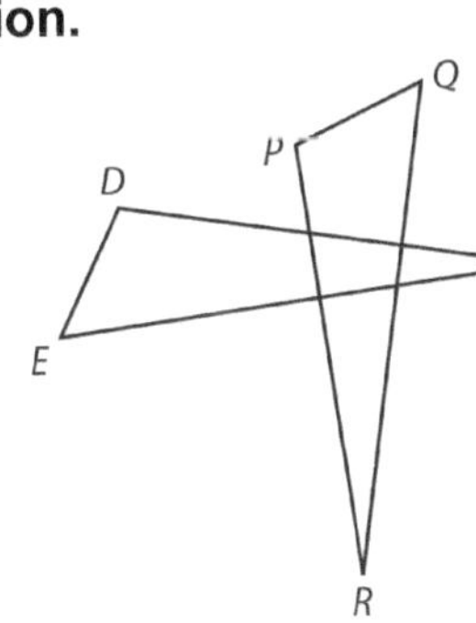

In the figure, $\triangle DEF \cong \triangle PQR$.

1

Which angle must be congruent to $\angle F$?

A) $\angle P$ C) $\angle Q$

B) $\angle R$ D) $\angle D$

2

Suppose $m\angle EDF = 3x + 18$ and $m\angle QPR = 4x - 12$. Find the value of *x*.

A) 108 C) 30

B) 56 D) 15

3

Suppose the perimeter of $\triangle DEF$ is 38. Find the value of *x* if $DE = x$, $QR = 3x + 1$, and $DF = 5x - 8$.

A) 5 C) 14

B) 7 D) 20

4

$\triangle NOP$ is similar to $\triangle JKL$, with $\angle N$ corresponding to $\angle J$ and $\angle O$ corresponding to $\angle K$. Suppose $\triangle NOP$ is the larger triangle and the scale factor is 4. If $m\angle P = 15°$, what is $m\angle L$?

A) 15° C) 60°

B) 30° D) 120°

5

$\triangle ACE$ is similar to $\triangle BDF$, with $\angle A$ corresponding to $\angle B$ and $\angle C$ corresponding to $\angle D$. Suppose $\triangle ACE$ is the smaller triangle and the scale factor is 3. If $AC = 6$, what is *BD*?

A) 2 C) 54

B) 18 D) 162

Name ______________________ Date ______________ Class______________

SAMPLE GRID-IN

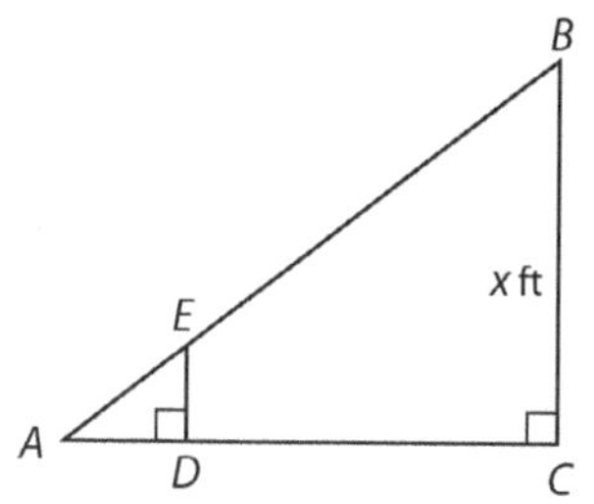

A 6-foot-tall man, represented by $\overline{DE}$, is standing in the shadow of a cell tower. Suppose DC is 24 feet and represents the distance from the base of the tower to where the man is standing, and AD is 8 feet and represents where his shadow and the shadow of the tower end. Find the height of the tower.

Note from the diagram that $\triangle ABC$ is similar to $\triangle AED$. Using $AD = 8$ and $DC = 24$, find AC and determine the scale factor.

$$AC = AD + DC = 8 + 24 = 32$$

To find the scale factor, divide AC by AD.

$$\frac{AC}{AD} = \frac{32}{8} = 4$$

To find x, use the length of $\overline{AC}$ and the scale factor.

$$\frac{BC}{ED} = 4$$

$$\frac{x}{6} = 4$$

$$x = 24$$

So, the tower is 24 feet tall.

Grid in 24.

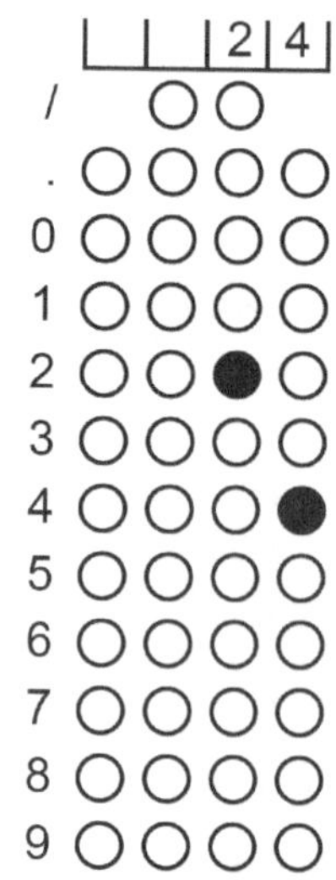

Questions 6–8 refer to the following information.

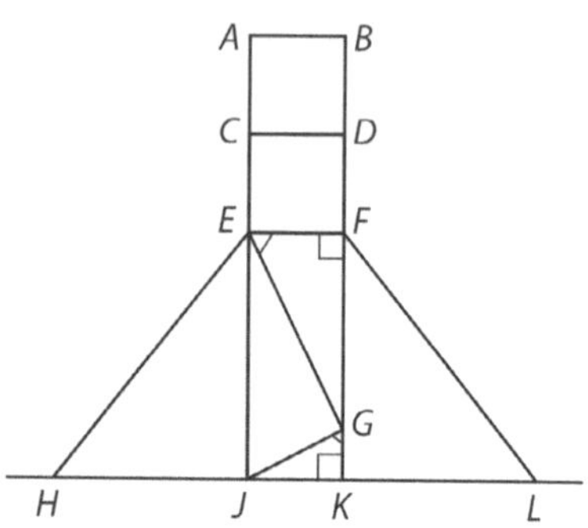

The figure represents a fire tower.

In the figure:

$\triangle EFG$ is similar to $\triangle GKJ$ and to $\triangle JGE$.

$\triangle HEJ \cong \triangle LFK$

$ABDC$ and $CDFE$ are congruent squares.

$EF = 20$ feet and $GK = 10$ feet

6

How tall, in feet, is the fire tower?

7

$\triangle EFG$ is similar to $\triangle GKJ$ with a scale factor of 2. If $m\angle GJK = 27°$, what is $m\angle EGF$?

8

It was given that $\triangle JGE$ is similar to both $\triangle EFG$ and $\triangle GKJ$, and that $EF = 20$ and $GK = 10$. What is the length of $\overline{EG}$ to the nearest tenth of a foot?

9

Jane is 1.6 meters tall and is standing on the shadow cast by a flagpole so that her shadow ends at the same spot as the shadow of the flagpole. The flagpole is 24 meters tall and its shadow is 18 meters long. How long, in meters, is Jane's shadow?

Name ______________________ Date ______________ Class ______________

Solve problems involving congruent and similar triangles using appropriate concepts and theorems.

ANSWER SHEET

1. A B C D

2. A B C D

3. A B C D

4. A B C D

5. A B C D

6.
/
.
0
1
2
3
4
5
6
7
8
9

7.
/
.
0
1
2
3
4
5
6
7
8
9

8.
/
.
0
1
2
3
4
5
6
7
8
9

9.
/
.
0
1
2
3
4
5
6
7
8
9

Name ______________________ Date ______________ Class______________

Determine the statements needed to prove relationships or satisfy theorems.

SAMPLE MULTIPLE CHOICE

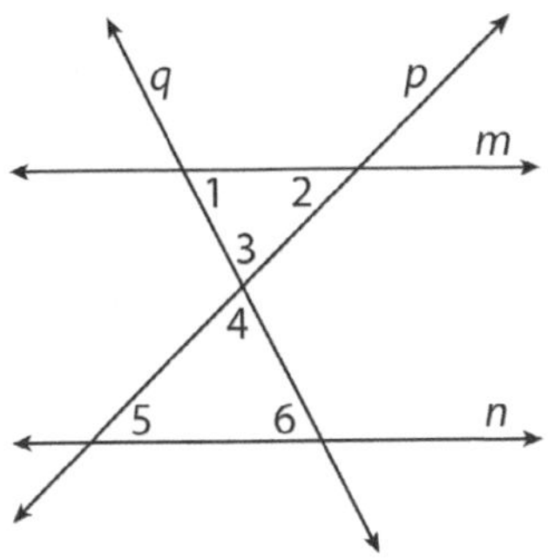

Which of the following statements is only true if $m \parallel n$?

A) $m\angle 1 + m\angle 2 + m\angle 3 = 180°$

B) $m\angle 1 + m\angle 5 + m\angle 3 = 180°$

C) $\angle 1 \cong \angle 5$

D) $\angle 3 \cong \angle 4$

The statement in choice A is always true by the triangle sum theorem, and the statement in choice D is always true because $\angle 3$ and $\angle 4$ are vertical angles. The statement in choice C might be true, but its truth does not depend on whether or not *m* and *n* are parallel. This leaves choice B as the statement that is true only if $m \parallel n$. Let's verify.

Start with the fact that $m\angle 6 + m\angle 5 + m\angle 4 = 180°$, by the triangle sum theorem. Since they are vertical angles, $\angle 3 \cong \angle 4$ and, therefore, $m\angle 3 = m\angle 4$. Using substitution, the equation above becomes $m\angle 6 + m\angle 5 + m\angle 3 = 180°$. This equation will become the equation in choice B if $m\angle 1$ can be substituted for $m\angle 6$.

Angles 1 and 6 are alternate interior angles, but their measures are only equal if $m \parallel n$. So, the equation $m\angle 1 + m\angle 5 + m\angle 3 = 180°$ is indeed only true if $m \parallel n$.

The correct answer is B. A ○ B ● C ○ D ○

Questions 1–3 refer to the following information.

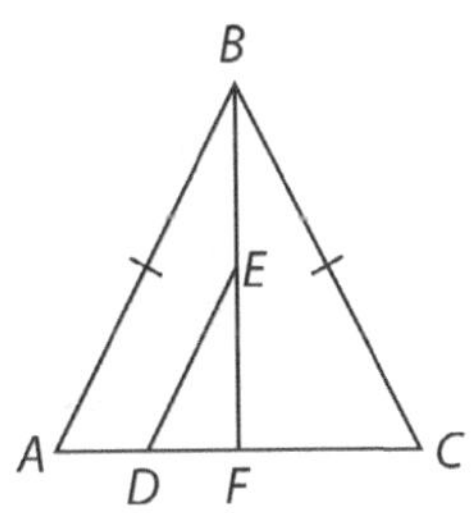

In the figure, $\overline{AB} \cong \overline{BC}$.

1

Which of the following must be true in order to prove $\triangle ABF \cong \triangle CBF$?

A) $m\angle ABF + m\angle AFB = m\angle BFC$

B) $m\angle AFB + m\angle CFB = 180°$

C) $m\angle BFC = 90°$

D) $2DF = FC$

2

If $\overline{BF} \perp \overline{AC}$, which of the following relationships does NOT have to be true?

A) $\triangle ABF$ is similar to $\triangle DEF$.

B) $m\angle ABC = 2m\angle ABF$

C) $\triangle ABF \cong \triangle CBF$

D) $FC = AD + DF$

3

If $\overline{AB} \parallel \overline{DE}$, which of the following statements needs to be justified in order to prove that $\triangle CBF$ is similar to $\triangle DEF$?

A) $\angle ABF \cong \angle DEF$

B) $\angle ABF$ and $\angle EDF$ are complementary.

C) $\angle BAF \cong \angle EDF$

D) $\angle AFB$ and $\angle BFC$ are supplementary.

Name ______________________ Date ______________ Class______________

Questions 4–9 refer to the following figure.

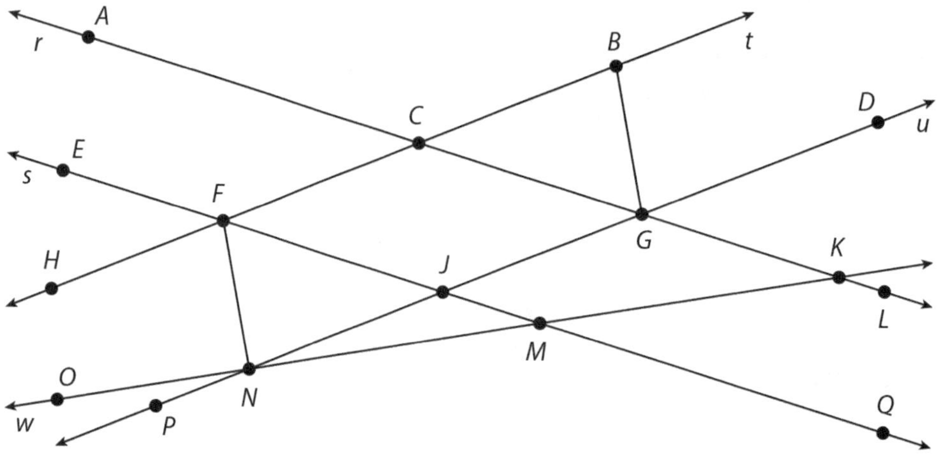

4

Using the fact that $\angle CGD$ and $\angle JGK$ are vertical angles, which of the following statements must be true?

A) $m\angle CGB + m\angle BGD = m\angle JGK$

B) $t \parallel u$

C) $\triangle CBG$ is isosceles.

D) $m\angle CGB + m\angle BGD + m\angle LGB = 180°$

5

If $\triangle NJM$ is similar to $\triangle NGK$, which of the following statements must be true?

A) $u \parallel t$

B) $\angle NMQ \cong \angle JGK$

C) $\frac{GK}{JM} = 2$

D) $r \parallel s$

6

If the measures of $\angle ACF$ and $\angle EFH$ are equal, then lines r and s must be parallel by the converse of which theorem?

A) Same-side interior angles theorem

B) Alternate interior angles theorem

C) Corresponding angles theorem

D) Vertical angles congruence theorem

7

Given that $u \parallel t$ and $r \parallel s$, it can be shown that $\overline{CG} \cong \overline{FJ}$. If it is given that $\angle NFJ \cong \angle BGC$, which statement can be justified in order to prove $\triangle FJN \cong \triangle GCB$?

A) $\angle NJF \cong \angle BCG$

B) $\overline{NJ} \cong \overline{BC}$

C) $FCGJ$ is a parallelogram.

D) $\overline{FN} \cong \overline{GB}$

8

Which theorem justifies the statement $m\angle NMQ = m\angle JMK$?

A) Same-side interior angles theorem

B) Alternate interior angles theorem

C) Corresponding angles theorem

D) Vertical angles congruence theorem

9

Given $u \parallel t$, which theorem is needed along with the triangle sum theorem in order to justify the statement $m\angle HFN + m\angle NFJ + m\angle FJN = 180°$?

A) Same-side interior angles theorem

B) Alternate interior angles theorem

C) Corresponding angles theorem

D) Alternate exterior angles theorem

Name ______________________ Date ____________ Class____________

Determine the statements needed to prove relationships or satisfy theorems.

ANSWER SHEET

1. A B C D ○ ○ ○ ○
2. A B C D ○ ○ ○ ○
3. A B C D ○ ○ ○ ○
4. A B C D ○ ○ ○ ○
5. A B C D ○ ○ ○ ○
6. A B C D ○ ○ ○ ○
7. A B C D ○ ○ ○ ○
8. A B C D ○ ○ ○ ○
9. A B C D ○ ○ ○ ○

Name ______________________ Date ______________ Class ______________

Understand that the scale factor *k* changes side lengths but not angle measures.

SAMPLE MULTIPLE CHOICE

Triangle *ABC* is similar to triangle *XYZ*, where vertices *A*, *B*, and *C* correspond to vertices *X*, *Y*, and *Z*, respectively. If triangle *XYZ* is related to triangle *ABC* by a scale factor of 1.5, what is the length in centimeters of $\overline{YZ}$?

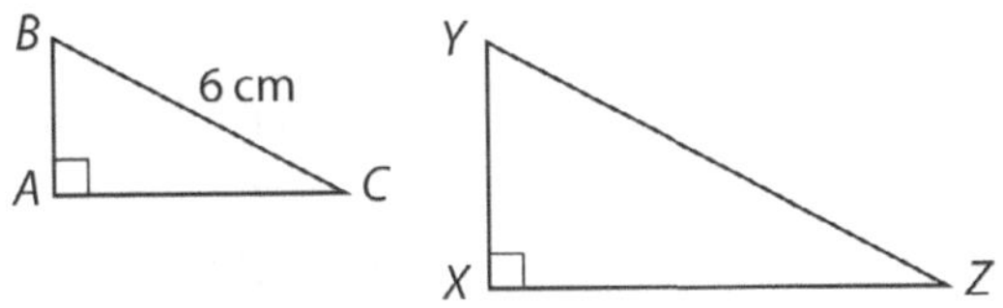

A) 15 C) 7.5
B) 9 D) 4

A scale factor relates the lengths of corresponding sides of similar figures. Since $\overline{BC}$ corresponds to $\overline{YZ}$, multiply 6 by 1.5 to find the length of $\overline{YZ}$.

$$6 \times 1.5 = 9$$

The correct answer is B. A ○ B ● C ○ D ○

Questions 1 and 2 refer to the following information.

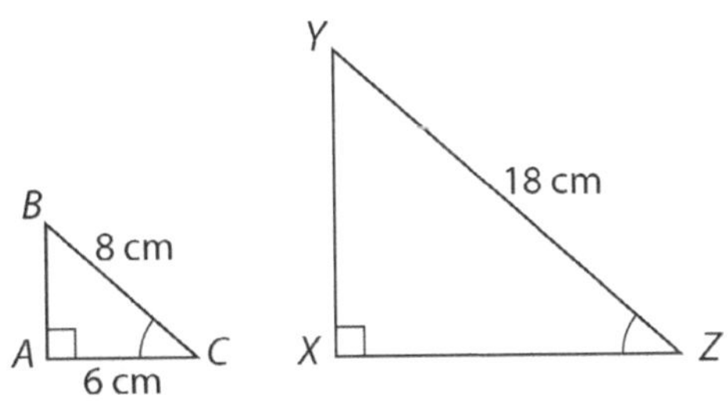

The two triangles above are similar, with $\triangle ABC \sim \triangle XYZ$.

1

What is the scale factor that relates $\triangle ABC$ to $\triangle XYZ$?

A) 1.5 C) 3
B) 2.25 D) 10

2

What is the length in centimeters of $\overline{ZX}$?

A) 12 C) 16
B) 13.5 D) 24

Questions 3 and 4 refer to the following information.

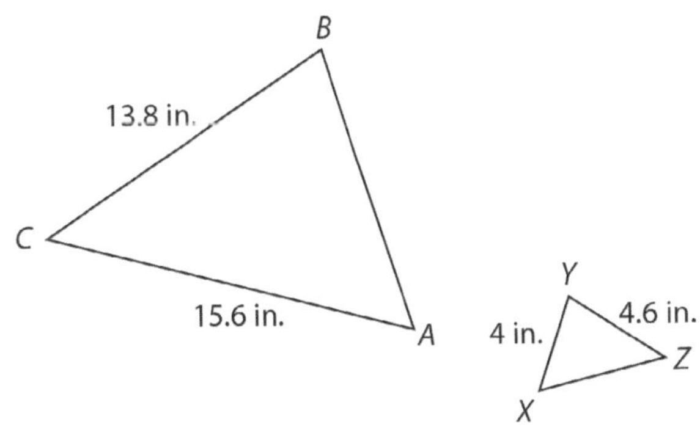

The two triangles above are similar, with $\triangle ABC \sim \triangle XYZ$.

3

What is the length in inches of $\overline{AB}$?

A) 9.2 C) 13.8
B) 12 D) 15

4

What is the length in inches of $\overline{ZX}$?

A) 12 C) 6.8
B) 9.2 D) 5.2

Name ______________________ Date ______________ Class ______________

SAMPLE GRID-IN

Triangles *ABC* and *XYZ* are similar triangles. Vertices *A*, *B*, and *C* correspond to vertices *X*, *Y*, and *Z*, respectively. What is m$\angle X$?

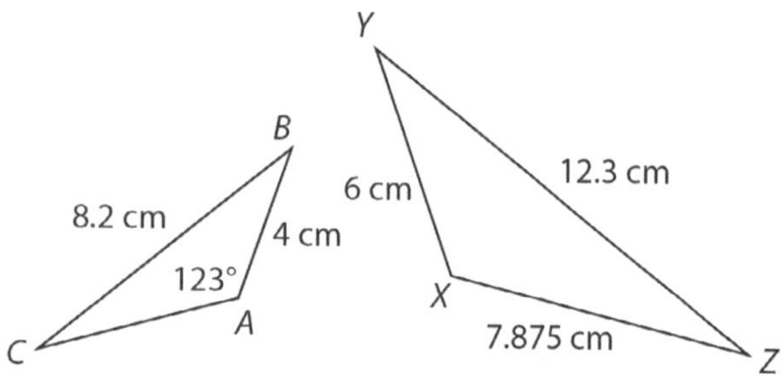

Recall that corresponding angles in similar figures are congruent.

$\angle X \cong \angle A$

$\angle Y \cong \angle B$

$\angle Z \cong \angle C$

Since congruent angles have equal angle measure, $m\angle X = m\angle A$. From the figure, $m\angle A = 123^\circ$. So, $m\angle X = 123^\circ$.

Grid in 123.

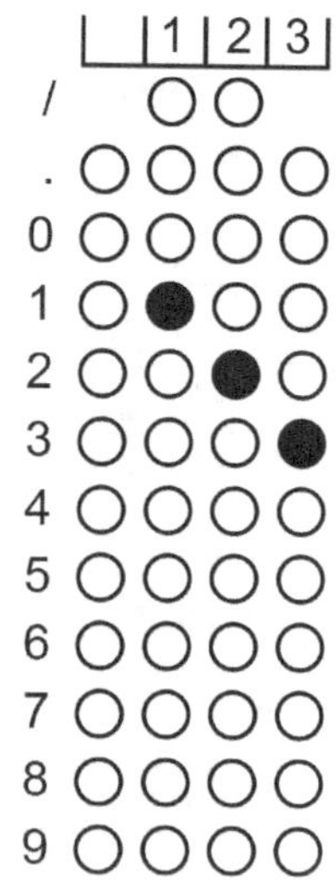

Questions 5–7 refer to the following information.

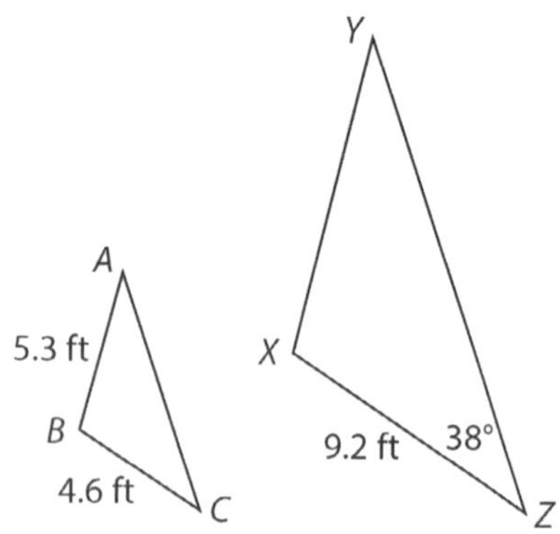

In the figure above, $\triangle ABC \sim \triangle YXZ$.

5

What is the length of $\overline{XY}$ in feet?

6

What is the measure of $\angle C$? Ignore the degree symbol when gridding your response.

7

If $m\angle A = 32^\circ$, what is the measure of $\angle X$? Ignore the degree symbol when gridding your response.

Questions 8 and 9 refer to the following information.

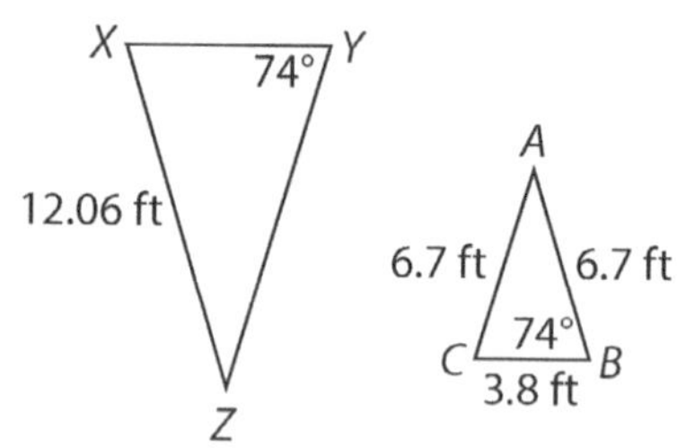

The triangles above are similar, with $\triangle ABC \sim \triangle ZXY$.

8

What is the length of $\overline{XY}$ in feet?

9

What is the measure of $\angle X$? Ignore the degree symbol when gridding your response.

Name ______________________ Date ______________ Class______________

Understand that the scale factor *k* changes side lengths but not angle measures.

ANSWER SHEET

1. A B C D

2. A B C D

3. A B C D

4. A B C D

5. / . 0 1 2 3 4 5 6 7 8 9

6. / . 0 1 2 3 4 5 6 7 8 9

7. / . 0 1 2 3 4 5 6 7 8 9

8. / . 0 1 2 3 4 5 6 7 8 9

9. / . 0 1 2 3 4 5 6 7 8 9

Name ______________________ Date ______________ Class ______________

Know and apply theorems about vertical angles, triangles, and parallel lines cut by a transversal.

SAMPLE MULTIPLE CHOICE

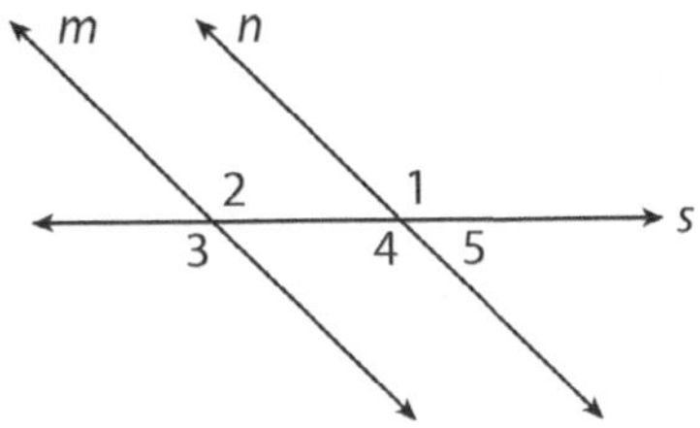

Given $m \parallel n$, which angle is congruent to $\angle 1$ by the vertical angle theorem?

A) $\angle 2$
B) $\angle 3$
C) $\angle 4$
D) $\angle 5$

Begin by recalling the definition of vertical angles. When two lines intersect, the angles that are opposite each other are called vertical angles. $\angle 1$ is formed by the intersection of lines n and s, as are $\angle 4$ and $\angle 5$.

$\angle 4$ is opposite $\angle 1$, so $\angle 1$ and $\angle 4$ are vertical angles. The vertical angle theorem states that vertical angles are congruent, so $\angle 1 \cong \angle 4$.

The correct answer is C. A ○ B ○ C ● D ○

Questions 1–4 refer to the following figure.

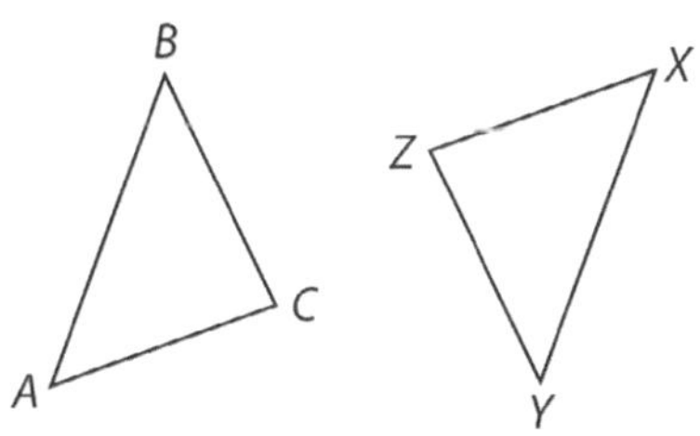

1

If $m\angle A = 75°$ and $m\angle B = 45°$, what is $m\angle C$?

A) 30°
B) 60°
C) 105°
D) 120°

2

Suppose $\triangle ABC$ is similar to $\triangle XYZ$ with $\angle A \cong \angle X$, $\angle B \cong \angle Y$, and $\angle C \cong \angle Z$. If $CA = 5$, $ZX = 15$, and $BC = 7$, what is YZ?

A) 12
B) 17
C) 21
D) 27

3

If $\angle C \cong \angle Z$, $\angle B \cong \angle Y$, $BC = 6$, and $ZY = 12$, which of the following statements is true?

A) $\triangle ABC \cong \triangle XYZ$

B) $\triangle ABC$ is similar to $\triangle XYZ$ with a scale factor of 2.

C) $\triangle ABC$ is similar to $\triangle XYZ$ with a scale factor of 4.

D) There is not enough information to determine a relationship between $\triangle ABC$ and $\triangle XYZ$.

4

If $\angle A \cong \angle X$, $\angle B \cong \angle Y$, and $\overline{AB} \cong \overline{XY}$, which triangle congruence theorem can be used to justify that $\triangle ABC \cong \triangle XYZ$?

A) Angle-side-angle theorem
B) Angle-angle-side theorem
C) Side-side-side theorem
D) Side-angle-side theorem

Name ____________________ Date ______________ Class ______________

SAMPLE GRID-IN

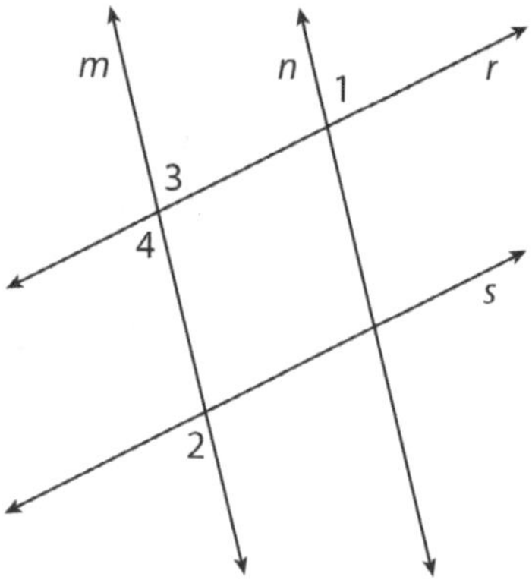

Given $m \parallel n$ and $r \parallel s$, what is the measure of $\angle 2$ if $m\angle 1 = 70°$?

Use what you know about parallel lines to determine the relationship between $\angle 1$ and $\angle 2$.

$\angle 1 \cong \angle 3$ because they are corresponding angles. $\angle 3 \cong \angle 4$ by the vertical angles theorem. $\angle 4 \cong \angle 2$ because they are corresponding angles. By the transitive property of congruence, we can conclude that $\angle 1 \cong \angle 2$. Therefore, the measure of $\angle 2$ is $70°$.

Grid in 70.

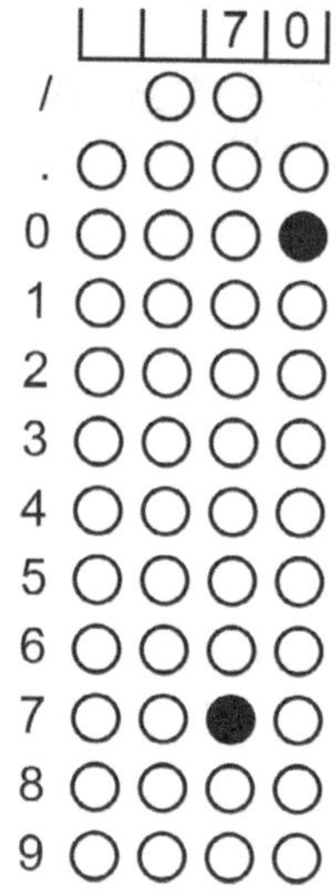

Questions 5–9 refer to the following information.

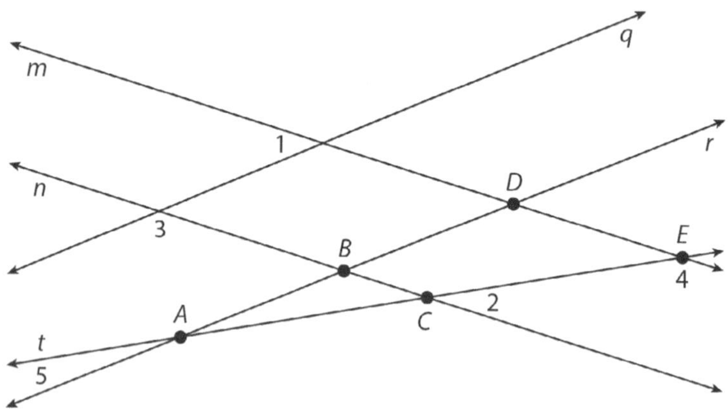

In the figure above, $m \parallel n$, $r \parallel q$, $m\angle 1 = 39°$, and $m\angle 2 = 26°$.

5

Find the measure of $\angle 3$. Ignore the degree symbol when gridding your answer.

6

Find the measure of $\angle BAC$. Ignore the degree symbol when gridding your answer.

7

If $BC = 4$, $DE = 10$, and $AC = 6$, what is CE?

8

Find the measure of $\angle 4$. Ignore the degree symbol when gridding your answer.

9

Suppose $AB = x - 3$ and $DB = 2x$. Find the value of x if the scale factor between $\triangle ABC$ and $\triangle ADE$ is 4.

Name ______________________ Date ______________ Class ______________

Know and apply theorems about vertical angles, triangles, and parallel lines cut by a transversal.

ANSWER SHEET

1. A B C D

2. A B C D

3. A B C D

4. A B C D

5.
/
.
0
1
2
3
4
5
6
7
8
9

6.
/
.
0
1
2
3
4
5
6
7
8
9

7.
/
.
0
1
2
3
4
5
6
7
8
9

8.
/
.
0
1
2
3
4
5
6
7
8
9

9.
/
.
0
1
2
3
4
5
6
7
8
9

Name ______________________ Date ____________ Class ____________

Solve real-world problems using the Pythagorean theorem and right triangle trigonometry.

SAMPLE MULTIPLE CHOICE

A taut cable extends at an angle from the top of a vertical pole to the ground. If the pole is 16 feet tall and the cable is 21 feet long, what is the distance from the base of the pole to the point where the cable touches the ground? Assume that the ground is horizontal. Round to the nearest tenth of a foot.

A) 12.9

B) 13.6

C) 14.1

D) 15.0

The pole, cable, and distance along the ground from the pole's base to the end of the cable form a right triangle. The Pythagorean theorem can be used to find the unknown distance *b*, where the length of the cable is the hypotenuse *c* of the right triangle.

$$a^2 + b^2 = c^2$$
$$(16)^2 + b^2 = (21)^2$$
$$256 + b^2 = 441$$
$$b^2 = 185$$
$$b \approx 13.6$$

So, the distance is about 13.6 feet.

The correct answer is B. A ○ B ● C ○ D ○

1

The Americans with Disabilities Act requires that a wheelchair and scooter ramp for business and public use has a minimum of 1 foot of ramp for each 1 inch of rise. What is the approximate angle of inclination of a ramp that has the maximum slope allowed?

A) 4.38°

B) 4.54°

C) 4.78°

D) 4.92°

2

A car leaves a parking lot and drives due north at a speed of 40 miles per hour. At the same time, a second car leaves the parking lot and drives due east at a speed of 50 miles per hour. Approximately how many miles apart are the two cars after 0.5 hour?

A) 27

B) 32

C) 41

D) 64

3

A television screen has an aspect ratio of 16:9 (the ratio of width to height). What is the height, to the nearest tenth of an inch, of a television screen with a 31-inch diagonal?

A) 14.8

B) 15.0

C) 15.2

D) 15.4

4

A 6-foot-tall observer stands 20 feet from the base of a tree. The angle of elevation from the observer's head to the top of the tree is 35°. What is the height of the tree to the nearest foot?

A) 14

B) 16

C) 18

D) 20

5

Two ships leave a port at the same time, one heading south and one heading west. After 1 hour, they are *x* miles apart. How many miles is each ship from the port?

A) x

B) $\frac{x\sqrt{2}}{2}$

C) $2x$

D) $\frac{x}{2}$

Name ________________________ Date ______________ Class ______________

SAMPLE GRID-IN

1 mile = 5,280 feet

A road is inclined at an angle of 5°. If you drive 1 mile along this road, by how much will your elevation increase? Round your answer to the nearest foot.

This situation can be modeled using a right triangle. The road forms the hypotenuse of the right triangle, and the angle between the hypotenuse and the horizontal leg is 5°. The length of the vertical leg is unknown.

Use the sine function to determine the length x of the vertical leg in feet.

$$\sin\theta = \frac{\text{opp}}{\text{hyp}}$$

$$\sin 5° = \frac{x}{5,280}$$

$$x = \sin 5° \cdot 5,280$$

$$\approx 460$$

So, you will gain 460 feet in elevation.

Grid in 460.

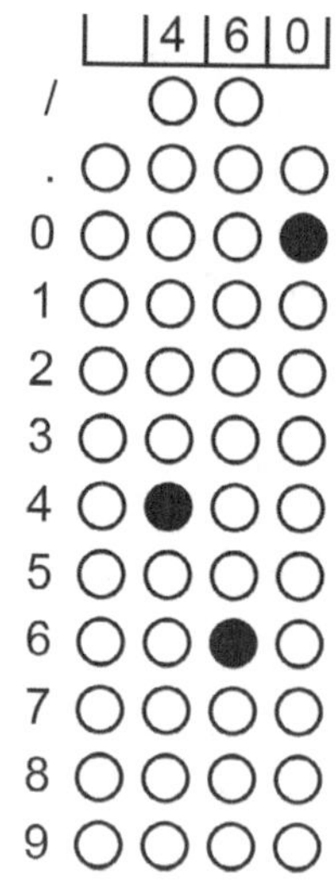

6

The Wolf Creek Pass on U.S. Highway 160 on the Continental Divide in Colorado has a maximum grade of 6.8%, where percent grade is the rise or fall per 100 horizontal units. What is the angle of inclination of the roadway where the maximum grade occurs? Round to the nearest tenth of a degree.

7

To get from Point A to Point B, an ant first walks in a direction perpendicular to the line through A and B. The ant then pivots and walks directly to B. Suppose the distance the ant walks in the direction perpendicular to the line through A and B is one-third of the total distance the ant walks. What is the angle measure of the turn the ant makes in order to head directly toward point B?

8

An ice cream cone has a diameter of 5 centimeters and a height of 12.5 centimeters. To the nearest tenth of a centimeter, what is the slant height of the cone?

9

The divergence of a laser beam is a measure of how much the beam expands as you move away from the transmitter. A certain beam has a divergence angle (full angle of opening) of 0.08°. To the nearest inch, what is the radius of the beam at a distance of 80 yards from the transmitter?

10

The Occupational Safety and Health Administration rules for portable ladder safety say that when leaning a ladder against a vertical wall, the base of the ladder should be one-quarter of the length of the ladder away from the wall. Suppose the upper end of a 12-foot ladder is to rest against a wall. To the nearest tenth of a foot, how high above the ground will that end be?

11

A guy wire is attached from the ground to the top of a tower. The tower is 100 feet high, and the guy wire makes an angle of 37° with the top of the tower. To the nearest foot, how long is the guy wire?

Name ______________________ Date ______________ Class ______________

Solve real-world problems using the Pythagorean theorem and right triangle trigonometry.

ANSWER SHEET

1. A B C D ○ ○ ○ ○

2. A B C D ○ ○ ○ ○

3. A B C D ○ ○ ○ ○

4. A B C D ○ ○ ○ ○

5. A B C D ○ ○ ○ ○

6. [grid-in: / ○○; . 0 1 2 3 4 5 6 7 8 9 ○○○○]

7. [grid-in: / ○○; . 0 1 2 3 4 5 6 7 8 9 ○○○○]

8. [grid-in: / ○○; . 0 1 2 3 4 5 6 7 8 9 ○○○○]

9. [grid-in: / ○○; . 0 1 2 3 4 5 6 7 8 9 ○○○○]

10. [grid-in: / ○○; . 0 1 2 3 4 5 6 7 8 9 ○○○○]

11. [grid-in: / ○○; . 0 1 2 3 4 5 6 7 8 9 ○○○○]

Name ______________________ Date ______________ Class ______________

Determine values of sine, cosine, and tangent by using similarity of triangles.

SAMPLE MULTIPLE CHOICE

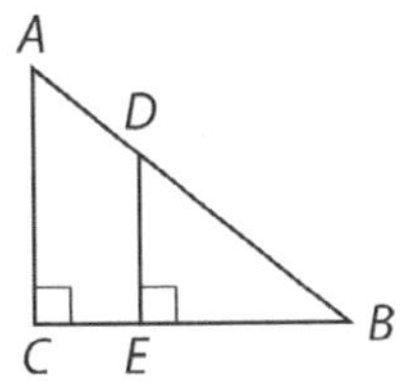

In the figure above, the length of $\overline{AC}$ is 6, the length of $\overline{DE}$ is 4, and the length of $\overline{EB}$ is 5. Find the value of $\sin A$ to the nearest hundredth.

A) 0.73
B) 0.78
C) 0.84
D) 0.88

To find the value of $\sin A$ directly, the lengths of $\overline{BC}$ and $\overline{AB}$ are needed. However, since $\triangle ABC$ and $\triangle DBE$ are similar, the measures of $\angle A$ and $\angle D$ are equal. Therefore, $\sin A = \sin D$. The value of $\sin D$ can be found using the given information. Begin by finding the length of $\overline{DB}$, the hypotenuse of $\triangle DBE$:

$$(DB)^2 = 4^2 + 5^2$$
$$(DB)^2 = 41$$
$$DB = \sqrt{41}$$

Then, find $\sin D$:

$$\sin D = \frac{EB}{DB} = \frac{5}{\sqrt{41}} \approx 0.78$$

The correct answer is B. A ○ B ● C ○ D ○

1

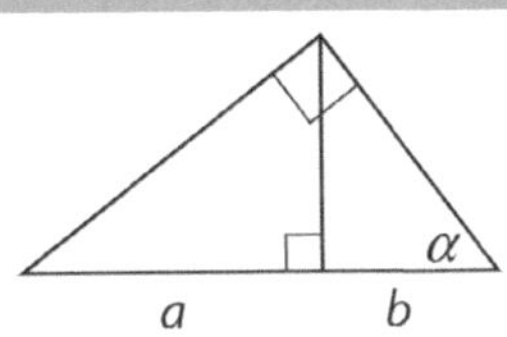

In the figure above, $a = 16$ and $b = 9$. Find the value of $\tan \alpha$.

A) $\frac{16}{9}$
B) $\frac{4}{3}$
C) $\frac{\sqrt{7}}{2}$
D) $\frac{\sqrt{5}}{2}$

2

The Eiffel Tower at the Paris Las Vegas Hotel is a half-scale replica of the Eiffel Tower in Paris, France. When the angle of elevation to the sun is 50°, the tower in France casts a shadow 272 meters in length. To the nearest meter, how tall is the replica tower in Las Vegas?

A) 162
B) 168
C) 172
D) 178

3

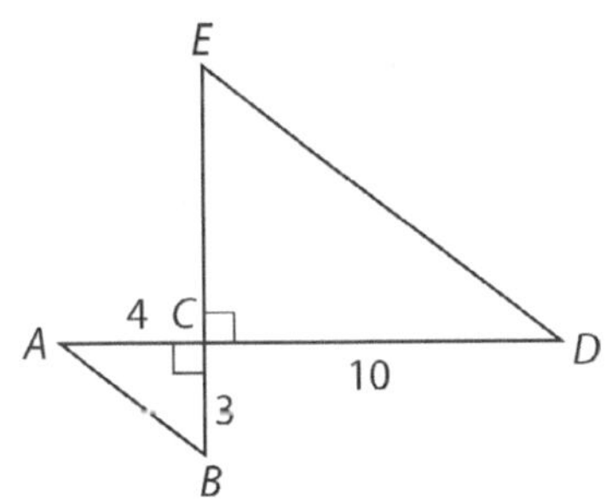

Right triangle ABC is similar to right triangle DEC. Find the value of $\sin D$.

A) 0.6
B) 0.67
C) 0.75
D) 0.8

4

When the angle of elevation to the sun is 61°, a building's shadow is 50 feet long. The shadow of a second building is three times as long. How tall is the second building, to the nearest foot?

A) 83
B) 90
C) 246
D) 271

Name ______________________ Date ______________ Class ______________

SAMPLE GRID-IN

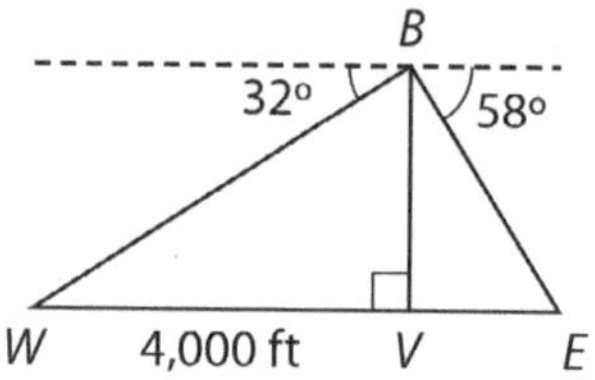

A hot air balloon is flying above a river, following its path. The angle of depression from the balloon B to the western edge W of the river is 32°, as shown in the figure. The angle of depression to the eastern edge E is 58°. The balloon is directly above a point V that is 4,000 feet east of the western edge of the river. What is the horizontal distance of the balloon from the eastern edge of the river (the distance EV), to the nearest foot?

Right triangle BVW has $\overline{BW}$ as its hypotenuse. Since the angle of depression to the western edge is 32°, the angle at vertex W is also 32°. From this, the height of the balloon can be calculated:

$$\tan 32^\circ = \frac{BV}{4{,}000}$$

$$BV = 4{,}000 \tan 32^\circ \approx 2{,}499$$

Observe that triangles BVW and EVB are similar:

$$\frac{EV}{BV} = \frac{BV}{WV}$$

$$\frac{EV}{2{,}499} = \frac{2{,}499}{4{,}000}$$

$$EV = \frac{2{,}499^2}{4{,}000} \approx 1{,}561$$

So, the distance is 1,561 feet.

Grid in 1561.

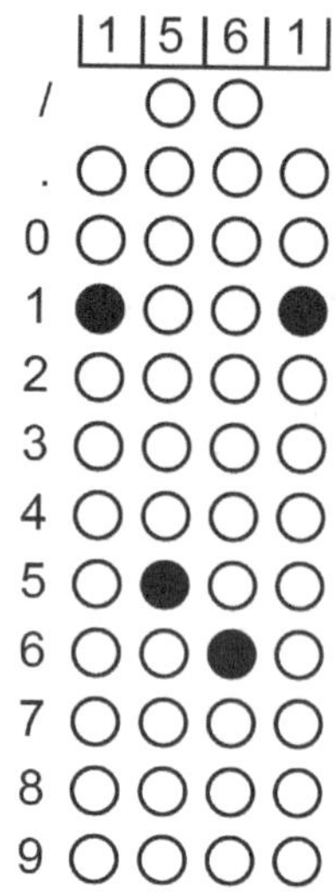

5

When the angle of elevation to the sun is 49°, Naomi's shadow is 5 feet long. The shadow of a nearby tree is eight times as long as her shadow. How tall is the tree, to the nearest foot?

6

Right triangle ABC is similar to right triangle EFG. Side BC has measure 40 and hypotenuse AC has measure 41. Find the exact value of $\sin G$.

7

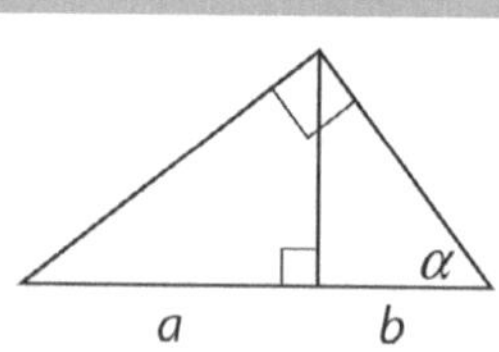

In the figure shown, $a = 10$ and $b = 8$. Find the exact value of $\cos \alpha$.

8

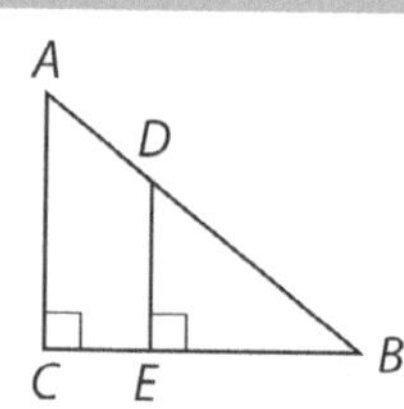

In the figure above, the length of $\overline{AC}$ is 7, the length of $\overline{DE}$ is 5, and the length of $\overline{EB}$ is 8. Find the value of $\cos A$ to the nearest hundredth.

9

A guy wire that is 27 feet long is attached to the top of a pole. The wire forms a 39° angle with the pole. Another wire that is parallel to the first wire is attached to the pole one-third of the way up from the ground. What is the distance from the ground to the point where this second wire is attached to the pole, to the nearest tenth of a foot?

Name ______________________ Date ______________ Class ______________

Determine values of sine, cosine, and tangent by using similarity of triangles.

ANSWER SHEET

1. A B C D

2. A B C D

3. A B C D

4. A B C D

5. / . 0 1 2 3 4 5 6 7 8 9

6. / . 0 1 2 3 4 5 6 7 8 9

7. / . 0 1 2 3 4 5 6 7 8 9

8. / . 0 1 2 3 4 5 6 7 8 9

9. / . 0 1 2 3 4 5 6 7 8 9

Name ______________________ Date ______________ Class______________

Calculate the remaining values in a right triangle when given one side length and one acute angle measure.

SAMPLE MULTIPLE CHOICE

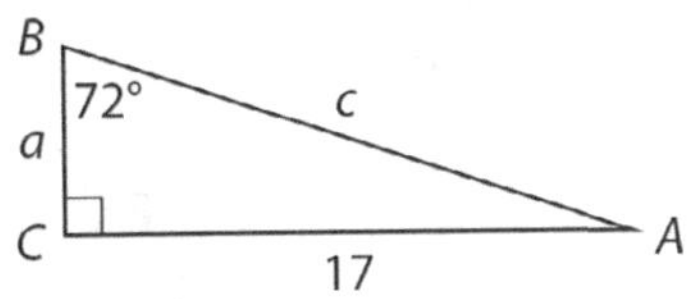

Find the value of c in the figure above. Round to the nearest tenth.

A) 18.1
B) 17.9
C) 17.7
D) 17.3

The measure of angle B is given, as is the length of the side opposite angle B. The length of the hypotenuse, c, must be found. The trigonometric function that involves an angle, the side opposite it, and the hypotenuse is the sine function. Use the sine function to find the value of c.

$$\sin \theta = \frac{\text{opp}}{\text{hyp}}$$

$$\sin 72^\circ = \frac{17}{c}$$

$$c = \frac{17}{\sin 72^\circ} \approx 17.9$$

The correct answer is B. A ○ B ● C ○ D ○

Questions 1–3 refer to the following figure.

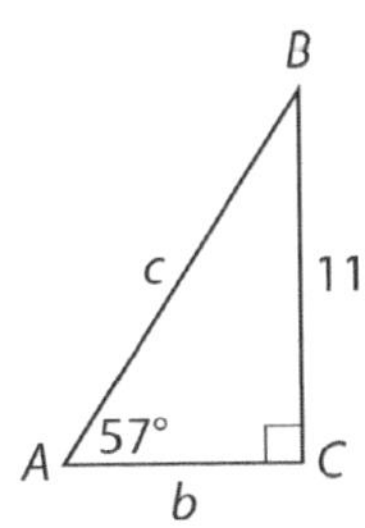

1

Find the value of c to the nearest tenth.

A) 7.1 C) 14.6
B) 13.1 D) 20.2

2

Find the value of b to the nearest tenth.

A) 7.1 C) 14.6
B) 13.1 D) 20.2

3

What is the measure of angle B?

A) 21° C) 29°
B) 23° D) 33°

Questions 4–6 refer to the following figure.

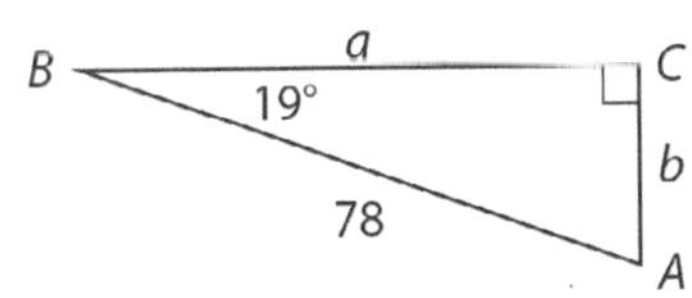

4

Find the value of b to the nearest tenth.

A) 25.4 C) 71.6
B) 26.9 D) 73.7

5

Find the value of a to the nearest tenth.

A) 25.4 C) 71.6
B) 26.9 D) 73.8

6

What is the measure of angle A?

A) 65° C) 71°
B) 68° D) 81°

Name ______________________ Date ______________ Class ______________

SAMPLE GRID-IN

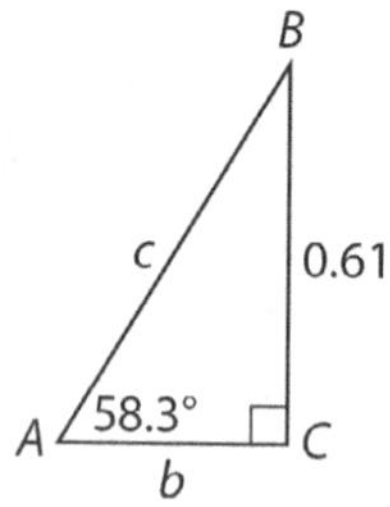

Find the value of b in the figure above. Round to the nearest hundredth.

The measure of angle A and the length of the side opposite angle A are both known. The length of the side adjacent to angle A is to be found. The trigonometric function that involves an angle, and both its opposite and adjacent sides is the tangent function. Use the tangent function to find the value of b.

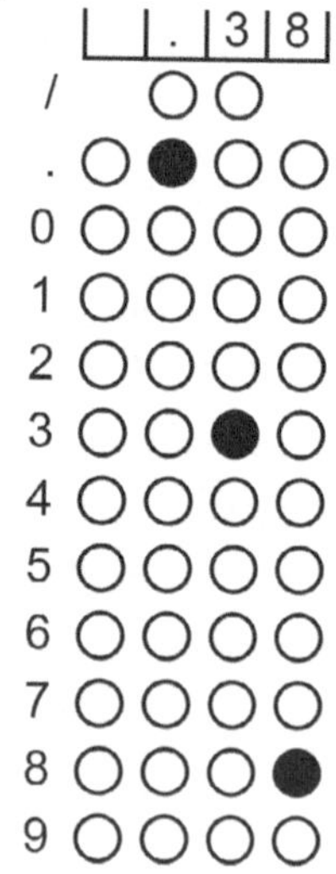

$$\tan\theta = \frac{\text{opp}}{\text{adj}}$$

$$\tan 58.3° = \frac{0.61}{b}$$

$$b \cdot \tan 58.3° = 0.61$$

$$b = \frac{0.61}{\tan 58.3°} \approx 0.38$$

The correct answer is 0.38.

Grid in .38.

Questions 7–9 refer to the following figure.

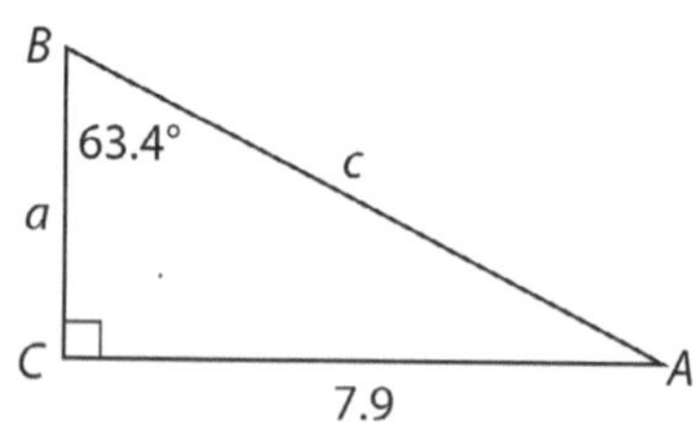

7

Find the value of c to the nearest tenth.

8

Find the value of a to the nearest tenth.

9

Find the measure of angle A. Ignore the degree symbol when gridding your answer.

Questions 10–12 refer to the following figure.

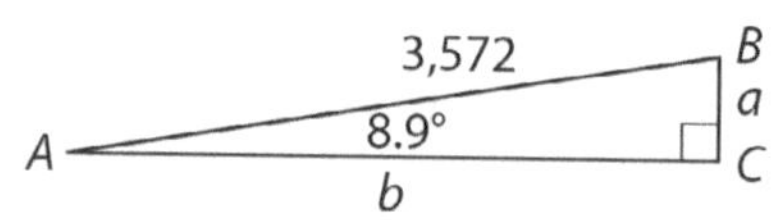

10

Find the value of b to the nearest whole number.

11

Find the value of a to the nearest whole number.

12

What is the measure of angle B? Ignore the degree symbol when gridding your answer.

Name ______________________ Date ______________ Class ______________

Calculate the remaining values in a right triangle when given one side length and one acute angle measure.

ANSWER SHEET

1. A B C D
2. A B C D
3. A B C D
4. A B C D
5. A B C D
6. A B C D
7. / . 0 1 2 3 4 5 6 7 8 9
8. / . 0 1 2 3 4 5 6 7 8 9
9. / . 0 1 2 3 4 5 6 7 8 9
10. / . 0 1 2 3 4 5 6 7 8 9
11. / . 0 1 2 3 4 5 6 7 8 9
12. / . 0 1 2 3 4 5 6 7 8 9

Name ______________________ Date ______________ Class ______________

Use the relationship between sine and cosine of complementary angles to solve problems.

SAMPLE MULTIPLE CHOICE

$\triangle DEF$ has a right angle at vertex D. If $\sin E = \frac{1}{5}$, what is the value of $\cos F$?

A) $90 - \frac{1}{5}$

B) $\frac{1}{5}$

C) $\frac{2}{5}$

D) $\frac{4}{5}$

Draw right triangle DEF with the side opposite vertex E having a length of 1 and the hypotenuse having a length of 5.

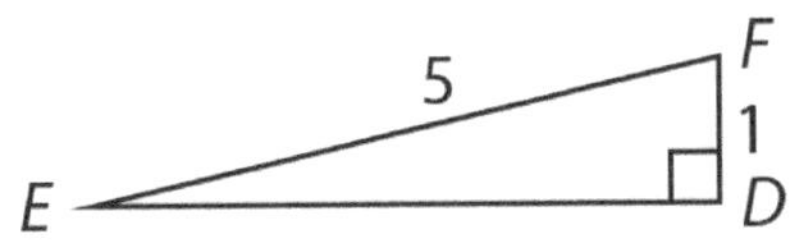

The cosine function involves the side adjacent to an angle and the hypotenuse. Notice that the side adjacent to vertex F is also the side opposite vertex E. Therefore, $\cos F = \sin E = \frac{1}{5}$.

The correct answer is B. A B C D

Time Saving Tip: The question can be quickly answered if you recognize that since angles E and F are the acute angles in a right triangle, then $\cos F = \sin E$.

1

In a right triangle, one of the acute angles has a measure of $\alpha°$. If $\cos \alpha° = 0.25$, what is the value of $\sin(90° - \alpha°)$?

A) 0.75 C) 0.25
B) 0.5 D) 0.125

2

$\triangle PQR$ has a right angle at vertex Q. If $\cos P = 0.38$, what is $\sin R$?

A) 0.38 C) $90 - P$
B) 0.62 D) $90 - 0.38$

3

Solve the following equation for θ.

$$\sin(\theta + 10°) = \cos \theta$$

A) 10° C) 40°
B) 20° D) 80°

4

$\triangle RST$ has a right angle at vertex S. If $\sin R = x$, what is $\cos T$?

A) $1 - x$ C) x
B) $1 - x^2$ D) $90 - x$

5

In a right triangle, one of the acute angles has a measure of $\beta°$. If $\cos \beta° = x$ and $\sin(90° - \beta°) = y$, what is the relationship between x and y?

A) $x^2 + y^2 = 1$ C) $x + y = 1$
B) $x + y = 90$ D) $x = y$

6

Solve the following equation for θ.

$$\sin(2\theta - 35°) = \cos(\theta + 5°)$$

A) 30° C) 50°
B) 40° D) 60°

Name ______________________ Date ______________ Class______________

SAMPLE GRID-IN

Solve the following equation for θ. Ignore the degree symbol when gridding your answer.

$$\sin \theta = \cos(\theta + 84°)$$

Complementary angles satisfy the relationship $\sin \theta = \cos(90° - \theta)$.

So the value of θ can be found by recognizing that the argument of the cosine function must be the complement of the argument for the sine function, θ. That is,

$$\theta + 84° = 90° - \theta$$

Solve this equation for θ.

$$\theta + 84° = 90° - \theta$$
$$2\theta = 90° - 84°$$
$$2\theta = 6°$$
$$\theta = 3°$$

So, the value of θ is 3°.

Grid in 3.

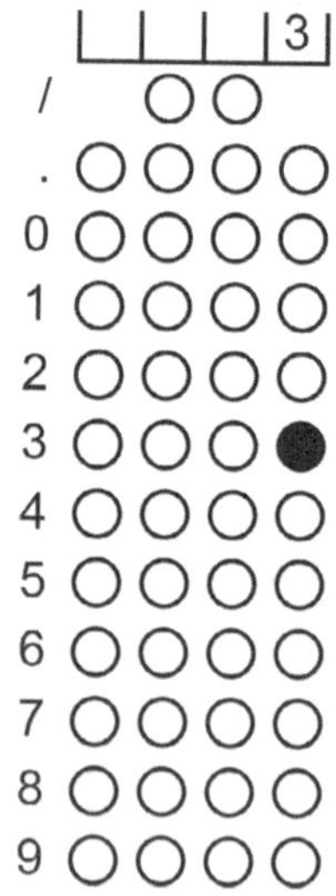

7

Solve the following equation for θ. Ignore the degree symbol when gridding your answer.

$$\sin(\theta - 18°) = \cos \theta$$

8

In a right triangle, one of the acute angles has measure $\alpha°$. If $\cos \alpha° = \frac{2}{7}$, what is the value of $\sin(90° - \alpha°)$? Give an exact answer.

9

$$\sin 62° = \cos \theta$$

Solve the equation above for θ. Ignore the degree symbol when gridding your answer.

10

$\triangle ABC$ has a right angle at vertex C. If $\cos A = 0.84$, what is $\sin B$?

11

Solve the following equation for θ. Ignore the degree symbol when gridding your answer.

$$\sin(\theta + 10°) = \cos(2\theta - 55°)$$

12

$\triangle EFG$ has a right angle at vertex E. If $\cos F = 0.3$, what is the value of $\cos F + \sin G$?

13

Solve $\sin(\theta + 26.2°) = \cos(3\theta - 58.6°)$ for θ. Ignore the degree symbol when gridding your answer.

14

In a right triangle, one acute angle has measure $(6° - \beta°)$. If $\cos(6° - \beta°) = 0.19$, what is the value of $\sin(84° + \beta°)$?

Name ______________________ Date ______________ Class ______________

Use the relationship between sine and cosine of complementary angles to solve problems.

ANSWER SHEET

1. A B C D ○ ○ ○ ○

2. A B C D ○ ○ ○ ○

3. A B C D ○ ○ ○ ○

4. A B C D ○ ○ ○ ○

5. A B C D ○ ○ ○ ○

6. A B C D ○ ○ ○ ○

7. |_|_|_|_|_|

/ ○○
. ○○○○
0 ○○○○
1 ○○○○
2 ○○○○
3 ○○○○
4 ○○○○
5 ○○○○
6 ○○○○
7 ○○○○
8 ○○○○
9 ○○○○

8. |_|_|_|_|_|

/ ○○
. ○○○○
0 ○○○○
1 ○○○○
2 ○○○○
3 ○○○○
4 ○○○○
5 ○○○○
6 ○○○○
7 ○○○○
8 ○○○○
9 ○○○○

9. |_|_|_|_|_|

/ ○○
. ○○○○
0 ○○○○
1 ○○○○
2 ○○○○
3 ○○○○
4 ○○○○
5 ○○○○
6 ○○○○
7 ○○○○
8 ○○○○
9 ○○○○

10. |_|_|_|_|_|

/ ○○
. ○○○○
0 ○○○○
1 ○○○○
2 ○○○○
3 ○○○○
4 ○○○○
5 ○○○○
6 ○○○○
7 ○○○○
8 ○○○○
9 ○○○○

11. |_|_|_|_|_|

/ ○○
. ○○○○
0 ○○○○
1 ○○○○
2 ○○○○
3 ○○○○
4 ○○○○
5 ○○○○
6 ○○○○
7 ○○○○
8 ○○○○
9 ○○○○

12. |_|_|_|_|_|

/ ○○
. ○○○○
0 ○○○○
1 ○○○○
2 ○○○○
3 ○○○○
4 ○○○○
5 ○○○○
6 ○○○○
7 ○○○○
8 ○○○○
9 ○○○○

13. |_|_|_|_|_|

/ ○○
. ○○○○
0 ○○○○
1 ○○○○
2 ○○○○
3 ○○○○
4 ○○○○
5 ○○○○
6 ○○○○
7 ○○○○
8 ○○○○
9 ○○○○

14. |_|_|_|_|_|

/ ○○
. ○○○○
0 ○○○○
1 ○○○○
2 ○○○○
3 ○○○○
4 ○○○○
5 ○○○○
6 ○○○○
7 ○○○○
8 ○○○○
9 ○○○○

Name ____________________ Date ____________ Class ____________

Apply properties of special right triangles to find lengths and trigonometric ratios for 30°, 45°, and 60° angles.

SAMPLE MULTIPLE CHOICE

A football is kicked into the air at an initial angle of 60° from level ground with an initial velocity of 18 meters per second. If the velocity is broken into its horizontal and vertical components, what is the vertical component of the velocity, in meters per second?

A) $18\sqrt{2}$

B) $9\sqrt{3}$

C) $9\sqrt{2}$

D) 9

The side lengths in a 30°-60°-90° triangle are related as shown in the figure. The initial velocity of 18 meters per second corresponds to the length of the hypotenuse, $2x$. The horizontal and vertical components of the velocity correspond to the horizontal and vertical legs, respectively.

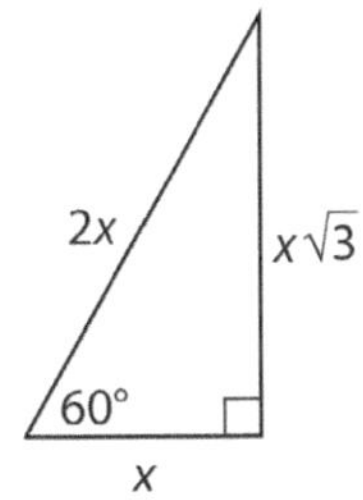

Since $18 = 2x$, the horizontal component of the velocity is $x = 9$ meters per second. Therefore, the vertical component is $9\sqrt{3}$ meters per second.

The correct answer is B. A B C D ○●○○

1

An equilateral triangle has a side length of 6 centimeters. What is the altitude of the triangle, in centimeters?

A) 3

B) $2\sqrt{3}$

C) $3\sqrt{2}$

D) $3\sqrt{3}$

2

Tracy is standing 2,000 meters from the base of a mountain. Suppose his eyes are at the same elevation as the base of the mountain. From his location, the angle of elevation to the peak of the mountain is 45°. How high, in meters, above the base is the peak of the mountain?

A) 2,000

B) $1{,}000\sqrt{3}$

C) $1{,}000\sqrt{2}$

D) 1,000

3

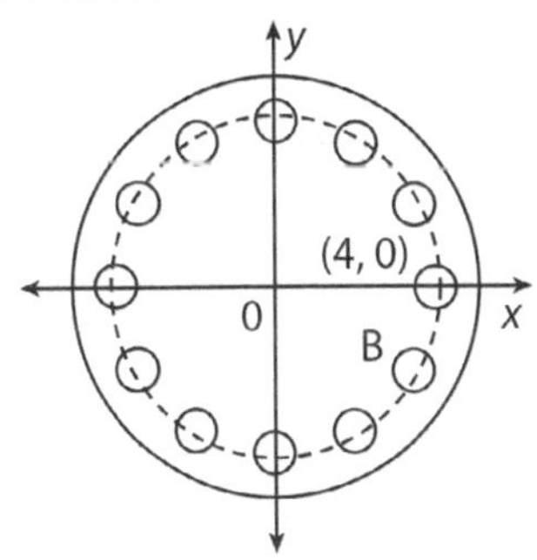

A machined part has holes in a circular pattern every 30°, as seen in the figure shown above. What is the x-coordinate of the hole in the location labeled B?

A) 2 C) $2\sqrt{3}$

B) $2\sqrt{2}$ D) $4\sqrt{3}$

4

Refer to the figure shown in Question 3. What is the y-coordinate of the hole in the location labeled B?

A) $-\sqrt{3}$ C) $-2\sqrt{2}$

B) -2 D) $-2\sqrt{3}$

Name ____________________ Date ____________ Class ____________

SAMPLE GRID-IN

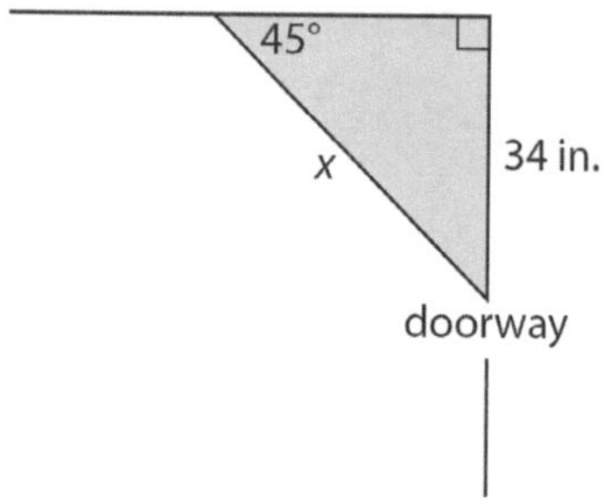

A homeowner plans to purchase a new flat-screen television. The television will sit on a stand built into the corner of a room. The top of the stand is represented by the shaded right triangle in the figure above. Due to a doorway, the top of the stand cannot have a side length greater than 34 inches. To the nearest tenth of an inch, what is the maximum length x of the long side of the top of the stand?

Recognize that the length x is the hypotenuse of a 45°-45°-90° right triangle. The ratio of the length of the hypotenuse to the length of a side in such a triangle is $\sqrt{2}:1$.

Set up a proportion to find the length x:

$$\frac{x}{34} = \frac{\sqrt{2}}{1}$$

$$x = 34\sqrt{2}$$

$$\approx 48.1$$

So, the maximum length of the long side of the top of the stand is approximately 48.1 inches.

Grid in 48.1.

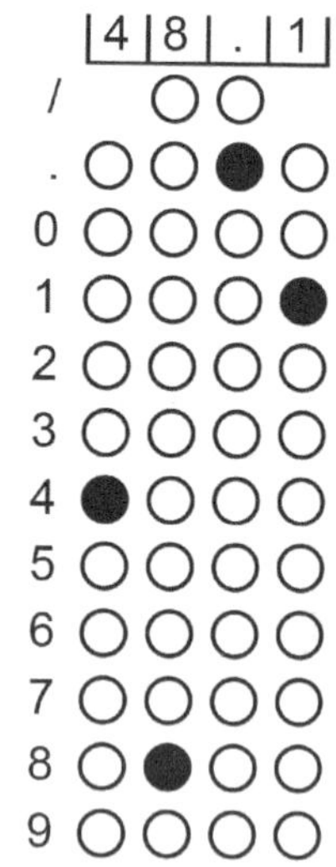

5

An escalator was built with an angle of depression of 30°. It descends at a rate of 100 feet per minute. If the vertical rise of the escalator is 60 feet, how many seconds does it take for a person riding the escalator to travel its full length?

6

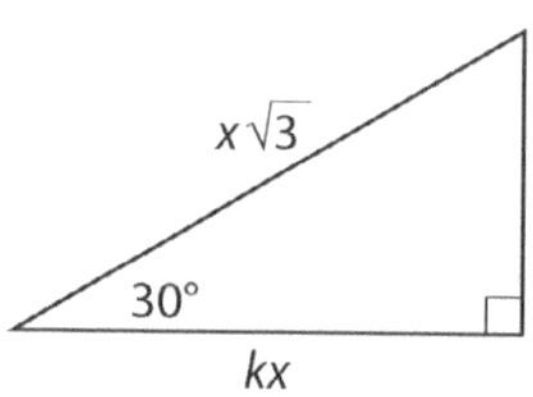

What is the value of k in the figure above?

7

A football is thrown with an initial velocity of 38 miles per hour at an angle of 30° from the horizontal. What is the vertical component of the velocity, in miles per hour?

8

A square has a diagonal of length 7. What is the area of the square?

9

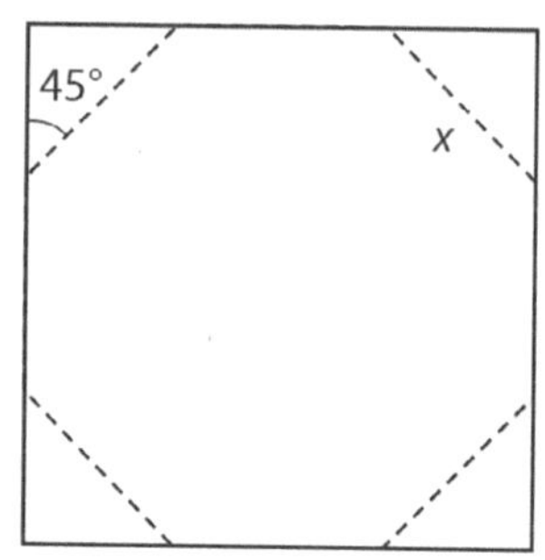

A square has sides 9 inches long. Its four corners are cut off at 45° angles, as shown in the figure above, to form a regular octagon. What is the value of x, the length of each side of the regular octagon? Round to the nearest hundredth of an inch.

Name ______________________ Date ______________ Class ______________

Apply properties of special right triangles to find lengths and trigonometric ratios for 30°, 45°, and 60° angles.

ANSWER SHEET

1. A B C D
○ ○ ○ ○

2. A B C D
○ ○ ○ ○

3. A B C D
○ ○ ○ ○

4. A B C D
○ ○ ○ ○

5. | | | | |
/ ○ ○
. ○ ○ ○ ○
0 ○ ○ ○ ○
1 ○ ○ ○ ○
2 ○ ○ ○ ○
3 ○ ○ ○ ○
4 ○ ○ ○ ○
5 ○ ○ ○ ○
6 ○ ○ ○ ○
7 ○ ○ ○ ○
8 ○ ○ ○ ○
9 ○ ○ ○ ○

6. | | | | |
/ ○ ○
. ○ ○ ○ ○
0 ○ ○ ○ ○
1 ○ ○ ○ ○
2 ○ ○ ○ ○
3 ○ ○ ○ ○
4 ○ ○ ○ ○
5 ○ ○ ○ ○
6 ○ ○ ○ ○
7 ○ ○ ○ ○
8 ○ ○ ○ ○
9 ○ ○ ○ ○

7. | | | | |
/ ○ ○
. ○ ○ ○ ○
0 ○ ○ ○ ○
1 ○ ○ ○ ○
2 ○ ○ ○ ○
3 ○ ○ ○ ○
4 ○ ○ ○ ○
5 ○ ○ ○ ○
6 ○ ○ ○ ○
7 ○ ○ ○ ○
8 ○ ○ ○ ○
9 ○ ○ ○ ○

8. | | | | |
/ ○ ○
. ○ ○ ○ ○
0 ○ ○ ○ ○
1 ○ ○ ○ ○
2 ○ ○ ○ ○
3 ○ ○ ○ ○
4 ○ ○ ○ ○
5 ○ ○ ○ ○
6 ○ ○ ○ ○
7 ○ ○ ○ ○
8 ○ ○ ○ ○
9 ○ ○ ○ ○

9. | | | | |
/ ○ ○
. ○ ○ ○ ○
0 ○ ○ ○ ○
1 ○ ○ ○ ○
2 ○ ○ ○ ○
3 ○ ○ ○ ○
4 ○ ○ ○ ○
5 ○ ○ ○ ○
6 ○ ○ ○ ○
7 ○ ○ ○ ○
8 ○ ○ ○ ○
9 ○ ○ ○ ○

Name ______________________ Date ______________ Class ______________

Solve problems using definitions, properties, and theorems involving circles and parts of circles.

SAMPLE MULTIPLE CHOICE

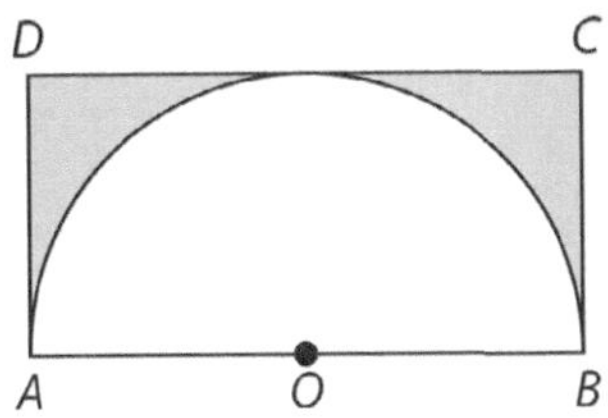

In the figure above, a semicircle with center O is inscribed in a rectangle. If $OB = 6.2$ inches, find the area of the shaded portion of the figure, to the nearest tenth of an inch.

A) 15.5
B) 16.5
C) 57.4
D) 60.4

The area of the shaded part will be the difference between the area of the rectangle and the area of the semicircle.

Since $OB = 6.2$ inches, then $AB = 2(6.2) = 12.4$ inches and $DA = 6.2$ inches.

The area of the rectangle is $AB \cdot DA = 12.4(6.2) = 76.88$ square inches.

The area of the semicircle is $\frac{1}{2}\pi r^2 = \frac{1}{2}\pi(6.2)^2 \approx 60.38$ square inches.

So, the approximate area of the shaded portion is $76.88 - 60.38 = 16.5$ square inches.

The correct answer is B. A B C D ○ ● ○ ○

Questions 1–4 refer to the following information.

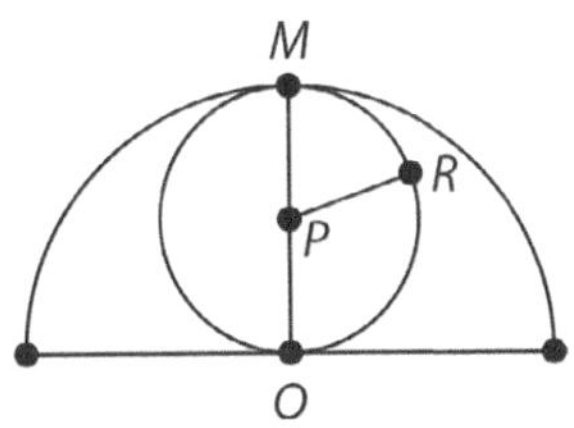

In the figure above, $MO = 50$ yards, point O is the center of the semicircle, point P is the center of the circle, and $m\angle OPR = \frac{11\pi}{18}$ radians.

1

What is the area, to the nearest square yard, of circle P?

A) 1,570
B) 1,963
C) 7,854
D) 8,000

2

What is the perimeter, to the nearest yard, of the semicircle centered at O?

A) 129
B) 157
C) 257
D) 314

3

What is the area, to the nearest square yard, of the sector OPR?

A) 600
B) 981
C) 1,078
D) 1,910

4

What is the length, to the nearest yard, of $\overset{\frown}{MR}$?

A) 31
B) 48
C) 61
D) 96

Name ______________________ Date ______________ Class ______________

SAMPLE GRID-IN

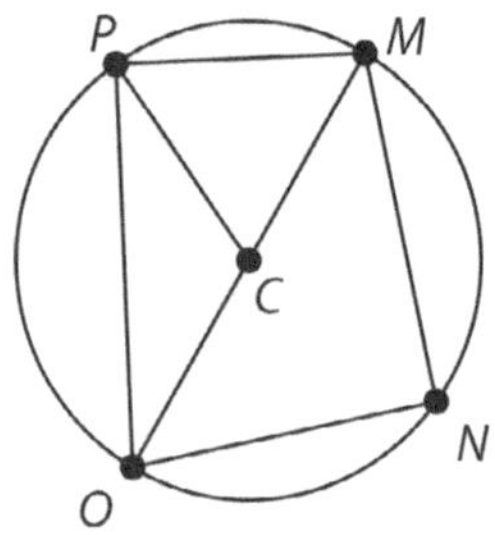

The quadrilateral *MNOP* is inscribed in the circle *C*. If $m\angle PCM = 65°$, what is the measure of $\angle POM$?

Notice that $\angle PCM$ is a central angle and $\angle POM$ is an inscribed angle. Then by the Inscribed Angle Theorem:

$$m\angle POM = \frac{1}{2} m\angle PCM$$
$$= \frac{1}{2}(65°)$$
$$= 32.5°$$

So, the measure of $\angle POM$ is $32.5°$.

Grid in 32.5.

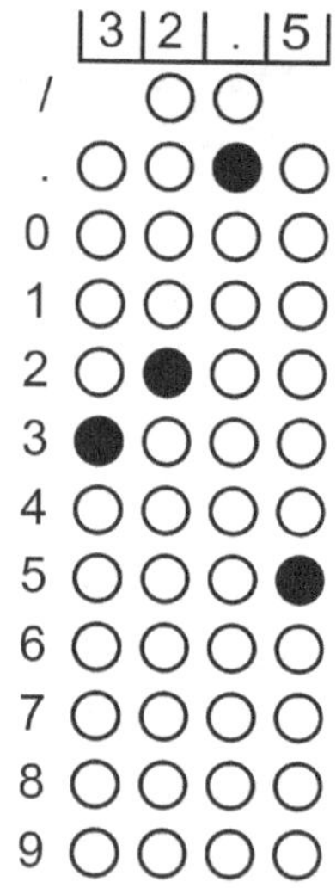

Questions 5–7 refer to the following information.

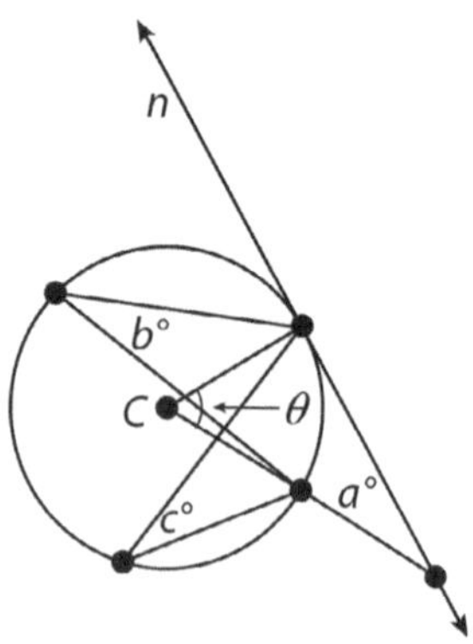

In the figure above, line *n* is tangent to the circle *C*, and $\theta = 26°$.

5

What is the value of *a*?

6

What is the value of *b*?

7

What is the value of *c*?

8

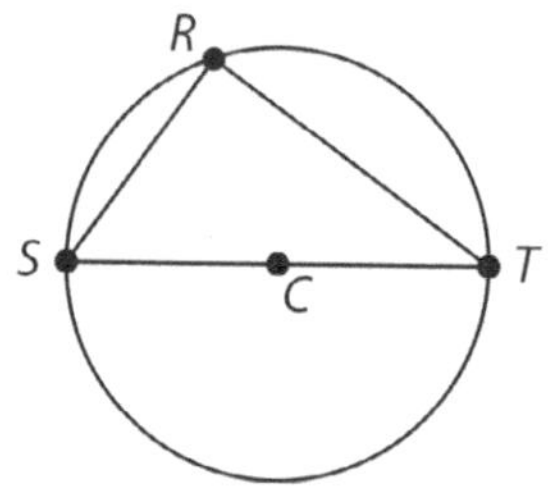

Given the circle centered at *C* above, if $m\angle SRT = 7x + 55$, determine *x*.

9

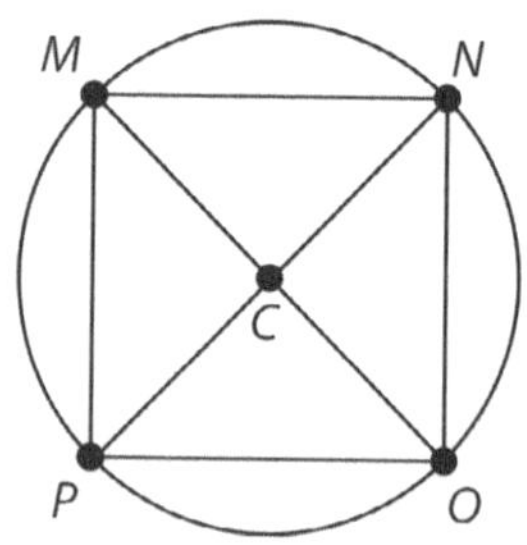

In the figure above, $CN = 4$ centimeters and $m\angle MCN = 90°$. What is the length, in centimeters, of the major arc *MPN*? Round to the nearest tenth.

Name ______________________ Date ____________ Class ____________

Solve problems using definitions, properties, and theorems involving circles and parts of circles.

ANSWER SHEET

1. A B C D
2. A B C D
3. A B C D
4. A B C D
5. / . 0 1 2 3 4 5 6 7 8 9
6. / . 0 1 2 3 4 5 6 7 8 9
7. / . 0 1 2 3 4 5 6 7 8 9
8. / . 0 1 2 3 4 5 6 7 8 9
9. / . 0 1 2 3 4 5 6 7 8 9

Name ______________________ Date ______________ Class______________

Use trigonometric ratios in the unit circle and radian measure to solve problems.

SAMPLE MULTIPLE CHOICE	
In a circle of radius 4, a central angle intercepts an arc of length 3. What is the measure of the central angle in radians? A) $\frac{1}{4}$ C) $\frac{3}{4}$ B) $\frac{1}{3}$ D) $\frac{4}{3}$	If *s* is the arc length intercepted by a central angle measuring θ radians in a circle of radius *r*, then $s = r \cdot \theta$. Substitute $s = 3$ and $r = 4$ into this formula and solve for θ: $s = r \cdot \theta$ $3 = 4 \cdot \theta$ $\frac{3}{4} = \theta$ The correct answer is C. A ○ B ○ C ● D ○

1

In a circle of radius 6, a central angle intercepts an arc of length 9. What is the measure of the central angle in radians?

A) $\frac{1}{3}$ C) $\frac{2}{3}$

B) $\frac{1}{2}$ D) $\frac{3}{2}$

2

The *y*-coordinate of a point on the unit circle is $-\frac{1}{2}$. Which of the following could be the *x* coordinate of the point?

A) $\frac{\sqrt{3}}{2}$ C) $\frac{1}{2}$

B) $\frac{\sqrt{2}}{2}$ D) 0

3

Let θ be the least positive angle measure, in radians, for which $\sin\theta = \cos\theta$. What is the measure of the angle that is supplementary to the angle with measure θ?

A) $\frac{\pi}{4}$ C) $\frac{3\pi}{4}$

B) $\frac{2\pi}{3}$ D) $\frac{5\pi}{6}$

4

In a circle of radius 8, what is the area of the sector formed by a central angle that measures $\frac{\pi}{2}$ radians?

A) 8π C) 32π

B) 16π D) 64π

5

In a circle of radius 18, a central angle measures $\frac{5\pi}{6}$ radians. What is the length of the arc the angle intercepts?

A) $\frac{5\pi}{108}$ C) 15π

B) $\frac{5\pi}{6}$ D) $\frac{108\pi}{5}$

6

A central angle is drawn in standard position on a unit circle in the *xy*-plane. The terminal side of the angle crosses the unit circle at the point (a, b). If $ab = \frac{\sqrt{3}}{4}$, which of the following could NOT be the radian measure of the central angle?

A) $\frac{\pi}{6}$ C) $\frac{2\pi}{3}$

B) $\frac{\pi}{3}$ D) $\frac{7\pi}{6}$

Name ______________________ Date ______________ Class______________

SAMPLE GRID-IN

In a circle with center O, the measure of central angle POQ is $\frac{3\pi}{4}$ radians. What fraction of the area of the entire circle is the area of the sector formed by $\angle POQ$?

The central angle associated with a full circle has measure 2π radians. Divide the radian measure of $\angle POQ$ by 2π to find the fraction:

$$\frac{m\angle POQ}{2\pi} = \frac{\frac{3\pi}{4}}{2\pi} = \frac{3\pi}{8\pi} = \frac{3}{8}$$

So, the area of the sector is $\frac{3}{8}$ of the area of the entire circle.

Grid in 3/8 or .375.

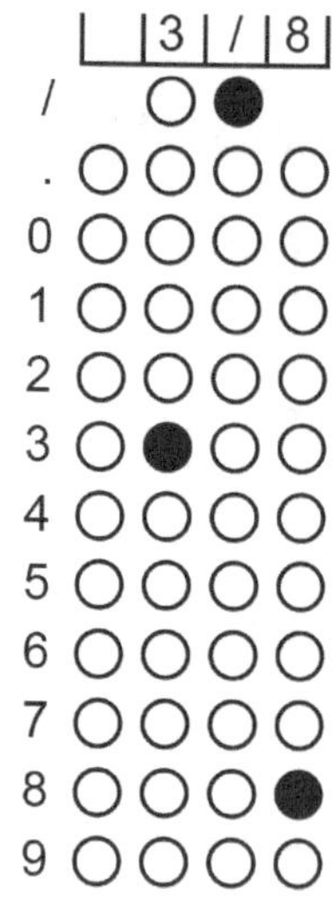

7

In a circle with center O, the measure of central angle XOY is $\frac{5\pi}{6}$ radians. The area of the sector formed by $\angle XOY$ is what fraction of the area of the circle?

8

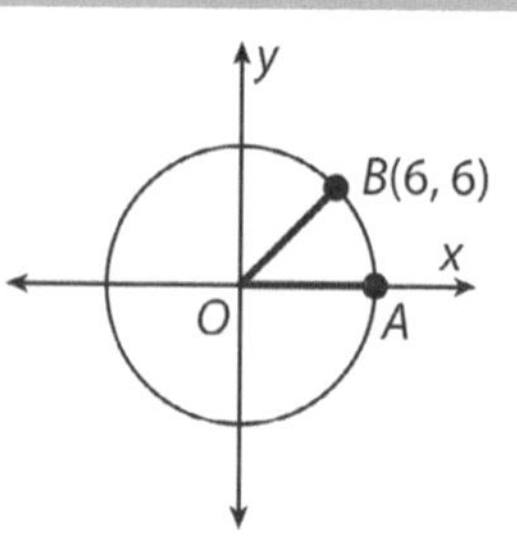

In the figure above, point O is the center of the circle and the measure of $\angle AOB$ is $\frac{\pi}{k}$ radians. What is the value of k?

9

A central angle of a circle measures $\frac{5\pi}{6}$ radians. It intercepts an arc of length 20π. What is the radius of the circle?

10

Circle C has radius 12. If central angle KCL forms a sector with area 180, what is the measure of angle KCL in radians?

11

Angles A and B are complementary. The measure of angle A is $\frac{5\pi}{16}$ radians. If the measure of angle B is $n\pi$, what is the value of n?

12

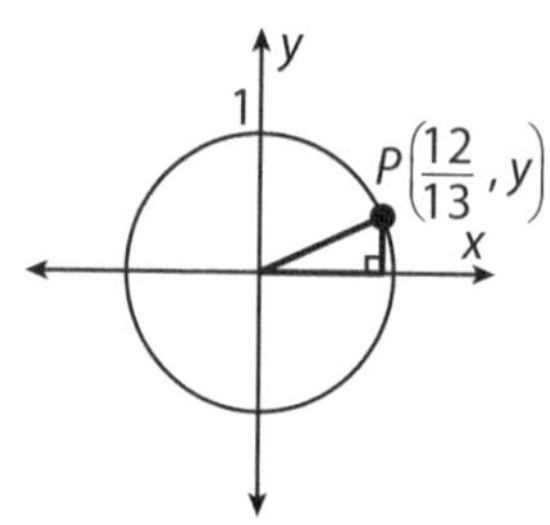

What is the y-coordinate of point P on the unit circle shown above?

13

$$\frac{\sin\left(\frac{\pi}{4}\right) \cdot \cos\left(\frac{\pi}{3}\right)}{\tan(0) + 2 \cdot \cos\left(\frac{\pi}{4}\right)}$$

If the unit circle is used to find the value of each trigonometric ratio in the expression above, what is the exact value of the expression?

Name ______________________ Date ______________ Class ______________

Use trigonometric ratios in the unit circle and radian measure to solve problems.

ANSWER SHEET

1. A B C D ○ ○ ○ ○
2. A B C D ○ ○ ○ ○
3. A B C D ○ ○ ○ ○
4. A B C D ○ ○ ○ ○
5. A B C D ○ ○ ○ ○
6. A B C D ○ ○ ○ ○

7. Grid-in: / ○○; . ○○○○; 0–9 ○○○○

8. Grid-in: / ○○; . ○○○○; 0–9 ○○○○

9. Grid-in: / ○○; . ○○○○; 0–9 ○○○○

10. Grid-in: / ○○; . ○○○○; 0–9 ○○○○

11. Grid-in: / ○○; . ○○○○; 0–9 ○○○○

12. Grid-in: / ○○; . ○○○○; 0–9 ○○○○

13. Grid-in: / ○○; . ○○○○; 0–9 ○○○○

Name ______________________ Date ______________ Class______________

Represent a circle in the *xy*-plane with an equation.

SAMPLE MULTIPLE CHOICE

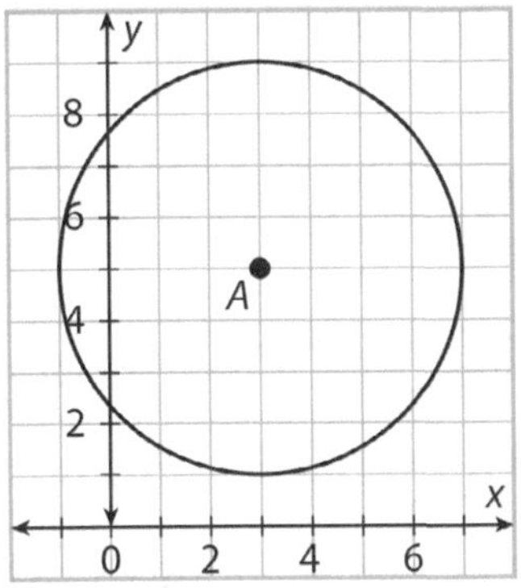

Which of the following is an equation for circle *A* shown in the figure above?

A) $(x-3)^2+(y-5)^2=4$

B) $(x-3)^2+(y-5)^2=16$

C) $(x+3)^2+(y+5)^2=16$

D) $(x+3)^2+(y+5)^2=4$

The given answer choices each show the equation of a circle written in standard form, where (h, k) is center and r is the radius.

$$(x-h)^2+(y-k)^2=r^2$$

The circle is centered at $(3, 5)$, so $h=3$ and $k=5$. So, either choice A or choice B is correct. Now determine the radius r of the circle. Using the figure, the distance from the center of the circle to the point on the circle directly to the right of the center appears to be 4 units. So $r=4$. Substitute for h, k, and r in the equation.

$$(x-3)^2+(y-5)^2=4^2$$
$$(x-3)^2+(y-5)^2=16$$

The correct answer is B.

A B C D
○ ● ○ ○

Questions 1 and 2 refer to the following figure.

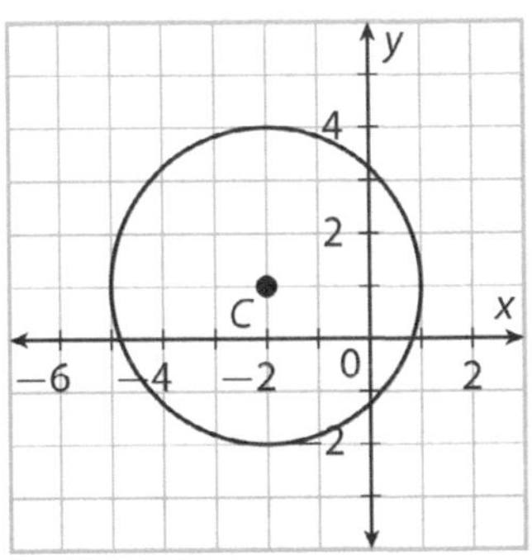

1

Which of the following is an equation for circle *C*?

A) $(x-2)^2+(y-1)^2=3$

B) $(x+2)^2+(y+1)^2=9$

C) $(x+2)^2+(y-1)^2=9$

D) $(x+2)^2+(y-1)^2=3$

2

If the center of circle *C* is moved 1 unit to the left and 3 units down and the radius of the circle is doubled, which of the following is an equation of the resulting circle?

A) $(x+3)^2+(y+2)^2=18$

B) $(x+3)^2+(y+2)^2=36$

C) $(x-1)^2+(y+3)^2=4$

D) $(x-3)^2+(y-2)^2=36$

3

Find the radius of a circle with center $(1, 4)$ that passes through the point $(13, -1)$.

A) 12

B) 13

C) 144

D) 169

Name ______________________ Date ____________ Class ____________

SAMPLE GRID-IN

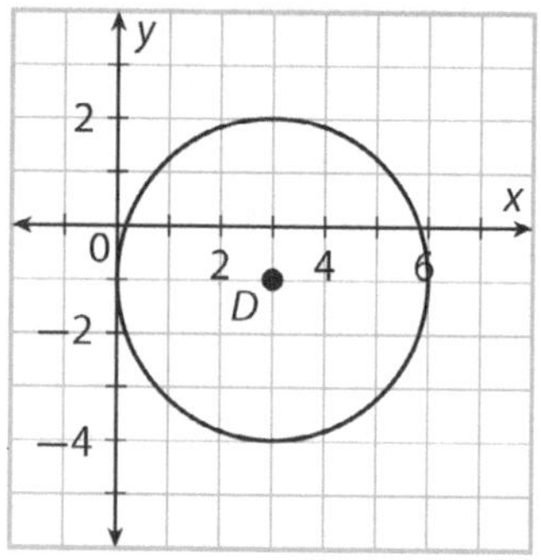

The equation of the circle graphed in the figure above can be written in the form $x^2 + y^2 + ax + by = c$. What is the value of b?

Use the figure to write an equation of the circle.

The center D of the circle has coordinates $(3, -1)$. The radius of the circle is 3 units. So the standard form of the equation is:

$$(x-3)^2 + (y+1)^2 = 9$$

Now rewrite the equation to match the form given in the problem.

$$(x-3)^2 + (y+1)^2 = 9$$
$$x^2 - 6x + 9 + y^2 + 2y + 1 = 9$$
$$x^2 - 6x + y^2 + 2y = -1$$

So, the value of b is 2.

Grid in 2.

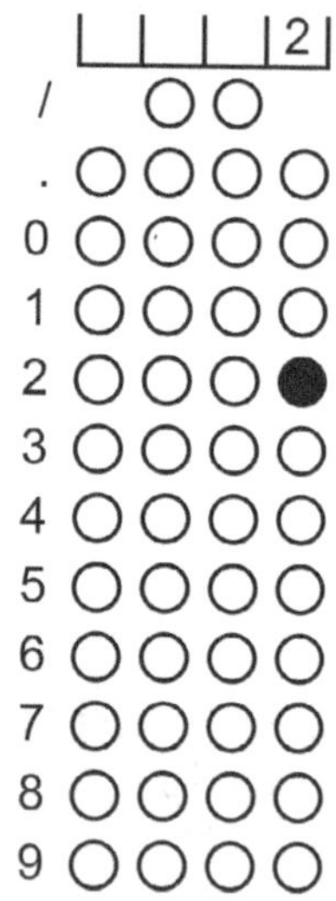

Questions 4–7 refer to the following information.

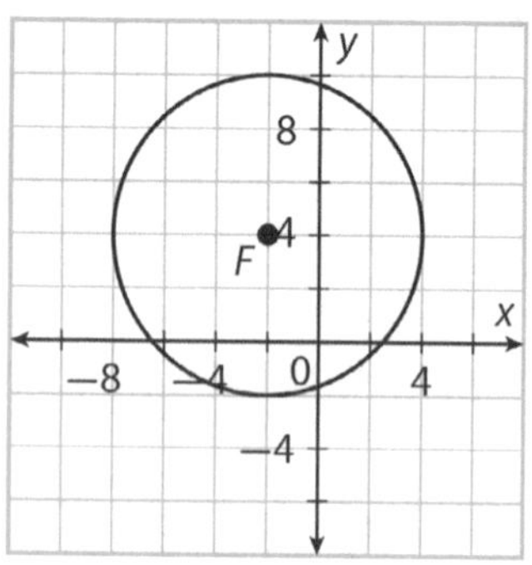

The equation of the circle has the form $x^2 + y^2 + ax - by = c$.

4

What is the radius of the circle?

5

Find the value of a in the equation.

6

Find the value of b in the equation.

7

What is the value of c in the equation?

Questions 8–10 refer to the following information.

$$x^2 + y^2 - 12x - 8y = 12$$

The equation of a circle in the xy-plane is shown above.

8

What is the radius of the circle?

9

What is the x-coordinate of the center of the circle?

10

What is the y-coordinate of the center of the circle?

Name ______________________ Date ____________ Class ____________

Represent a circle in the *xy*-plane with an equation.

ANSWER SHEET

1. A B C D

2. A B C D

3. A B C D

4.
/
.
0
1
2
3
4
5
6
7
8
9

5.
/
.
0
1
2
3
4
5
6
7
8
9

6.
/
.
0
1
2
3
4
5
6
7
8
9

7.
/
.
0
1
2
3
4
5
6
7
8
9

8.
/
.
0
1
2
3
4
5
6
7
8
9

9.
/
.
0
1
2
3
4
5
6
7
8
9

10.
/
.
0
1
2
3
4
5
6
7
8
9

Name ______________________ Date ______________ Class ______________

Understand the relationship between equations and graphs of circles.

SAMPLE MULTIPLE CHOICE

The graph of $x^2 + y^2 = 9$ is a circle. Suppose the circle is translated 2 units right and 1 unit down. What is the equation of the circle in its new position?

A) $(x-2)^2 + (y+1)^2 = 9$

B) $(x+2)^2 + (y-1)^2 = 9$

C) $x^2 + y^2 = 25$

D) $x^2 + y^2 = 4$

The standard form of the equation of a circle with center (h, k) and radius r is $(x-h)^2 + (y-k)^2 = r^2$.

The given circle has center (0, 0) and radius 3. After the translation, the resulting circle has center (2, – 1). So, for the translated circle, $h = 2$ and $k = -1$. Since translations do not affect lengths like the radius of the circle, the circles have the same radius, $r = 3$.

Substitute into the equation of a circle:

$$(x-h)^2 + (y-k)^2 = r^2$$
$$(x-2)^2 + (y-(-1))^2 = 3^2$$
$$(x-2)^2 + (y+1)^2 = 9$$

The correct answer is A. A ● B ○ C ○ D ○

1

The graph of $x^2 + y^2 = 49$ is a circle. Suppose the circle is translated 4 units left and 3 units down. What is the equation of the resulting circle?

A) $(x+4)^2 + (y-3)^2 = 49$

B) $(x-4)^2 + (y-3)^2 = 49$

C) $(x+4)^2 + (y+3)^2 = 49$

D) $(x-4)^2 + (y+3)^2 = 49$

2

Micah draws two circles on an *xy*-plane. The equation of the first circle is $x^2 + y^2 = 4$. The equation for the second circle is $x^2 + y^2 = 16$. The second circle is the result of applying which transformation to the first circle?

A) Dilation by a factor of 2

B) Dilation by a factor of 4

C) Translation 12 units left

D) Translation 12 units up

3

Tamara draws a circle on an *xy*-plane. She then applies a transformation to the circle. The resulting circle has the same radius as the original circle. Which of the following transformations could NOT be the one that Tamara used?

A) Vertical translation of 2 units

B) Horizontal translation of 5 units

C) Reflection over the *x*-axis

D) Dilation by a factor of 3

4

One circle is modeled by the equation $(x+4)^2 + (y-3)^2 = 49$. A second circle is modeled by $(x-4)^2 + (y-3)^2 = 49$. The second circle can be viewed as the result of applying what translation to the first circle?

A) 8 units left

B) 8 units right

C) 4 units left

D) 4 units right

Name ______________________ Date ______________ Class______________

SAMPLE GRID-IN

The graph of $x^2 + y^2 = 25$ is a circle centered at the origin of the xy-plane. Suppose the circle is translated 3 units left and 4 units up. What is the radius of the new circle?

The equation of the resulting circle is $(x+3)^2 + (y-4)^2 = 25$. This is in the form $(x-h)^2 + (y-k)^2 = r^2$. Since $25 = 5^2$, the radius is 5.

Grid in 5.

Time Saving Tip: This question can be answered quickly if one recognizes that translations do not affect a length like the radius of the circle. Since the original circle has radius $\sqrt{25} = 5$, the new circle also has radius 5.

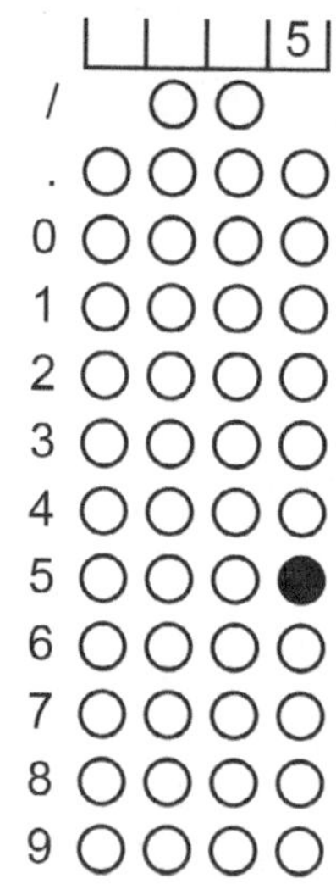

5

The graph of $x^2 + y^2 = 72.25$ is a circle centered at the origin. Suppose it is translated 9 units right and 1 unit up, and then reflected across the x-axis. What is the radius of the new circle?

Questions 6–8 refer to the following information.

Sue draws a circle with radius $\frac{7}{4}$ units centered at $(7, -4)$ in the xy-plane. She translates it 5 units left and 8 units up to draw a new circle. Then she writes the equation of the new circle in the form $(x-h)^2 + (y-k)^2 = r^2$.

6

What is the value of h?

7

What is the value of k?

8

What is the value of r?

9

Kevin draws the circle modeled by the equation $(x-7.5)^2 + (y+10)^2 = 9$. He wants to translate it so that the center is at the origin. What straight-line distance should he translate the circle to do this?

Questions 10 and 11 refer to the following information.

Two circles are described by the equations $(x+1)^2 + (y+2)^2 = 4$ and $(x-7)^2 + (y+5)^2 = 4$. The circle modeled by the second equation is the image of the circle modeled by the first equation after a horizontal translation and a vertical translation.

10

How many units to the right is the horizontal translation?

11

How many units down is the vertical translation?

Name ______________________ Date ______________ Class ______________

Understand the relationship between equations and graphs of circles.

ANSWER SHEET

1. A B C D

2. A B C D

3. A B C D

4. A B C D

5.
/
.
0
1
2
3
4
5
6
7
8
9

6.
/
.
0
1
2
3
4
5
6
7
8
9

7.
/
.
0
1
2
3
4
5
6
7
8
9

8.
/
.
0
1
2
3
4
5
6
7
8
9

9.
/
.
0
1
2
3
4
5
6
7
8
9

10.
/
.
0
1
2
3
4
5
6
7
8
9

11.
/
.
0
1
2
3
4
5
6
7
8
9

Name ______________________ Date ______________ Class ______________

Understand the relationship between the standard form of the equation of a circle and its graph.

SAMPLE MULTIPLE CHOICE

Which of the following is an equation of a circle in the *xy*-plane that has center $(-4, -2)$ and passes through the point $(-1, 2)$?

A) $(x-4)^2+(y-2)^2=25$

B) $(x+4)^2+(y+2)^2=25$

C) $(x-4)^2+(y-2)^2=5$

D) $(x+4)^2+(y+2)^2=5$

The equation $(x-h)^2+(y-k)^2=r^2$ is the standard form of the equation of a circle with center (h, k) and radius r. In this case, $h=-4$ and $k=-2$. Substitute these values into the equation.

$$(x-(-4))^2+(y-(-2))^2=r^2$$
$$(x+4)^2+(y+2)^2=r^2$$

Now substitute the coordinates of the point $(-1, 2)$ in the equation and find the value of r^2.

$$(x+4)^2+(y+2)^2=r^2$$
$$(-1+4)^2+(2+2)^2=r^2$$
$$25=r^2$$

The correct answer is B. A B C D ○ ● ○ ○

1

Which of the following is an equation of a circle in the *xy*-plane that has center $(-2, 4)$ and passes through the point $(1, 4)$?

A) $(x+2)^2+(y-4)^2=3$

B) $(x-2)^2+(y+4)^2=3$

C) $(x+2)^2+(y-4)^2=9$

D) $(x-2)^2+(y+4)^2=9$

2

Which of these is an equation of a circle in the *xy*-plane that has a diameter with endpoints $(-3, 6)$ and $(7, 4)$?

A) $(x+3)^2+(y-6)^2=104$

B) $(x-2)^2+(y-5)^2=26$

C) $(x-7)^2+(y-4)^2=104$

D) $(x-2)^2+(y-5)^2=676$

Questions 3–5 refer to the following information.

A circle has a diameter with endpoints $(-0.25, -0.75)$ and $(1.75, -0.75)$.

3

What point is the center of the circle?

A) $(0.75, -0.75)$ C) $(1.5, -0.75)$

B) $(0.75, -1.5)$ D) $(1.5, -1.5)$

4

Through which quadrant of the *xy*-plane does the graph of the circle NOT pass?

A) Quadrant I C) Quadrant III

B) Quadrant II D) Quadrant IV

5

How many *x*- and *y*-intercepts does the graph of the circle have?

A) 1 C) 3

B) 2 D) 4

Name ______________________ Date ____________ Class ____________

SAMPLE GRID-IN

A circle with its center at $(2, 5)$ has a radius of 5. Anna needs to find a point on the circle that has x-coordinate 6 and a y-coordinate greater than 6. She starts by expressing the coordinates of the point as $(6, b)$. What could be the value of b?

Begin by using the radius and the coordinates of the center to write the equation of the circle:

$$(x-2)^2+(y-5)^2=25$$

Now substitute $x=6$ and $y=b$ into this equation and solve for b:

$$(x-2)^2+(y-5)^2=25$$
$$(6-2)^2+(b-5)^2=25$$
$$16+(b-5)^2=25$$
$$(b-5)^2=9$$
$$b-5=\pm 3$$
$$b=5\pm 3$$
$$b=8 \text{ or } 2$$

Since b must be greater than 6, choose $b=8$.

Grid in 8.

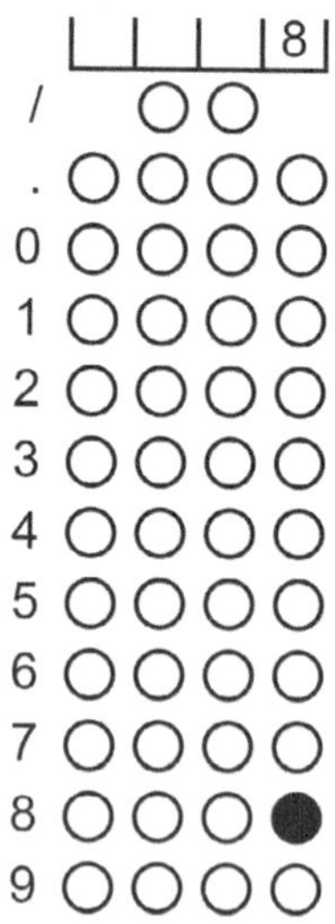

6

A circle has center $(9, 12)$ and radius 10. Mike must find a point on the circle with y-coordinate 18 and x-coordinate less than 5. He starts by writing the coordinates of the point as $(a, 18)$. What could be the value of a?

7

The points $(-1, 3)$, $(-2, -4)$, $(5, 3)$, and $(6, 2)$ all lie on a circle centered at $(2, -1)$. What is the radius of the circle?

8

One diameter of a circle has endpoints $\left(3, \frac{1}{2}\right)$ and $\left(3, -\frac{9}{2}\right)$. If the equation of the circle is written in the form $(x-p)^2+(y+q)^2=r^2$, what is the value of the expression $\frac{pq}{r}$?

Questions 9–12 refer to the following information.

A circle with center located in Quadrant II passes through exactly one point on each axis. The diameter of the circle is 6 units. Its equation can be written in the form $(x+a)^2+(y-b)^2=c$, where a, b, and c are all positive.

9

What is the value of a?

10

What is the value of b?

11

What is the value of c?

12

The circle passes through at least one point of the form $(-3, t)$. What is the value of t if $t>0$?

Name ______________________ Date ______________ Class ______________

Understand the relationship between the standard form of the equation of a circle and its graph.

ANSWER SHEET

1. A B C D

2. A B C D

3. A B C D

4. A B C D

5. A B C D

6.
/
.
0
1
2
3
4
5
6
7
8
9

7.
/
.
0
1
2
3
4
5
6
7
8
9

8.
/
.
0
1
2
3
4
5
6
7
8
9

9.
/
.
0
1
2
3
4
5
6
7
8
9

10.
/
.
0
1
2
3
4
5
6
7
8
9

11.
/
.
0
1
2
3
4
5
6
7
8
9

12.
/
.
0
1
2
3
4
5
6
7
8
9

Name ______________________ Date ____________ Class ____________

Convert angle measurements between degrees and radians.

SAMPLE MULTIPLE CHOICE

Convert 38° to radians, as a decimal to the nearest hundredth.

A) 0.73
B) 0.66
C) 0.23
D) 0.21

To convert from degrees to radians, multiply the given degree measure by $\frac{\pi}{180^\circ}$.

$$38^\circ\left(\frac{\pi}{180^\circ}\right) = \frac{38\pi}{180} = \frac{19\pi}{90} \approx 0.66$$

38° is approximately 0.66 radian.

The correct answer is B. A ○ B ● C ○ D ○

1

Convert $\frac{4\pi}{3}$ radians to degrees.

A) 30° C) 210°
B) 60° D) 240°

2

Which of these is the measure, in radians, of the angle that is complementary to an angle of 48°?

A) $\frac{7\pi}{30}$ C) $\frac{11\pi}{15}$
B) $\frac{4\pi}{15}$ D) $\frac{26\pi}{15}$

3

If an angle in standard position on the unit circle has measure $\frac{17\pi}{15}$ radians, in what quadrant does the terminal side of the angle lie?

A) Quadrant I C) Quadrant III
B) Quadrant II D) Quadrant IV

4

Convert $-1{,}260^\circ$ to radians, as an exact value in terms of π.

A) -7π C) $-\pi$
B) $-\frac{7\pi}{2}$ D) $-\frac{\pi}{7}$

5

An obtuse angle with its terminal side in Quadrant II has a radian measure of $\frac{41\pi}{45}$.

What is this measure in degrees?

A) 91° C) 160°
B) 106° D) 164°

6

Which of these is the measure, in radians, of the angle that is supplementary to an angle of 135°?

A) $\frac{\pi}{8}$ C) $\frac{2\pi}{3}$
B) $\frac{\pi}{4}$ D) $\frac{3\pi}{4}$

Name ______________________ Date ______________ Class______________

SAMPLE GRID-IN

For a circle of radius r, the arc length intercepted by a central angle of measure θ is given by the formula $s = r\theta$, when θ is in radians. Suppose that $\theta = 56°$ and $r = 3$ inches. What is the value of s, rounded to the nearest hundredth?

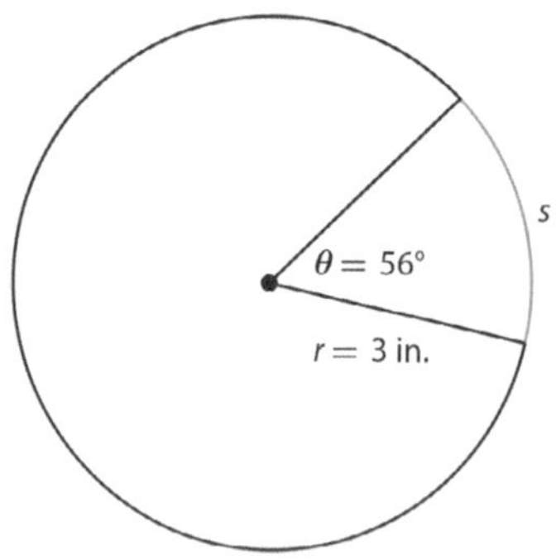

First, convert θ from degrees to radians.

$$56°\left(\frac{\pi}{180°}\right) = \frac{56\pi}{180}$$
$$= \frac{14\pi}{45}$$

Next, evaluate the formula with the given values for r and θ.

$$s = 3\left(\frac{14\pi}{45}\right)$$
$$= \frac{14\pi}{15}$$
$$\approx 2.93$$

So, the arc length is 2.93 inches.

Grid in 2.93.

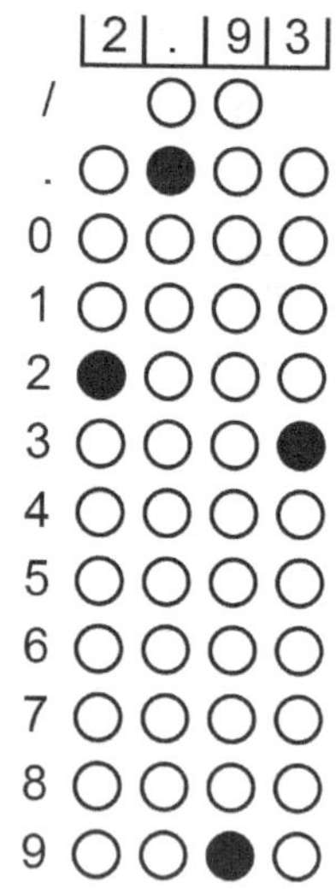

7

Given arc length $s = \pi$ feet and radius $r = 12$ feet, what is the measure, in degrees, of the central angle θ?

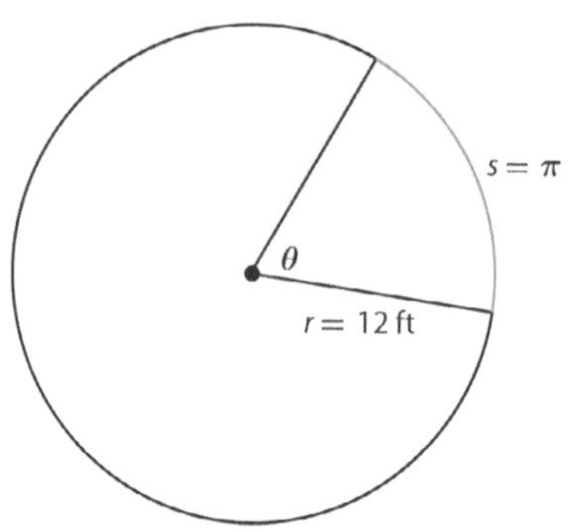

8

Convert 175° to radians.

9

If an angle has a radian measure of 0.392, what is its approximate degree measure?

10

The area A of a sector of a circle can be found using the formula $A = \frac{1}{2}r^2\theta$, where r is the radius and θ is the measure of the central angle in radians. What is the area, in square inches, for a sector of a circle with a radius of 2 inches if $\theta = 12°$?

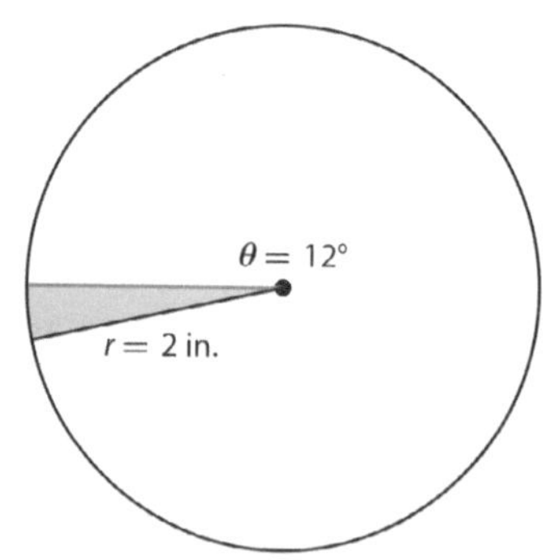

11

In radians, what is the measure of the angle supplementary to a 122° angle?

Name ______________________ Date ______________ Class ______________

Convert angle measurements between degrees and radians.

ANSWER SHEET

1. A B C D

2. A B C D

3. A B C D

4. A B C D

5. A B C D

6. A B C D

7.

/
.
0
1
2
3
4
5
6
7
8
9

8.

/
.
0
1
2
3
4
5
6
7
8
9

9.

/
.
0
1
2
3
4
5
6
7
8
9

10.

/
.
0
1
2
3
4
5
6
7
8
9

11.

/
.
0
1
2
3
4
5
6
7
8
9

Name ______________________ Date ______________ Class ______________

Solve problems about circles in the *xy*-plane using the distance formula or by completing the square in *x* and *y*.

SAMPLE MULTIPLE CHOICE

$$8x^2 + 16x - 32y + 8y^2 = 40$$

The equation of a circle is shown above. Find the coordinates for the center of the circle on the *xy*-plane.

A) (1, 2)

B) (−1, 2)

C) (2, 1)

D) (−2, 1)

Complete the square in both x and y to write the equation in the form $(x-h)^2 + (y-k)^2 = r^2$, where (h, k) is the center of the circle and r is the radius.

$$8x^2 + 16x - 32y + 8y^2 = 40$$

$$x^2 + 2x - 4y + y^2 = 5$$

$$x^2 + 2x + \left(\frac{2}{2}\right)^2 + y^2 - 4y + \left(\frac{-4}{2}\right)^2 = 5 + 1 + 4$$

$$(x+1)^2 + (y-2)^2 = 10$$

In this equation, $h = -1$ and $k = 2$, so the center of the circle is (−1, 2).

The correct answer is B. A B C D ○ ● ○ ○

1

$$9x(x-4) + 9y^2 - 8y + 9 = 36$$

What is the center of the circle whose equation is given above?

A) $\left(2, \frac{4}{9}\right)$ C) $\left(2, \frac{64}{81}\right)$

B) (44, 2) D) (2, 44)

2

To the nearest hundredth, what is the radius of the circle whose equation is $3x^2 + 15x - 4 + 3y^2 - 6y - 5 = 0$?

A) 13.25 C) 3.64

B) 10.25 D) 3.20

3

$$x^2 + 12x + 32 + y^2 + 6y - 8 = 0$$

Find the exact radius of the circle whose equation is shown above.

A) $2\sqrt{10}$ C) $\sqrt{21}$

B) 7 D) $7\sqrt{3}$

4

Find the center and radius of the circle with equation $x^2 + \frac{1}{3}x + y^2 + \frac{2}{3}y = 0$.

A) $\left(-\frac{1}{6}, -\frac{1}{3}\right)$, $r = \frac{\sqrt{5}}{6}$

B) $\left(-\frac{1}{6}, -\frac{1}{9}\right)$, $r = \frac{\sqrt{17}}{36}$

C) $\left(-\frac{1}{9}, -\frac{4}{9}\right)$, $r = \frac{\sqrt{5}}{6}$

D) $\left(\frac{1}{9}, \frac{4}{9}\right)$, $r = \frac{\sqrt{17}}{36}$

5

What is the center of the circle whose equation is given below?

$$4x^2 + 3x - \frac{21}{2} + 4y^2 - 28y - 8 = 0$$

A) $\left(\frac{3}{8}, \frac{7}{2}\right)$ C) $\left(\frac{7}{2}, -\frac{3}{8}\right)$

B) $\left(-\frac{3}{8}, \frac{7}{2}\right)$ D) $\left(-\frac{7}{2}, \frac{3}{8}\right)$

Name ____________________ Date ____________ Class ____________

SAMPLE GRID-IN

What is the shortest distance between the point $P(10, 7)$ and any point on the circle whose equation is $(x+2)^2+(y-2)^2=36$?

In the equation of the circle, $h=-2$ and $k=2$, so the center of the circle is $(-2, 2)$. The radius of the circle is $r=\sqrt{36}=6$.

The point on the circle closest to $P(10, 7)$ will lie on the line segment from P to the center of the circle. Use the distance formula to find the distance d between the center $(-2, 2)$ and the point $(10, 7)$.

$$d=\sqrt{(10-(-2))^2+(7-2)^2}$$
$$=\sqrt{12^2+5^2}$$
$$=\sqrt{169}=13$$

The point on the circle closest to P lies at a distance r from the center of the circle. So subtract the radius r from the distance between the center and point P: $13-6=7$.

So, the shortest distance is 7.

Grid in 7.

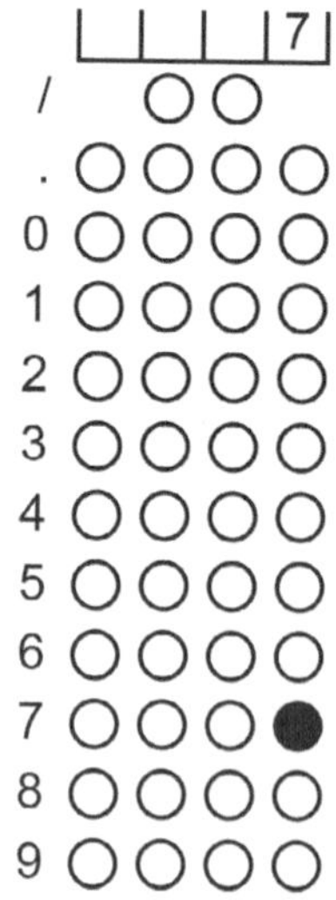

6

The equation of a circle is $x^2+y^2=196$. To the nearest hundredth, what is the shortest distance between the point $P(2, 9)$ and any point on the circle?

7

Suppose the center of a circle is the point $C(h, 14)$ and the point $P(1, 11)$ lies on the circle. If the circle has radius 3, what is the value of h?

8

A circle has its center at $C(3, -4)$. The point $P\left(-\frac{3}{2}, 1\right)$ lies on the circle. What is the radius of the circle, rounded to the nearest tenth?

9

Suppose the point $P(-5, 1)$ lies on a circle whose center is $C(-4, -6)$. Find the radius of the circle, rounded to the nearest tenth.

10

$$2x(x+4)-30=-2y(y+8)-20$$

The equation of a circle is shown above. What is the shortest distance between the circle and the point $P(7, 6)$. Round the distance to the nearest tenth.

11

Find the y-coordinate of the center of the circle whose equation is $y^2+x^2-13y-11x=100$.

Name ______________________ Date ______________ Class ______________

Solve problems about circles in the *xy*-plane using the distance formula or by completing the square in *x* and *y*.

ANSWER SHEET

1. A B C D

2. A B C D

3. A B C D

4. A B C D

5. A B C D

6.
/
.
0
1
2
3
4
5
6
7
8
9

7.
/
.
0
1
2
3
4
5
6
7
8
9

8.
/
.
0
1
2
3
4
5
6
7
8
9

9.
/
.
0
1
2
3
4
5
6
7
8
9

10.
/
.
0
1
2
3
4
5
6
7
8
9

11.
/
.
0
1
2
3
4
5
6
7
8
9

Name ______________________ Date ______________ Class ______________

Add, subtract, multiply, and divide complex numbers and solve problems.

SAMPLE MULTIPLE CHOICE

What is the product of $8+5i$ and its complex conjugate?

A) 89

B) 39

C $64-25i$

D) $5i-8$

The conjugate of a complex number $z=a+bi$ (denoted $\overline{z}$) is $\overline{z}=a-bi$. So, the conjugate of $8+5i$ is $8-5i$.

The product of a complex number z and its conjugate $\overline{z}$ is given by $z\cdot\overline{z}=a^2+b^2$.

$$\begin{aligned}(8+5i)(8-5i)&=8^2+5^2\\&=64+25\\&=89\end{aligned}$$

The correct answer is B. A ○ B ● C ○ D ○

1

What is the difference for $(6-11i)-(-3+2i)$?

A) $9-9i$

B) $3+13i$

C) $9-13i$

D) $-8+8i$

2

Simplify $-5-(4-7i)$.

A) $-12-4i$

B) $-9-12i$

C) $-1+2i$

D) $-9+7i$

3

What is the conjugate of the sum $(16-13i)+(7+25i)$?

A) $12-23i$

B) $23-12i$

C) $23-38i$

D) $-23-12i$

4

Find $(-4i)(-5+3i)$.

A) $12+20i$

B) $-20-12i$

C) $-5-i$

D) $-20i+12$

5

Find the product of $2-7i$ and $-6+9i$.

A) $75+60i$

B) $-24i+51$

C) $12-63i$

D) $51+60i$

6

Write $\dfrac{-6i}{10-13i}$ in standard form $a+bi$.

A) $\dfrac{60}{269}-\dfrac{78}{269}i$

B) $-\dfrac{26}{23}+\dfrac{20}{23}i$

C) $\dfrac{6}{13}-\dfrac{3}{5}i$

D) $\dfrac{78}{269}-\dfrac{60}{269}i$

Name ____________________ Date ____________ Class____________

SAMPLE GRID-IN

Simplify i^{240}.

Since the complex number i is defined as $i = \sqrt{-1}$, then

$$i^2 = \left(\sqrt{-1}\right)^2 = -1$$

$$i^3 = \left(\sqrt{-1}\right)^3 = -i$$

$$i^4 = \left(\sqrt{-1}\right)^4 = 1.$$

From this pattern, according to the laws of exponents, $(i^4)^n = (1)^n = 1$, for $n \geq 0$.

Using this rule:

$$\begin{aligned} i^{240} &= (i^4)^{60} \\ &= (1)^{60} \\ &= 1 \end{aligned}$$

Grid in 1.

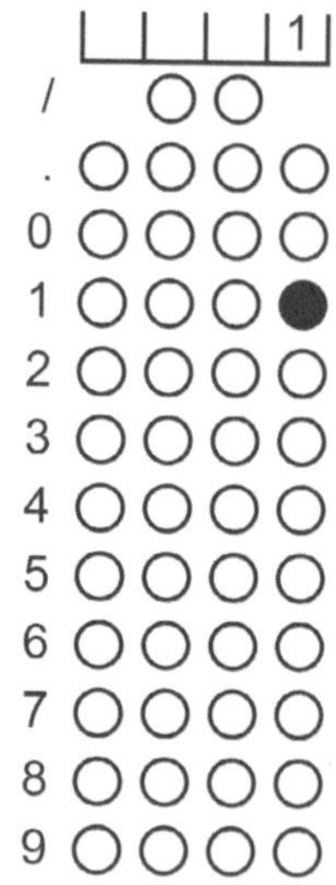

7

Divide $\dfrac{1-3i}{4-12i}$.

8

If $(3+2i)^2$ is written in the form $a+bi$, what is the value of a?

9

If $\dfrac{2}{3+4i}$ is written in the form $a+bi$, what is the value of a?

10

Simplify $i^{1,432}$.

11

Calculate $i^{11} - i^7$.

12

Simplify $\dfrac{(1-i)^3}{(1-i)^5}$. What is the coefficient of the imaginary part of the complex number?

13

If $\dfrac{5}{2-6i}$ is written in the form $a+bi$, what is the value of b?

14

If $(3+2i)(9+i) = x+yi$, what is the value of xy?

Name ______________________ Date ______________ Class ______________

Add, subtract, multiply, and divide complex numbers and solve problems.

ANSWER SHEET

1. A B C D

2. A B C D

3. A B C D

4. A B C D

5. A B C D

6. A B C D

7.

8.

9.

10.

11.

12.

13.

14.

4500939733-0607-2026

Printed in the U.S.A